The Recording, Mixing, and Mastering Reference Handbook

The Recording, Mixing, and Mastering Reference Handbook

Karl Pedersen and
Mark Grimshaw-Aagaard

OXFORD

UNIVERSITY PRESS

Oxford University Press is a department of the University of Oxford. It furthers the University's objective of excellence in research, scholarship, and education by publishing worldwide. Oxford is a registered trade mark of Oxford University Press in the UK and certain other countries.

Published in the United States of America by Oxford University Press
198 Madison Avenue, New York, NY 10016, United States of America.

Library of Congress Cataloging-in-Publication Data
Names: Pedersen, Karl, 1952- author. | Grimshaw-Aagaard, Mark, 1963– author.
Title: The recording, mixing, and mastering reference handbook /
Karl Pedersen and Mark Grimshaw-Aagaard.
Description: New York, NY : Oxford University Press, 2019. |
Includes bibliographical references and index.
Identifiers: LCCN 2018013006 | ISBN 9780190686635 (hardcover) |
ISBN 9780190686642 (pbk.)
Subjects: LCSH: Sound recordings—Production and direction. |
Sound—Recording and reproducing. | Sound studios.
Classification: LCC ML3790.P407 2019 | DDC 781.49—dc23
LC record available at https://lccn.loc.gov/2018013006

1 3 5 7 9 8 6 4 2

Paperback printed by Sheridan Books, Inc., United States of America
Hardback printed by Bridgeport National Bindery, Inc., United States of America

CONTENTS

ABOUT THE COMPANION WEBSITE

www.oup.com/us/rmmrh

Oxford has created a website to accompany *The Recording, Mixing, and Mastering Reference Handbook*. Material that cannot be made available in a book, namely, audio examples, is provided here. Additionally, all images in the book are reproduced in color on the website. The reader is encouraged to consult this resource in conjunction with the chapters. Examples available online are indicated in the text with Oxford's symbol ⊙.

The Recording, Mixing, and Mastering Reference Handbook

Read Me First!—A quick guide to using *The Recording, Mixing, and Mastering Reference Handbook*

This handbook has been written with two groups of readers in mind: those who are new to the art and craft of audio engineering and require a practical and theoretical guide for use while learning, and those who are experienced engineers who, from time to time and while on the job, need a handy reference book to remind them quickly and efficiently of particular techniques for specific situations. The handbook covers predominantly the production of popular music recordings in a broad sense, and so, while it does give information on the recording of specific orchestral instruments and small ensembles, it deals neither with the recording of large ensembles such as symphony orchestras nor with the live mixing of concerts.

Whichever group you belong to, it is likely that you are learning or have learned to be an audio engineer through one of two pathways. The first is the learning-by-doing approach, and, whether you have a home studio or are fortunate enough to be an apprentice to an experienced engineer, you will have found yourself thrown in at the deep end, being confronted, for example, with the immediate and pressing need to record an unfamiliar instrument or ensemble. The second is the new approach to training in the art and craft of the recording studio that gradually emerged in the 1980s—that is, a specialist education, and there are now many such educations across the world of variable length and at various levels in schools, colleges, and universities.

In *The Recording, Mixing, and Mastering Reference Handbook*, we have taken from the best of both these worlds and have provided you with a hands-on practical section backed up by a theoretical section. The practical section details how to record virtually any acoustic or electronic instrument and shape it using EQ, compression, reverb, and so on, and it comes first in the book as you would expect it—instant recording and mixing techniques at your fingertips!

The second, theoretical section provides valuable information on EQ, reverb, compression, mic specifications, acoustics, and so forth. If you are new to audio engineering, once you have gained some experience you will benefit from an understanding of the theory and principles of recording tools—how they are constructed and how they function—as well as an understanding of basic instrument and room acoustics. For example, by understanding the principles of microphone characteristics, the properties of the room acoustics, and the acoustics of the individual instruments, you can improve your recordings, and you can easily and efficiently track problems and minimize compromises and frustrations. As your experience and knowledge deepen, you can let your creative juices flow—you may start playing ping-pong with the compressor, using it creatively to shape the sound, or you may find yourself having fun juggling with complementary

EQ. If you are an experienced engineer, looking for tips on how to record the djembe or background information on the history of mechanical and electronic reverberation in order to achieve that retro sound your client so desires, then you will likewise find both sections of the handbook to be informative and helpful.

So there are at least two ways to make use of this book in order to speed up your craft of audio, develop your creative audio side, or brush up on your existing knowledge:

1. Start with the practical section; for example, in order to read about the techniques and equipment required for the instrument you are going to record in the next minute.
2. Go directly to the theoretical section to obtain an understanding of EQ or how to shape the mix, for instance, and then apply this knowledge practically.

Most likely, you will end up combining the two approaches, because the book is structured as a practical reference handbook, to be kept close at hand in your studio for you to dip into as and when you wish.

Glossary

In addition to an index, a glossary is found at the end of the handbook. The glossary provides a quick reference to selected essential terms and concepts with brief explanations or definitions.

PART I
The Instruments

The Voice

Unless the music is instrumental, it is the voice that establishes the personality of the song, and so the voice is what we pay the most attention to when listening to music.

The vocal track should therefore be given extra attention—both in the recording and in the mixing process—and it's one of the reasons why it is normally recorded as an overdub. During the recording of the basic tracks, the musicians must deal with a cue or scratch vocal: in their headphones, they hear a rough vocal track giving the cues and creating the initial musical atmosphere to play along with.

Acoustics and Microphone Settings

(This section gives specific advice on microphone settings for the voice—similar sections are found in those chapters dealing with other instruments throughout the first section of the book. You can find further general advice on using and setting up microphones in chapter 14.)

Recording the vocal is relatively simple: a quality, large-diaphragm condenser microphone (LDC, see p. 123) in cardioid mode placed 10–20 cm from the singer, a pop filter, a mic stand placed on a carpet, and no reflective surfaces in the near surroundings. This setup always works.

Of course, a Neumann M49, U47, or Telefunken ELA M251 (see figure 1.3) would be the perfect choice, but in the real world lots of LDCs would do the job—even some of the cheap ones will function just as well as well as many dynamic mics. Michael Jackson used a Shure SM7b to record his voice on the singles "Billie Jean" and "The Way You Make Me Feel" and if you sell just a fraction of what the album *Thriller* did, you'll have done very well indeed.

In many cases, a tube microphone is chosen because of its rich sound and because it makes the voice distinct and full bodied in the mix without being sharp. The choice of microphone also depends on the musical genre. Often, an aggressive microphone is used when recording, for example, a rap vocal, emphasizing the midrange—the microphones often used for this purpose (Shure SM58, Beyerdynamic M88, and similar dynamic mics) also appear on a lot of rock recordings. At the same time, dynamic mics tolerate high sound pressure levels (SPL) without distorting or capturing shocks, and they are

Figure 1.1

Before the condenser microphones arrived on the scene, the RCA 44 ribbon microphone, introduced in 1931, was the most commonly used vocal mic. © RCA/Ribbon Mics

less sensitive to spill than condenser mics; placing a dynamic mic in the right spot facilitates the recording of the voice live with the band.

The choice of microphone is paramount to making the vocal cut through in the mix, and matching the voice with the right mic makes the use of EQ almost redundant. A bright microphone is not the choice for a female soprano, but it might be the right choice for a dark male voice, and nasal voices cut through the mix like a knife through butter when using microphones that highlight the 2–4 kHz frequency range.

A good preamp is important because it highlights the vocals in the mix and it can deal with the large dynamic range of the voice without distortion. It is common to use the low-cut filter of the preamp (normally set at 60 Hz) at the recording stage, because content below the cutoff frequency would "cloud" the mix; it is, however, more flexible to postpone low-cut equalization until mixing.

The recording room must either be completely dampened or have controlled acoustics. Room acoustics are almost never recorded onto the vocal track, as any reverberation or echoes are then impossible to remove from the recording.

Use close-miking and be sure to keep a good distance (at least 2 m) away from reflecting walls and the control room window, as these will cause early reflections and comb filtering, which are evident even in small doses (see p. 272). The voice is a strongly dynamic instrument, and often the compressor or the limiter is used to tame the dynamics during recording, thus avoiding distorting the equipment used at the input stage. Light compression (or limiting if the singer's vocal levels are completely out of control) solves the problem of singers giving in to their own enthusiasm. A mild ratio of 2:1 and a threshold set to 6–8 dB below peaks takes the top off most fluctuations in level—and there will still be enough dynamics left to deal with in the mix.

Vocal Psychology

The vocal is rarely recorded in one take, and the perfect vocal has become a matter of production. From the 1970s, it became normal procedure to transfer part of the composition process to the studio, and overdubs became the most commonly used recording method for the vocal, the track being built up over several takes consisting of individual phrases or even single words. Sometimes the vocal is edited from perhaps twenty to thirty single takes, and plug-ins like Audio Suite and VocAlign can correct the timing of the overdubbed tracks to the edited track.

Figure 1.2
The Neumann TLM49 adds a boost in the 2–7 kHz range which makes it a perfect match for vocals. Moreover, a 2 dB boost at 11–13 kHz makes it sound transparent.

In the real world, "first takes" are often the best, because they preserve expression and vitality. Singing is very personal, and especially when compared to instrumental overdubs, the ability to sing well depends on empathy and mood. It is crucial that the singer let loose on those emotions that create a great vocal performance, so psychology is one the most important tools when recording vocals.

Simple and basic preparations can be crucial. Some singers do not want to be seen, while others demand a control room crowded with hangers-on to deliver their performance to. Making the technology invisible is a good start, so that the singer can work his/her way into the song, and this can be achieved in many cases simply through good preparation. Set up a balanced headphone mix of previously recorded tracks in advance and quietly adjust the recording levels and the like. If different microphones are to be tested, set them up in a row and let the singer try them out during the warm-up.

If the singer is nervous, it is important to create a secure atmosphere—anything from flowers and candles in the studio to throwing others out of the studio if their presence causes the singer to be self-conscious. A good vocal requires empathy so that the singer can have his/her confidence boosted and deliver the required performance.

If a handheld dynamic microphone makes the singer feel at home in the anxiety-provoking surroundings of the studio, then use it—a good performance is more important than using a Neumann U67.

It is important to start recording while the singer is fresh and ready to go. Keep your hands off the talkback and let the singer concentrate on singing. Record everything from the start—often the best take is delivered when the singer doesn't think there is a recording taking place.

A singer typically makes the most vibrant performances within the first takes, and after a few run-throughs they often fall back on routine and lose focus (as anyone can do). If concentration does drop, pausing the session or shifting the approach might bring the singer back into the flow and presence of the song.

The Headphone Mix

The headphone mix is not just an almost-good-enough mix: it's the mix that should motivate the singer to make the best take in recording history. Listen to the mix yourself and customize it to the singer's wishes.

- If the singer does not hear themselves clearly in the headphones, a phase reversal (at the mic preamp or the vocal track) often solves the problem. The reason is that singers hear themselves both directly (the inner ear) and through the headphones, and if the two signals have the opposite phase, they will cancel out at certain frequencies.

- If the singer is out of tune or tempo, it may be due to too crowded a headphone mix. Too many instruments may confuse the pitch and the groove, and the solution might be to restrict the mix to drums, bass, and a harmony instrument. (The same

---

Box 1.1 Mythical Microphones

Like many a committed professional, musicians and technicians love to tell stories about themselves and their great achievements. Expensive and rare vocal mics are important parts of this mythology—classical heavyweights like the Neumann M49, U47, U67, and AKG C12 and Telefunken ELA M251.

A real-world budget is more likely to be suited to an AKG C414, Studio Projects C1, MXL V89, or Røde NT1A, and these are often equally good choices. Even a low-budget mic like the sE Electronics X1 sounds stunning on vocals and acoustic guitars. And a humble dynamic mic like the Sennheiser MD441 contributed to the success of Prince's "Kiss."

The myths about magical equipment creating great music out of almost nothing are numerous, the reason being that it is very difficult to figure out where such magic occurs in the recording process—if indeed it does. In particular, it is unclear exactly what produces a striking performance in the studio, but if a Telefunken ELA M251 excites a singer enough to make her give everything she's got, then go right ahead.

In the real world, though, it is often the opposite that is the case. Inexperienced singers have often started taking singing lessons as a result of meeting their first Neumann U67, because the studio technology renders their voice mercilessly transparent, revealing insecure intonations, sloppy pronunciation, disjointed phrasing, and an often comprehensive lack of vocal technique; the weaknesses become chiseled in granite via the studio monitors.

But studio technology *can* be used to enhance the musical performance. During recording, you can work for hours building the vocal track, correcting the details, and crafting a single phrase to the point where it becomes much better than a live recording; tricks using overdubbing, autotuning, producing a fuller and larger timbre, and so forth are all elaborated in this chapter.

applies when recording instruments such as brass, woodwind, and string instruments that, like the voice, require the performers to pitch their intonation.)

- Use little or no reverb in the headphone mix, because it makes the singer's intonation shaky. A vocal that sounds good without reverb will sound even better with reverb added into the mix later on. However, a little reverb might inspire a vocalist to sing at their best.

Various Vocal Techniques

Vocal Doubling

Vocal doubling—also known as double-tracking—involves separate performances of the same vocal melody each recorded onto its own track. Since no two musical performances will be the same, doubling makes the voice sound fuller when the tracks are played simultaneously. For this reason, it is often used in mainstream pop and with inexperienced singers. Vocal doubling is rarely used in rock, folk, and jazz, as the two combined tracks are perceived as "flattened out"— without strength and emotional impact because small-scale dynamic fluctuations over small periods of time in the one track can often be canceled out when combined with another track that has dynamic fluctuations in other places.

Figure 1.3
Telefunken ELA M251. Some mythical mics appear in song lyrics. On "Crew End" and "Sy Borg" (from the 1979 album *Joe's Garage*), Frank Zappa sings about a Telefunken U47— both as a phallic reference and as the tool capturing the upper body. The Telefunken ELA M251 was actually manufactured by Neumann in 1947. The mic was distributed by Telefunken under that brand name, while Neumann named it the U47. It is tube-based and one of the most sought-after vocal mics. © Telefunken

---

Box 1.2 Automatic Double-Tracking

Automatic double-tracking was invented at Abbey Road Studios (then EMI Studios) during the recording of the Beatles' *Revolver* album (1966). John Lennon was not happy with his voice and wanted to double it, making it sound bigger, but he did not like the flattening effect of double-tracking either. Engineer Ken Townsend modified a two-track Revox tape recorder that he then used to delay the original vocal by a few milliseconds (equivalent to the distance between the tape deck's recording and playback heads). Moreover, the tape speed was varied a little with an oscillator. Combining this signal with the original track created a vibrant and full timbre—without the neatness of the double-tracking. It was called automatic double-tracking (ADT), and the effect was used on "Doctor Robert," "Here There and Everywhere," "Eleanor Rigby," and, later on, "I Am the Walrus."

ADT was used by Pink Floyd on "The Piper at the Gates of Dawn" (1967) and later by Simon and Garfunkel, Jimi Hendrix, and many others.

Figure 1.4

By copying a tape recording and intentionally making the copy wobble using the frequency oscillator, the speed of the second tape machine was varied to make it sound like a separate take. The Waves plug-in Reel ADT emulates double-tracking, with varispeed and tape saturation included. © Waves

Pitch Shift

Pitch shift is another technique used to make the vocals sound larger and fuller.

Add a pitch shift plug-in to a copy of the vocal track and set L (left) to −20 cents and R (right) to −30 cents. Leave dry at 0 and wet at 100. In this way, only the pitch-processed sound is heard from the track copy. Pan is set to C (center) for both tracks. Because pitch shifting creates different results for different voices, you should gradually add the pitch-shifted track to the mix in order to determine the appropriate level for the particular singer's voice.

The Mix Settings and Effects

The voice is the most prominent element in the mix—it is the part that the average listener relates to—and so the vocal is granted special attention not only during recording but also during mixing.

Level

The golden rule for balancing a pop vocal is that it should sit just enough above the snare drum that it does not drown in the beat. For recordings without a drum kit, balance the voice in relation to the most prominent non-vocal instrument in the mix.

Many engineers still mix vocals manually, because they feel this creates a performance that is impossible to recreate by editing. On the analog mixer, this was called "gain riding"—adjusting the levels while the tracks play back. Gain riding is easily adapted to the workflow of the DAW by recording level changes (level automation), with the prerequisite that you are completely familiar with the vocal track. Furthermore, the DAW has the advantage of enabling you to come back repeatedly and make fine adjustments. Gain riding is similar to using an invisible compressor, but without the compressor's "opening and closing" artifacts (arising from sudden shifts in level, thereby changing the timbre and expression of the vocal). Such artifacts derive from the compressor's amplification and attenuation characteristics and, in extreme cases, are colloquially known as "pumping" and "breathing." If the vocal changes character within the song's development, then gain riding is a particularly good solution.

Instead of making numerous fine edits, manual gain riding allows for a creative approach to the mixing of levels—play the faders like a musician plays an instrument. That this method works so well is probably due to the organic interplay between the instruments and the melody line, which is only achievable with a human performance.

EQ

When recorded with quality equipment, the vocal needs very little EQ—sometimes only a boost of a few dB at the top end and a small cut somewhere in the 200–500 Hz area. If more extensive EQing is needed, then be aware of particular frequency ranges giving the basic character to the vocal: male vocals have fullness and body in the 125–300 Hz range and females in the 200–350 Hz range.

Often it is necessary to cut between 200 and 500 Hz to remove the muddy/boomy or "woolly" frequencies, and if the vocal sounds too deep in the mix, this is not necessarily because of lack of top end.

Nasal, whiny, and tinny sound sits in the range 1–1.5 kHz, which is why classic EQ designs always have 1 kHz as one of their fixed frequencies. A cut at 1 kHz of 6–12 dB (Q, the bandwidth of the EQ, should be quite narrow) creates space for the other instruments, and this means that the vocals can be powerful without sounding harsh and metallic.

Presence and articulation are located in the 2–5 kHz area. Both the text clarity and impact are located here, but excessively boosting in this range does not sound pleasant, because it makes the vocal sharp and sibilant.

Sibilance resides in the 5–9 kHz area, creating both clarity and explosive sibilants especially on the consonants p, s, and t (see de-essing, p. 14). The English [ʃ], as in "shoe," forms very pronounced sibilants, an effect that is created by an air current hitting the front teeth and creating a powerful hissing noise that distorts the operation of the mic diaphragm.

Air and openness are between 10 and 16 kHz, and this frequency range only affects the harmonics of instruments (see p. 167). Boosting within this range enhances transient harmonics, while dampening within the range is like putting a veil over the instruments.

A low-shelf dampening or a low-cut filter will highlight the dynamics of the vocal while reducing the "boomy" bass area; attenuate with a low-shelf filter somewhere from 150 Hz and downwards (according to the vocalist's gender, timbre, and the pitch) and combine, if necessary, with a low-cut filter from 70 Hz (see pp. 156–158 on the EQ).

Pan and EQ

It is often difficult to make space for the vocals in a recording with powerful guitars, because both the guitar and the vocal are located close to each other in the midrange area from 300 Hz to 3 kHz.

Boosting guitars in these frequencies will steal from the vocals, so instead let the guitars range over the sides of the stereo image (pan completely L and R). The guitars can be attenuated 2–3 dB in this midrange and still be heard distinctly, while at the same time a space is cleared for the vocal in the center.

Compression

It is almost always necessary to smooth out the levels of the vocal using compression.

Start with the loudest passage of the recording and set a ratio of 2.5:1 to 3:1 for a natural sound. Set the threshold so that gain reduction is 2–4 dB (see pp. 171–179 on the compressor).

Attack should be medium to slow at 20–50 ms and release at 200 ms to avoid pumping, and often the auto setting will work perfectly well because the vocal is a relatively simple signal. The combination of medium to slow attack and fast release makes the vocal stand out from any powerful backing tracks, though afterwards it is often necessary to boost EQ in the presence area because compression attenuates transients.

Experiment with the threshold until the vocal track stands out clearly in the mix with a balance that is natural and a compression that matches the song.

The UREI 1176 and LA-3 are classic compressors widely used for vocals because they are capable of both "invisible" yet powerful compression of the dynamics. Choose the compressor for the character you want it to add to the track: optical, FET, or variable mu (see p. 243).

Reverb and Delay

Vocals normally need reverb or delay to thrive in the mix, but the choice of spatial effects depends on the role the vocal plays in the song and on the music genre. Guitar, bass, and drums provide the solid foundation to the song, while the vocals should float on top of the mix. To this end, reverb and delay are used to create a space around the vocal.

Reverb makes the vocal blend into the mix while at the same time placing it slightly to the back (distance is always a side effect of using reverb); keep reverb time and level low enough that the vocal stays forward in the mix. Often, it needs a bright reverb such as plate or slap back, and if this creates a whistling sound, then put a de-esser in front of the input to the reverb unit.

Often a short delay is better than reverb, because this keeps the vocal up front in the mix. Delays preserve presence and text clarity; in particular, this can be accomplished by a short delay that fits into the pulse and groove of the song.

Multing

Multing is the distribution of the vocal/instrument over two tracks in which, normally, the original track maintains a full/natural sound while the copy is given an aggressive twist. Give the copy a powerful boost in the 3–5 kHz region and an aggressive compression. Use a UREI 1176–type compressor, LA-3A, or LA-2A (or an emulation thereof). The UREI 1176 has an "all buttons in" setting (all the ratio buttons activated) providing highly aggressive compression to vocals. The copy is balanced beneath the original track, adding character and pushing the vocal forward in the mix.

Box 1.3 Vintage Compression

The Teletronix LA-2A and LA-3A are two of the most popular vocal compressors in rock history, because they add powerful gain reduction to vocals without crushing the dynamics to death. The LA-3A from 1969 is a transistor-based optical compressor based on the 1962 LA-2A, which was tube-based. The LA-2A and the LA-3A both have soft-knee characteristics and a program-dependent release. The optical element provides a slow and nonlinear reaction to transients, resulting in a more musical performance because the musical dynamics are preserved. When driving the input hard, the LA-2A provides a pleasant, harmonic tube distortion as well. This can be heard quite distinctly on the White Stripes' vocals, which utilize the distortion as a powerful effect along with the compression.

A similar optical behavior is found in the Tube Tech CL1B and the Avalon VT737SP.

The LA-3A has been the workhorse of the major studios due to its transparent compression and discreet harmonic distortion. With the LA-3A, the vocal track can withstand a 10–20 dB compression (the gain reduction meter hitting the limits), without completely losing transients. At the same time, the LA-3A adds character by boosting the midrange, making it suitable for drums, bass, and vocals (for example, on Prince's "Purple Rain"). The LA-3A's attack is a fast 1.5 ms with 50% release at 60 ms. The combination of optical-based compression and fast time constants (attack and release) is the secret to its ability to soak up ambiences from overhead and room mics and to make vocals stand out in the mix. On the snare drum, which can be difficult to compress without destroying its transients, a 3 dB LA-3A compression provides distinctiveness in the mix with a good resonance from the bottom skin.

The fixed time constants make the LA-2A and LA-3A simple to use:

- Gain determines output.
- Peak reduction controls the degree of compression (i.e., both ratio and threshold).

Both are available as plug-ins, including Waves and Universal Audio.

Automating EQ on Harsh Vocals

Singers who do not use abdominal support and the main resonance of the body cavities but instead are singing from the throat often sound cutting and trumpet-like—piercing and shrill. This sound can be made less offensive to the ears by using EQ, but compression triggered by the unpleasant frequencies will yield a better result.

Use a compressor with a side chain function (see p. 246) controlled by an EQ that boosts the offensive frequencies somewhere between 2.5 and 4 kHz. It is set up exactly as with the de-esser (see below) but slightly lower in the high midrange (the de-esser usually works in the 4–6 kHz frequency range), and the ratio is set to 4:1 (a slightly more moderate ratio than the de-esser). Alternatively, use a graphic EQ as the side chain instead of a parametric EQ, as it allows for boosting 2.5 kHz with +6 dB and 15.3 kHz with +12 dB, and set 4 kHz to +4 dB. On top of that, a de-esser can be added to the chain controlled by a high-shelf filter from 5 kHz and up. Thus, nothing below 2.5 kHz is affected. This setup reduces sibilance along with the harsh "aaa" vowels (in rock and pop music, this is the inevitable and spontaneous emotional outburst "ba-aaa-by!").

The advantage of the side chain technique is that it only attenuates the selected frequency range when excessive hard vowel sounds are present; the rest is left unaffected. Reducing these frequencies only with EQ would affect the entire vocal track.

De-essing

The de-esser is used to remove sibilance from vocal tracks, especially the ʃ-sibilance ("shoe") that sounds like distortion and appears everywhere in the signal chain from the mixer to the effect units. It is set up by means of a peak limiter (or a compressor) with a side chain fed by an EQ that is boosted in the frequencies where the sibilance resides.

Raising the level of the problem frequencies in the side chain EQ makes them more effective triggers for the threshold that, if exceeded, the compressor will respond to with attenuation. Only when sibilance exceeds the threshold will the compressor kick in and reduce the level of the vocal track.

For de-essing purposes, the quality of the equalizer is not critical, since the vocal track does not become equalized, the side chain being a control signal that only triggers the compression by amplifying the problem frequencies.

Start setting the EQ a little wider than usual; for example, the frequencies from 5 kHz up to 12 kHz, which more than cover the area of potential sibilance. Set the Q bandwidth to wide (see pp. 158–160) and make a 6–12 dB boost. Then gradually narrow Q, and when the unpleasant frequencies are identified, make Q even narrower and add a low-cut below the sibilant frequencies so that the low frequencies do not trigger compression.

Start setting the compressor ratio to ∞:1 (limiting) and then reduce it to a more musical setting—down to 3:1 for a discreet de-essing.

Since the side chain is a control signal for the compressor, it is important to set release so that the gain of the input signal recovers quickly, letting the vocal through uncompressed when sibilance stops. Set attack to 0.05 ms and release to between 50 and 60 ms.

Of course, it is better to avoid sibilance at the recording stage. Try the following:

- Place the singer further away from the microphone (this also creates less proximity effect; see pp. 131–132) so that powerful air currents are avoided.
- The tongue directs sibilants forward and a little downwards, and so a good solution is to place the microphone capsule at eye level, pointing down a little; this has the additional advantage that it makes the singer straighten up, thereby improving the quality of the vocals.
- Make the singer place a tiny piece of chewing gum on the back of the front teeth, where sibilants are formed.
- Select a microphone that does not emphasize sibilant frequencies.

Special Uses of Vocal Microphones

- *Kiss an omni*—Cardioid microphones have an innate Proximity Effect: the closer the microphone, the more the bass boost. It usually sounds fine on rock vocals, adding a full-bodied timbre to both dark and bright vocals, but in other genres it is often too powerful an effect. The proximity effect also becomes a problem if the singer does not keep a consistent distance from the microphone. Even small movements result in varying bass levels, and in the mix this may require tedious equalization, phrase by phrase, to clean up the recording. An omni microphone exhibits no proximity effect—even at "kissing distance" from the microphone, the omni is still crystal clear and detailed (use the −10 dB pad to avoid overdriving the electronics). Because of this, omnis are also used to avoid the varying proximity effect resulting from when the singer moves.
- *Sub a cardioid*—Cardioid microphones highlight deep vocals (the dub bass and Leonard Cohen / Barry White effect). Keep the distance to the microphone consistent at 15 cm. In the mix, a parametric EQ is used to cut 3–6 dB at 150 Hz (medium Q at 1.2), cleaning up the muddiness from the proximity effect but leaving the lowest frequencies alone. Boost strongly at 60 Hz with narrow Q to highlight the sub bass and at 4–5 kHz as well in order to highlight presence. The result: a clear and detailed vocal track with tons of deep low end.
- *Think small*—Small-diaphragm mics generally capture more detail than large diaphragm mics, but their light diaphragms also tend to pop when exposed to vocal plosives and the air currents of close-miking. If you want a vocal with lots of detail, place an omni 90° off-axis and a little to the side of the singer (removing a little high frequency energy and avoiding air currents hitting the microphone capsule). Placing the omni slightly above or below the singer's mouth has a similar effect but retains more of the high-frequency energy. Use a proper pop filter—not one of the foam shields that come with cheap mics, because these absorb high frequencies. If you combine the omni with a cardioid, remember to check for out-of-phase coloration.

Harmony Vocals as Overdub

Harmony vocals are recorded as overdubs, usually one singer at a time.

While the lead vocal is always recorded without ambience, the harmony vocals can benefit from some good acoustic ambience, providing depth and width.

Often, the harmony vocals are doubled (or tripled) to create fullness. Be aware that the proximity effect stacks the same frequencies on top of each other and might make the overall sound boomy and bass-heavy. Normally, a cut is needed between 100 and 250 Hz along with a low-cut that removes the woolly sound, making the harmony vocals distinct in the mix. Consider a roll-off of a few dB between 300 and 800 Hz as well.

When the harmony vocals have been balanced (both volume and EQ), they should be sent (via a bus) to an aux channel controlling the overall volume of the harmony vocals in the mix, both in relation to the lead vocal and the backing. On the aux, the same amount of compression, reverb, and delay can be added to all the harmony vocals. A group does pretty much the same, but here the tracks do not share the same compressor or the levels of the effect sends.

A compressor usually reduces the transients that are located at the bright end of the frequency spectrum, and they should be revitalized with a high-shelf boost above 5–6 kHz.

The same vocalist singing all the harmony parts provides a very dense and rich choral timbre (the repetition being almost identical). In the mix, the harmony parts are distributed across the stereo image—for example, by panning doubled parts opposite to each other.

The rock band Queen developed the artistic possibilities of this technique on "Bohemian Rhapsody" (1975) with Freddy Mercury overdubbing himself 20–25 times in order to make both the full choir sound in the rock ballad at the beginning and the song's operatic choir sound in the middle section.

On most recordings, extra time is spent to make one perfect and thoroughly functioning choir, which is then used throughout the entire song. This requires that the basic tracks have either been recorded to click track or are based on a sequencer recording if the same choir should fit completely into all chorus sections.

Experienced singers, members of a gospel choir for example, normally prefer to record the entire choir in one take, and this might provide a denser sound as they adjust to each other while singing. Shure Beta 58 mics or the equivalent are suitable for recording several vocals in one take, leaving an opportunity to balance each voice in the mix. Set up the microphones according to the 3:1 principle (see p. 275). If used, the headphone mix imposes demands on singers, making it difficult to hear both their own voices and the other voices clearly; this often causes problems in adapting their vocal performance, as they easily would without headphones. Often, the solution of wearing only one side of the headphones works best with the ear outside the headphones hearing the other singers naturally.

Further information on processing the vocal is dealt with in Part 3, Processors and Effects and in Part 4, Mixing and Mastering.

TIPS

✓ If the singer does not do it herself, ask her to pull back a little on ex plosive bursts—changing the distance from the microphone depending on the passage: from 5–10 cm distance in soft passages to 25–40 cm distance in loud passages. If you feel the singer's confidence will wilt under such a request, an other solution is to set the mic preamp gain low enough to avoid clipping, though this does not eliminate the bursts and whistles that make the mic membrane pop.

✓ The distance required to pull back from a dynamic mic is usually slightly less than for a condenser. Close-miking provides a fuller and more intimate sound because of the proximity effect of dynamic mics, an effect that ends at 25–30 cm.

✓ Dead and deader . . . If the room is small and has poor acoustics, the vocal will benefit greatly from dampening the ceiling and the walls. A Reflexion Filter on the microphone will also exclude most of the reflections; such filters come in varying qualities, and using them is always cheaper than acoustically treating the room.

✓ An acoustically tuned space can be created with acoustic dampening material, such as Rockfon, Ecophon, or Auralex. (The manufacturer specifies on the material which frequen cies are dampened.) However, frequencies below 400 Hz cannot be dampened this way.

✓ A pop filter is required to filter the bursts created typically by the consonants p, t, and b. If the microphone is angled slightly off-axis (see p. 135), less airflow will be directed toward its diaphragm. Another solution is to place the microphone tilting down, a little above the airflow.

✓ The singer should avoid coffee and dehydrating sugary fluids (water good, Coca-Cola bad).

✓ Intonation problems can be reduced by wearing only one side of the headphones. This way singers also hear the direct sound of their voices. Fretless instruments (e.g., double bass and violin, and instruments with less precise intonation in general) can also be the cause of a singer's pitch confusion. Leave them out of the headphone mix.

✓ After working for a long time on a vocal recording, changing the mood provides new insights. Adjust the accompaniment by, for example, reducing it to an acoustic guitar. This provides a fresh perspective so that the singer can make a "first take" performance.

✓ Contrasts between the verse and the chorus can be enhanced by using different microphones. For example, a condenser mic slightly compressed in the verse and a dynamic microphone such as a Shure SM57 with loads of compression and an overdriven tube preamp in the chorus. This is more efficient than attempting to create contrast in the mix.

✓ De-essing can be fine-tuned by adding an extra de-esser. Choose an optical com pressor (which is quite lazy in attack and release) and set it to an additional 3–4 dB of gain reduction on the problem frequencies so as to smooth the sibilants a little more.

✓ To avoid the side effects of de-essing (which may result in lisping artifacts), start with reducing the volume in the problem areas. If it only concerns a limited number of sibilant effects and you are using a DAW, reducing them by drawing a dip in the DAW's level automation is a fine solution. Alternatively, they can be reduced at the sample level (waveform editing).

2

The Drum Kit

A basic principle of the sound studio is "Garbage in, garbage out." Fixing a defective recording will never be as good making a good recording in the first place, and a good basic recording will save you time later on in the mix.

The drum kit is one of the most difficult instruments to record, not only because it creates its sound in interaction with the acoustics but also because it has so many different sounds combined in the one instrument.

There are no definite rules for the use of microphones on an acoustic instrument other than first becoming familiar with the hows and whys of the interactions of your microphones and the recording room and then choosing the mic that best captures a certain instrument; place it in "the sweet spot," the spot where the sound seems natural, or where the mic provides the coloring you are going for. Like any other acoustic instrument, without acoustics, drums do not breathe, and they become weightless and confined.

It is not just a matter of having the right studio equipment; the acoustics and the sound of the drum set are just as important, and the most important studio assets are the musicians. It is your task to be attentive to the way they play their instruments, and the musicians will have a sound that they have developed over many years' experience.

The Instrument and the Acoustics

The drum kit sound is strongly influenced by the room in which it is recorded. A small room dominated by hard materials (e.g., a stone wall with wooden floors) is used to achieve a dense sound, while large recording rooms with wooden linings provide very vibrant and ambient acoustics. Professional studios have a dedicated drum room with appropriate acoustics—even better, certain areas of this recording space are acoustically designed for different kinds of reverberation.

On the other hand, a dampened room with carpets and lots of soft furnishings will make the drums sound as if the drummer is hitting cardboard boxes. Therefore, experiment with the best location in the room available to you—the place where the drum kit sounds best. Each individual drum should sound right in itself, and it might take hours to find the right snare, to change skins, and to tune or eliminate ringing and rattling noises. For this reason, bands having the financial resources to spare often have a drum technician who repairs, replaces, and tunes the drum kit before recording.

Box 2.1 The History of Drum Sound

Until the mid-1960s, normally only one microphone was used for recording the drum kit. When the tape recorder increased its tracks from 2 to 4 to 8 tracks, the idea of sculpting the sound of the individual instruments in the mix process began to take shape. The idea was fascinating, but still a little unrealistic, because mixers with more than just a few channels were not produced at that time.

Around 1964, some technicians began to place a microphone about 50 cm in front of the bass drum to add bottom end in the beat music of that time. The classic Ringo drum sound (the Beatles after 1965) comes from three microphones: a Coles 4038 ribbon as overhead, an AKG D19 on the snare, and an AKG D20 in front of the bass drum. Motown Studios also began to apply a similar microphone technique, because the soul genre had a rich bottom end as part of its sound, and already in 1964 Motown Studios had acquired an 8-track tape recorder. Before then, studios had implemented technical regulations for how much bottom end could be recorded (deep bass caused problems in the mastering of LPs) and how much sound pressure the microphones might be exposed to, thus preventing that kind of excess. In point of fact, most mics are capable of handling the sound pressure of the bass drum, and technical improvements in the lacquer gradually allowed for more bottom end in the mastering of LPs.

However, when the studios' capabilities grew to 16 and 24 tracks, this did not lead to a better drum sound. Most often, the drums became duller sounding, because recordings of the drum kit were now made in isolation rooms insulated with rockwool; previously, drums had been recorded in large, acoustically live rooms like Abbey Road's Studio 2.

Fortunately, not everyone was recording in the duller rooms. The Led Zeppelin drum sound of the early 1970s was recorded in the hall of the English manor Headley Grange. This produced an acoustically vibrant sound and was in sharp contrast to the 1970s' dry, dampened sound of the studios. "When the Levee Breaks" was recorded with only two microphones and powerful compression soaking up the acoustics of the hall. This created a large, ambient drum sound and became the ideal for the 1980s' gated drum sound and the ambient drum sound of the 1990s.

From the late 1970s, digital recording technology provided new opportunities. One of the first practical achievements was the gated reverb of the 1980s, frequently used on the snare drum. On "In the Air Tonight," Phil Collins combined gated recordings with strong compression and the ambient acoustics of the Stone Room in the Townhouse Studio (see also box 21.5). This drum sound was extensively copied by producers and sampled by the new techno groups, and it subsequently found its way into new contexts.

In 1984, the English producer Trevor Horn went back to the roots of this drum sound and sampled John Bonham's drums on "Whole Lotta Love" (1969) to use them in "Relax" (which became a million-selling record for Frankie Goes to Hollywood).

Around 1990, a new drum ideal began to surface: the dry sound of drum machines in the hip-hop and dance-music genres. Because of the sequencer, the grooves and fills no longer needed to relate to how a drummer with two arms and two legs could overcame the body's physical limitations to create great art.

Since 2000, the drum ideal seems to be "adapt or die." Retro drum sound, mechanical and industrial drums, natural and digital dynamic drums, and so forth coexist as elements within a wide variety of genres.

With a great-sounding drum kit, a good drummer, and an appropriate recording space, the sound setup and check will last no more than a few hours, but if some of these are missing, this can easily take half a day and more.

A widespread mistake is to excessively dampen the drums to prevent resonances; dampening removes sound that cannot be recreated. Instead, use O-rings or tape very small pieces of foam to the top and/or bottom of the drumheads as this reduces the resonances effectively with only slight dampening.

Generally, drums that are deeper than they are wide tend to ring, while drums having the same depth and width will have more tone and fewer unusual noises and resonances. There are no absolute rules for the tuning of the drums; some drummers tune in fifths and octaves, while others prefer thirds. You can also tune the drumheads to the resonance tone of the drum, but whatever tuning you choose, it is important that the top and bottom heads are tuned close to each other and preferably with a little detuning applied to the bottom head of each drum.

Make sure that the heads have an even tension. On a bad sounding drum, slacken off the lugs on the top head and gradually tighten them up one by one until the tone seems to match the size and frequency of the shell. Repeat this with the bottom head, though this should be tuned slightly lower. Use your ears—and keep on trying! Drum emergency assistance takes plenty of time, as many kits can be in really bad shape.

Mic Setup

When the kit itself sounds great in the room, position the microphones according to the sound you intend to capture. The key to getting an ambient drum sound with minimal technical complexity is the use of overhead microphones (OH mics); together with a microphone each on the bass drum and the snare, they capture the essence of the kit.

In multi-miking, the mics are placed so that they capture the individual drums as best as possible, preferably one mic capturing one drum (close-miking) so its sound can be processed individually in the mix. Close-miking is normally complemented by ambient miking (OH and room mics).

Positioning the mic is part of designing the sound of the individual drum. You can emphasize or attenuate the attack, decay, sustain (on ADSR see p. 175), and so forth by listening to and trying out the mic position. The microphone's spacing and angle is vital when it comes to spill from the other drums; spill onto the snare particularly must be minimized so that its sound can be shaped in the mix without coloring the sound of the rest of the kit. For this reason, experienced drummers hit the snare heavily and the hi-hat more weakly.

A microphone setup can range from two microphones (stereo mics that capture the entire drum kit) to 6–8 mics or even 12–15 mics for larger drum kits, if the goal is total control over all its individual parts, the cymbals and toms included. A large number of mics on the drum kit has both advantages and disadvantages. It certainly provides control over the individual drums, but at the same time it increases the risk of phase problems (the comb filter effect; see p. 272) that reduce the dynamics and degrade the sound quality. As spill cannot be avoided with this form of multi-miking, many sound engineers deliberately use the leakage to create a bigger drum sound. Apart from the snare drum, phase problems can be dealt with because of the different frequency ranges of the drums, and spill from multiple microphones might appear in the form of fullness and depth and as unexpected coloring in the sound palette.

▶ Audio examples 02.1a–02.1d demonstrate four different microphone setups for the drum kit.

Box 2.2

See also box 14.2, "The Basic Rules of Microphone Placement."

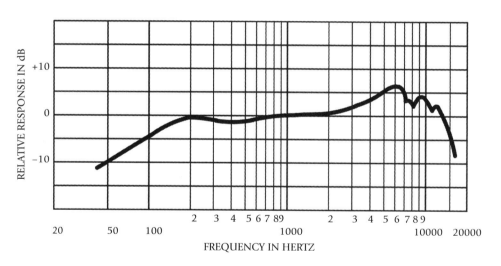

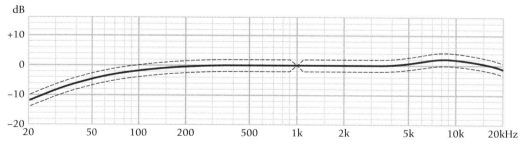

Figure 2.1

Frequency response of the Shure SM57 and the Neumann 184 (both cardioids). Frequency is shown on the horizontal axis (20 Hz to 20 kHz). The vertical axis displays the deviation from a linear representation in dB. The Neumann 184 covers a wider frequency range and is more linear because it is a condenser mic. It is therefore suitable for all sorts of acoustic instruments and for use as an overhead mic. © Shure © Neumann

Mic Technique: The Individual Drums in the Kit

Any microphone colors the sound it picks up, and so certain microphones are traditionally chosen to highlight particular parts of the drum kit. The fact that a Sennheiser 421 or a Shure Beta 57A is often used for the toms is due to their frequency response (see p. 124), which emphasizes both the body and the attack of most toms. Likewise, an ordinary Shure SM57 is often the first choice for the snare because it withstands high sound pressure levels, emphasizes the fullness of the snare drum (its proximity effect), and provides definition in the high-mid frequencies.

The Bass Drum

The bass drum loves a large diaphragm mic with cardioid characteristics. An AKG D12 or D112 is the classic choice, but dynamic mics like a Sennheiser 421, Audix D6, or Shure Beta 52A will also do the job well. Placed inside the drum (through a hole in the rear skin) and pointing toward where the beater hits the beater head, the mic captures a distinctive attack. Close up to the beater, the sound is precise and defined, while it has more body and depth further away. Placed outside the bass drum, a condenser is the best choice; this captures the resonant tone and longer sustain of the front skin but less of the attack (see figure 2.2).

Figure 2.2
A Neumann TLM103 outside the drum captures sustain and fullness. If at the same time a mic is placed on the beater head, this adds attack. When mixed, the phase is reversed on the one mic.

TIPS
✓ Remove the rear skin to get a full, rich sound with lots of attack. A pillow or a blanket against the beater head makes the attack tighter. Boosting EQ at 2.5 kHz provides additional punch.
✓ Aim the mic downward if it picks up too much of the snare drum.
✓ A mic with figure-of-eight characteristics located inside the drum picks up both the impact from the beater head and reverberations from the front skin.
✓ An additional mic on the beater head (next to the foot pedal) provides definition, but it might also pick up the snare drum, which then has to be removed using a gate. If the snare track is fed into the key chain so that the gate closes on the snare attacks, this will work well except when the snare hits at the same time as the bass drum, in which case the gate must be turned off in such passages.

Figure 2.3

The Yamaha Subkick on the bass drum; a resonator device capturing the low-end frequencies. Here, it is used together with an AKG D112 (in the hole of the drum head). © Yamaha Corp.

The Snare Drum

The snare drum requires a mic able to cope with very high sound pressure levels. Normally, a dynamic cardioid mic is placed at the edge of and 5–10 cm above the skin, angled so that it picks up as little sound as possible from the rest of the kit. Close to the outer edge, there are more overtones (great for jazz and acoustic music), while a muscular rock snare (with powerful bottom end) is the result when aiming the mic toward the center of the snare.

One of the most commonly used microphones is the Shure SM57, but alternatives are increasingly used, for example the Sennheiser 441, Audix i5, and Audio Technica ATM650. Even the AKG C414 is used; being a condenser, this mic picks up more of the other drums. However, it provides a more nuanced sound, making the spill from the other drums useful as depth in the mix.

Figure 2.4
Two mics on the snare. In addition to the classic Shure SM57 there is a Royer R-101 ribbon on the side of the snare. Ribbon mics have a figure-of-eight pattern and capture almost nothing from the sides (called a "null"). Such a mic, therefore, is placed so that the hi-hat is exactly in the null and thus is not recorded onto the snare track. A cardioid does not have a null; its back is less sensitive, though, and it has a nonlinear frequency response. © Royer Labs

✓ The snares (the rattling metal wires along the bottom head) are best captured at the outer edge of the snare drum.

✓ Alternatively, place a second mic beneath the bottom head to capture more of the snares, as this will brighten up the sound. Use a condenser, as it reproduces the overtones better. Remember to reverse the phase of the bottom mic, as it catches sound in opposite phase to the top mic.

✓ A light towel over the snare drum may provide a tighter sound; to compensate, boost its attack in the 4–6 kHz range.

✓ A piece of cardboard of about 15 × 15 cm might dampen some of the spill from the hi-hat. Make a hole in the middle and wrap it around the mic 4–5 cm behind its membrane.

✓ A snare drum tuned higher is usually easier to position in the mix, while a lower-tuned drum overlaps with, and risks being drowned by, the other instruments of the rhythm section.

✓ If the snare drum recording is too thin-sounding, the track itself can be re-recorded and the two tracks then mixed. Send the snare recording to a small monitor (e.g., an Auratone) placed on the snare head pointing down. The level of the playback determines how much the snare will resonate. Record this with a good condenser microphone and use it in the mix to add definition and fullness.

✓ An old Abbey Road technique: record the snare drum with a Neumann 87 placed 40–60 cm above the snare drum. Then add hard compression through an UREI-type compressor (this is often done on a separate mixer channel, i.e., as parallel compression), thus providing plenty of richness, depth from the rest of the kit, and ambience from the room.

✓ Pitch shift can tune the snare drum up slightly (or down), placing it better in the mix. Always add a bit of reverb too.

The Hi-Hat

Most of the time, there is more than enough hi-hat in the overhead tracks and, through spill, on the snare mic. If the sound of the hi-hat is important (and to be edited separately), try to screen its mic from the snare drum sound (without restricting the mobility of the drummer). Avoid placing it so that the air flow is picked up by the microphone when the hi-hat closes. Placement is best at a distance of 15–30 cm, pointing between the edge and the center of the hi-hat at a 45° angle, and a supercardioid captures less of the snare drum.

Figure 2.5

Above the hi-hat is an AKG c451b and, below, a DPA 4011. © DPA Microphones

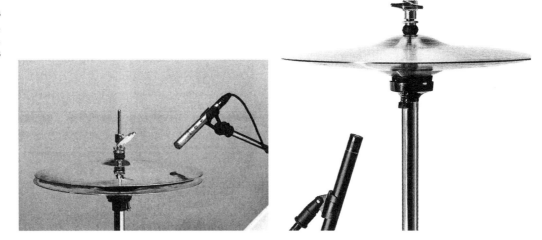

Select the microphone that best captures the required sound. A condenser can be selected for its purity and detail, for example, an AKG C451 or Shure SM81, while dynamic microphones provide more gritty highs that might fit when a thrashy midrange is the aim. Ribbon mics attenuate the aggressive midrange and the sharp highs and provide ample opportunity for later EQing.

TIPS

✓ The spill from the hi-hat to the other mics often causes problems. A screen can be set up supported by the microphone stand so that the hi-hat's sound is dampened relative to the other mics.

✓ Do not make a low cut until the mix, at which point it is easier to determine how much should be cut from the low-frequency spill coming from the other drums.

The Toms

For the toms, dynamic cardioid or supercardioid microphones are most often used, and, being dynamics, they also have the best chances of surviving direct hits from the sticks. The mics are placed at the top edge of each skin, or just one between the two toms (see the right in figure 2.6), 5–10 cm above and angled so that they capture the least spill from the rest of the kit.

Figure 2.6
Sennheiser 421
pictured inside the
tom and between
two toms.

27

If a cardioid microphone is raised 25 cm (or more) above the heads, the rumble of the proximity effect is avoided, but, in return, more spill from the other drums is captured. The Sennheiser MD421 is the most used mic for the toms, but the Audix D2 and D4, Audio Technica ATM25, and Shure Beta 56/57 are all equally suitable while being different in tonal character. Alternatively, most large diaphragm mics can be used to capture a more detailed sound.

TIPS
- ✓ Remove the bottom skins and place the microphone inside the drum (see the left in figure 2.6). This provides good isolation from the spill from other drums but with slightly less attack.
- ✓ Remember to eliminate rattling from loose bolts on the toms before recording. Likewise, mic stands touching the drums may ruin a good recording.
- ✓ A figure-of-eight microphone can be placed between two toms, capturing the toms and almost nothing from the snare and hi-hat because of the null characteristics at the mic's sides.

The Overhead Mics

OH mics are used for capturing cymbals and the entirety of the drum kit. They are placed right above, behind, or in front of the drum kit at different heights. In jazz and acoustic music, the OH mics are particularly important and, together with a microphone on the bass drum and an optional mic on the snare, are all that is needed, because they provide a natural balance over the entire kit (albeit with a remote and thin-sounding bass drum).

Figure 2.7
DPA d:dicate 4011. Cardioid mics used as OH mics. This setup is called spaced stereo. © DPA microphones

Small diaphragm mics are often used (Neumann KM184, Røde NT5, Audio-Technica AT4041, DPA 4009, Oktava MK012, and AKG C-451B), but the AKG 414 also perfectly fulfills the OH mic role.

The location of the mics should be where they sound best in the room (ranging in height from 40 to 100 cm above the tom height). The distance makes a great difference: close placement provides a tight and punchy sound; further away, a more open and ambient sound. With high ceilings, the mics have to be placed higher (and vice versa), because the early reflections (see p. 198) from the ceiling create comb filter effects. The various stereo configurations (see p. 141) are all proven stereo techniques, each with its strengths and limitations in capturing the entirety of the kit. Spaced omnis or cardioids are the most commonly used configurations, because they are easily positioned relative to the cymbals.

TIPS

✓ The X-Y setup (see p. 145) is a good start, because it does not create phase problems between the two OH mics.

✓ With the spaced omni (or cardioid; see p. 142), it is easy to control the width of the stereo image. Here, it is important to place them so that they sound good together with the snare mic.

✓ Two condenser mics on each side of the drums—pointing toward the floor—can be used to capture a full and broad image of the entire drum kit with only a relatively small part of the cymbals.

✓ The ABBA drum sound was nearly always only bass drum and snare drum. Producer Michael Tretow did not use OH mics. Instead, he placed two PZM boundary mics (see p. 61) on the floor in front of the kit, pointing upward. These mics capture the fullness of the bass drum and toms but only a little of the cymbals.

✓ If the objective is the sound of a jazz kit in a small club, you have to put the drums in a slightly dampened room and reduce the mic setup down to the OH mics, one mic on the snare, and one on the bass drum.

Figure 2.8
Producer Bruce Swedien uses two Royer R-122 ribbons as OH mics. There is also an R-122 on the ride cymbal and the hi-hat. On toms is a Neumann U87 and on snare a Shure SM57. © Royer Labs

The Cymbals

The cymbals are usually captured by the OH mics. If the microphones are to only pick up the cymbals, place one on each cymbal (if possible pointing from below, as this will screen off everything else). Condenser mics best reproduce the rich sound of the cymbals, and the most percussive sound is to be found near the bell, while further out the after-ringing is more pronounced. Remember, clean the tracks of unwanted material or automate Mute Track when not in use. In particular, it is important that the snare is removed in this cleaning process in order to avoid phase problems.

Room Mics

Room mics color the drum kit with room acoustics (ambience), and they are placed behind, in front of, or beside the drum kit, sometimes at several meters' distance. Room mics add a richer and more live sound if used judiciously to spice up the mix. The location is determined by the space and by personal preference, so experiment by moving the microphone while wearing headphones. Unusual locations, such as an adjacent room, below or inside a grand piano, and so forth, might contribute to that huge drum sound you have in mind.

For this type of room mic, you can use a single condenser microphone (omnis capture more acoustics and provide deeper bottom; cardioids are directional). However, with two microphones (stereo), a wider, more spacious sound is captured. Often, it is easiest to place a few around the space and then use the most suitable.

If a room mic needs to capture fullness, then place it in front of or behind the kit and just 20–30 cm above the floor to capture mostly the bass drum, toms, and the snare. When placed close to the floor, it picks up more early reflections, thus enhancing the low frequencies; when emphasized with EQ and hard compression in the mix, this adds power and energy to the drums.

Advanced Mic Setups

Glyn Johns (an engineer at Abbey Road Studios) developed a particular microphone setup consisting of one microphone above the center of the drum kit, between the tom and snare drum, and one meter above the drum heads. Another microphone is placed 20–30 cm away from the floor tom, pointing across its top toward the hi-hat. The two microphones should have the same distance to the snare drum's center (which you can measure quickly with a mic cable). Then, all that is needed is to add a microphone on the bass drum and another on the snare drum to get a great drum sound.

The Holy Trinity is a second approach that uses only three microphones. The main mic is a ribbon just above the drummer's head capturing the entire kit as the drummer hears it. This microphone is compressed hard using an 1176-type compressor (which is capable of hard compression without completely strangling the attacks from the drumsticks) so that it sucks up the entire kit sound together with the ambience of the room. A condenser mic can also be used, as this one mic is capable of capturing a large amount of the kit. Finally, two mics are added to the cymbals (OH mics), and it is important that they have the same distance to the main microphone (measured with a mic cable). If you get the balance between the three mics right, you have the Holy Trinity, capturing the entire kit. This can optionally be complemented with a microphone on the bass drum.

Mix Settings and Effects

EQ

EQ is used to position each of the drums in the mix, but, here too the rule applies that the less equalization—both during recording and mixing—the more dynamic the sound. The extent of EQing, of course, will depend on the specific drum kit used, acoustics, microphones, and the recording technique, but in the following you will find some general recommendations.

The Bass Drum

The bass drum has its deep end in the 40–80 Hz range (sub-bass)—the frequencies that you feel physically in the chest and abdomen at live concerts.

A specialized plug-in is often used on the bass drum to enhance the sub-bass in the range below 60 Hz and to position it relative to the bass (in Logic it is called the Sub Bass—the Sony Transient Modulator and SPL Transient Designer do the same and more). Fullness is found between 80 and 250 Hz.

It is quite common to cut a few dB (medium Q) around 200–600 Hz where muddiness tends to build up.

Often, a cut between 100 and 200 Hz is needed in order to make space for the bass guitar.

The upper midrange provides definition for the attacks (2–4 kHz).

The bass drum EQ varies considerably depending on the genre and the trends of the time. For example, in the dance genre, the bass drum is boosted at 200–300 Hz and also compressed hard to enhance the dry and cardboard-like character popular in this genre. Along with a low cut, this creates space for the synth bass, which in the dance genre is always deeper than the bass drum. In the metal genres, by contrast, the bass drum is allocated lots of sub-bass and attack.

The Snare Drum

The snare drum preferably should be recorded so that it requires only a little bottom end (a 2–4 dB boost at 100–300 Hz) and a little high-mid (4–6 kHz) to provide clarity and definition in the mix with perhaps an attenuation around 500–700 Hz. The open sound is captured mainly by a microphone placed below the snare. It is important that the tone of the snares—the skin, the tuning, and the quantity of ambience—is dealt with before recording, as these parameters can only be changed to a small extent with EQ.

If the snare mic is boosted at 3–4 kHz, this will also increase the spill from the hi-hat.

Where previously gates were used to remove spill from other drums, with the DAW it has become common to clean up the tracks manually or to use gate-like tools such as Strip Silence. The gate on the snare track is set up with a threshold so that it only opens up on the snare hits, while the more distant (and weaker) drums do not surpass the threshold. The setup can be improved by means of a side chain (see p. 246). Gate techniques only work if the drummer mainly plays on the 2 and 4 beats; on the softer beats and dynamic fills this will not work. A (cumbersome) alternative is to clean the snare track manually, but the hits on the hi-hat that coincide with snare hits will still remain, and, in this case, subsequent EQing and the like will affect the hi-hat sound. The result is the hi-hat changing its tone and level on every snare hit.

An expander, which increases the difference between the weakest and the strongest recorded signal, provides a more organic result when dealing with spill (see p. 106). But in any case the best solution is to reduce the spill to the snare mic early on during recording through careful placement of the microphone.

The Hi-Hat

The hi-hat is equalized so that not only its own sound sounds right but also that of the snare drum that spills onto the same track. To this end, everything below 150 Hz can be cut away with a high-pass filter. However, when the drummer is using the hi-hat pedal, a very useful punch is found in the 200 Hz area.

The hi-hat sound is very genre-dependent too:

*   Nice, brilliant highs between 7 and 12 kHz in pop productions.
*   Rattling midrange around 2–4 kHz in guitar rock.
*   A slightly nasal EQ between 1.5 and 4 kHz on the hi-hat in the dance genres.

The Toms

The toms have fullness (fundamentals) at 120–250 Hz (floor toms, however, are slightly lower at 60–120 Hz) and attacks around 5–8 kHz.

In the range from 400 Hz to 1.5 kHz, a cut is often made to remove the all-too frequent sound that is a bit like someone hitting a cardboard box.

Toms frequently ring, and so in order to both have an in-your-face presence when they play and avoid this ringing when the other drums in the kit are hit, the solution might be to only open up the track on the DAW when the toms are being played. Sometimes, however, a complete mute of the tom tracks can create the effect of a drum machine sound on the other drums. Accordingly, automating the levels of the tom tracks might be better. First, find the level where they add fullness and depth to the mix without the ringing being heard. Then find their level when the drums are playing; it is then simple to set the levels of automation on the tom tracks based on the waveforms.

Overhead Mics

OH mics need only be equalized to a limited extent if good condenser mics have been used. EQing the OH mics should contribute specifically to the snare sound. The bottom end below 200 Hz should often be boosted by a few dBs, and any rumbling and muddy sound can be cut away at 200–400 Hz so that the whole becomes more transparent. A few dB with narrow Q at 8 kHz will open up the kit, and high-shelf EQ from 12 kHz adds air, but be careful, since cymbals easily become sharp or thin when you are boosting the mid and high frequencies.

Box 2.3

See chapter 19, "EQ and Instruments," for more suggestions on EQing the drums.

Compression

Drums and compressors are in a permanent love-hate relationship. On the one hand, compression adds punch and presence; on the other, it soon destroys the subtle transients generated by the attacks.

Compression always modifies the natural dynamics, especially those of the acoustic instruments. This can be addressed to a certain extent by setting the compressor attack so that the transients pass through uncompressed—that is, use a slow attack.

In addition, set the release so that the compressor releases before the next attack. This is particularly important for the snare drum, which will sound like a cardboard box if compressed on the attack.

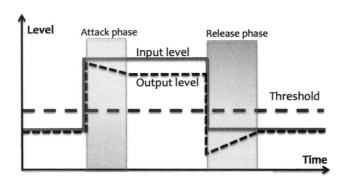

Figure 2.9
The effect of compression. The short-dashed line (red on the companion website) shows the output after compression, the solid line (green on the companion website) the input. Attack and release take place over time as the signal goes over and then below the threshold.

For the snare, there are basically three scenarios for the attack and release times:

1. A fast attack and fast release, the effect being that the transients are compressed (flattened out) while the compression releases before the snare sound ends. Therefore, the tail of the sound, the decay, is not boosted by the compressor gain makeup.
2. Fast attack and slow release times, the effect being that transients are compressed (flattened out) as with 1 above but the compression continues until the snare sound ends. The tail is thus relatively stronger and the sound is sustained.
3. Longer attack and slow release times, the effect being that (a part of) the transients slip through before compression takes place. Since the tail is compressed, the difference in level between the transient and the rest of the sound is increased.

Generally, medium to slow attack and slow or medium release (depending on the rhythm and tempo) is used for the drums. This means that the sustain and decay levels will be raised up toward the next attack, providing a fuller sound while preserving the attacks and transients to some extent.

The dynamics of the snare will survive a fast attack at 4–10 ms, a quick release at 200 ms, and a maximum ratio of 4:1. If the attack is increased to 15–20 ms and the release reduced to 40–60 ms, compression takes place over the richer-sounding part of the snare; this sounds good but is difficult to use to advantage in the mix, since the transients are so powerful that the gain makeup cannot be raised.

Compression works fine on a mic placed under the snare, where it is shielded from the hi–hat spill.

On the bass drum, compression can generally be used without problems—if the track does not contain too much spill (which must be removed with a gate or Strip Silence)—making it defined and solid and also longer and fuller sounding. Start with a 3:1 ratio and a medium to slow attack of 40–80 ms. If the bass drum has to sit right up in the front and at the same time have a substantial decay, then increase to a 6:1 ratio and a faster attack.

On the OH track, only a mild compression of 2–3 dB, set to slow release (80–150 ms) and medium to slow attack (30–60 ms), should be used to make the attacks a little more present and the timbre slightly wider by sucking up the acoustic ambience.

The cymbals are even more sensitive to compression. Because of their long decays, they react relatively strongly to compression, and therefore compression should be avoided unless the cymbals are part of the OH tracks.

If you go for an in-your-face drum sound, parallel bus compression is normally better. In this case, you only need to compress very slightly on the individual tracks so that they preserve their dynamics and attacks.

Parallel Bus Compression

If you want the benefits of compression—density, sustain, and an in-your-face sound—without destroying the natural dynamics of the drums, parallel bus compression (also called drum bus compression) is the tool.

A parallel bus is a copy of the drums being played in parallel with the original track. It is set up by busing the drums via a send (set to unity gain for each track send) to an aux channel. Normally, the overhead tracks are omitted in order to avoid the compression making the cymbals pump. Insert the compressor on the aux channel; if possible, use an 1176-type compressor. Compress the drums very hard in order to suck up the sustain and the ambience picked up from the room by the microphones.

Figure 2.10

The 1176 compressor is particularly suitable for the parallel bus because it has almost no sound of its own. It does not attenuate the treble like most compressors do, and it smooths out the signal without completely destroying the attacks—a real benefit for the snare drum. Shown here is the Universal Audio plug-in. © Universal Audio

The aux channel is added to the mix, so that it brings substance and power to the original, dynamic drum kit; sometimes the drum bus can even be the main drum sound. Using a good compressor also adds harmonic distortion, which contributes to a fuller sound in addition to an increased sustain.

Drum bus compression also works on drum loops, especially those recorded in a studio with good acoustics.

▶ Audio example 02.01e demonstrates the effect of parallel bus compression on the drum kit.

Box 2.4

Read more about setting up parallel bus compression on p. 178.

TIPS

✓ The TG, the SSL bus compressor, the Teletronix LA-2A Silver, and 1176 compressors are all suitable for drums. Likewise, the Fatso Sr. compressor (and its digital modeling) is suitable because of its attenuation of the top end (kill the cymbals), making for a smooth and full sound.

✓ An alternative to using the gate to eliminate spill between the drums is an expander, which increases the difference between the weakest and the strongest signal. A well-chosen threshold and a high ratio (over 8:1) will reduce the spill without the side effects that come from gating, since the expander does not cut attacks and decays away. The gate merely reduces the weak signals (spill) and enhances the more powerful drum signal. Fast attack settings cause a sudden attenuation, while slow attack settings make for a softer feel. Fast release times provide an effective elimination of spill.

✓ Gating the bass drum with fast attack and release will change the envelope (ADSR, see p. 175) and completely alter the dynamics of the bass drum. This also tightens the bass range, creating more space for the bass guitar.

✓ Make a copy of the snare drum. While the original track is EQed to the desired sound, the copy track is boosted strongly in the 1 kHz range and given heavy compression. When added discreetly to the mix, this provides definition and, if exaggerated, aggression.

Reverb

Close-miking is used to separate each of the drums in the kit and removes the acoustics that are usually perceived as part of their sound. But even such dry drums must blend or merge with one another and the other instruments in the mix. The acoustics are captured by the OH and room mics in a great sounding room, but occasionally you can get by using reverb to restore some of the acoustics.

Reverb need not be clearly heard. In the first place, it works as the necessary glue that binds the drums together. Only if it is removed can you hear that it is missing, because the drums will sound small and boxy.

Reverb is usually only noticeable on the snare and toms. Plate reverb provides bite and definition and is virtually indispensable, for example, in those slow songs characterized by lots of reverb. Plenty of great reverb units and plug-ins are available, and sometimes even a mediocre reverb will make it, one example being Pro Tool's D-verb, which in itself sounds awful but will make drums sit well in the mix.

For a dry drum sound, an ambience reverb is sufficient. The room reverb is more perceptible, yet discreet, since the drums are still felt close by. The hall reverb places the drums in a larger location such as a stadium, because the long reverb tails (i.e., long reverb times) give a feeling of distance.

If a distinct snare reverb is needed, it is best to make a copy of the snare track and strip everything but the snare away from the track. This track is taken out of the stereo bus and only used as a send to the reverb unit. This is done by fully turning down the volume of the stripped track and then setting the reverb send to pre-fader.

The great classic (rock) drum sound cannot be created using reverb alone. The powerful drums found on Audioslave's *Revelations* (2007) are the combination of an ambient recording space, compression sucking up the ambience (OH and room mics), and reverb added to the mix. The same applies in varying degrees to the drum sound found on the recordings of Nirvana, Rage Against the Machine, Pearl Jam, Soundgarden, and so on—all of them bands that have developed the sound that started with the ambient drums recorded by Led Zeppelin.

Box 2.5

See chapter 24, "Ambience and Reverb," for more on the reverb types and their uses.

Drum Sampling

EQing reduces the dynamics of music and adds resonances to some extent in the boundary frequencies. This happens particularly when using additive EQ (boosting); subtractive EQ (attenuation) is less destructive to the dynamics and is therefore recommended whenever possible (read more p. 162).

Rather than EQing a drum track to death, it is better to fatten up thin drums using samples. One approach is to sample the drums individually when recording in order to have some quality samples to replace the less good ones with. The advantage is that they will have the same ambience as the rest of the recording, and therefore they will blend well. If it comes to a limited number of indistinct bass drum beats, the samples can be placed manually by zooming in on the waveform until you can see where to place them. In the same way, imprecise beats can be shifted into place.

Always remember to maintain the original length of the track. When copy-pasting on the sample level, be sure to paste in the exact number of samples being cut out. If they do not match, the timing of the following material is offset. You will get used to remembering strange numbers like 34,682 or 786,421 samples.

World renowned mix stars such as Chris Lord-Alge and Bob Clearmountain use samples to improve the bass drum in most of the songs they mix. The objective is consistency and a tight bottom end—and a good sample sounds better than EQing and compressing an inferior recording. If samples are added to the original drums, pay attention to double-hits and flanger-like effects due to inaccurate placing.

Replacing the snare drum is a lot more demanding. In simple pop and rock songs, dominated by a regular 2 and 4 snare beat, it can be done, but in most other rhythmic genres the snare has greater variation. With such a varying velocity and drum pattern, the same snare sample cannot be used all the way through the song without making the drumming less dynamic and thus sterile. And since the snare changes timbre with the strength of the impact, the problem cannot be addressed by boosting or reducing levels.

Only in the hip-hop and dance genres are the same samples used throughout a song, providing the special synthetic sound that is evident when, for example, a sixteenth-note snare swirl is gradually turned up.

The economic costs—a large studio with variable acoustics—and the difficulty of attaining an increasingly sophisticated drum sound means that many choose to completely replace the recorded drums with sampled drums in the mix. In the DAW, there are a number of tools that will identify each drum event in the track and replace it with a sample from a library. Often, the samples are added on top of the original recording, thus providing a richer and more powerful mix. Drumagog, Slate Drums, Sound Replacer, and so forth maintain the timing and dynamics of the acoustic drums they replace if the threshold (which determines when a sound event will trigger a sample) is set precisely in relation to the strength of the recorded acoustic drums.

Audio Quantizing

Just as the drums can be replaced with samples, they can also be quantized, so that all of the beats are placed precisely in relation to the DAW's tempo grid.

Beat Detective, Drum Rehab, and the like are the updated version of the click track from the 1980s and 1990s and have the same advantages and disadvantages. They provide an immediately stunning and completely tight rhythm section, but in the long run it often becomes a little boring because it robs (good) musicians of some of their character and personality. Placed exactly in a metric grid, the timing becomes perfect but also predictable. Such tools destroy the interaction between musicians by chopping up the music into uniform slices, and so the music loses some of its verve, especially if the rhythm section is capable of excellent ensemble playing.

With an imprecise drummer who does not keep the beat well, however, audio quantizing is a great tool for reducing this human element. Although the musicians may be less proud of it, it is beneficial to those who have to listen to the recording repeatedly. Here, there are probably some elements of musical listening habits at stake: if you are used to listening to the interplay and synergy of the music, over-editing will destroy human variations, so that the music takes on a mechanical character, but to people who are used to DAW-produced synth- and sample-based music, this may be just fine.

3

The Bass Guitar

The Instrument

In recordings with rhythm sections, the bass guitar lays the foundations of the sound image and provides both the harmonic and rhythmic pulse: together with the drums, the bass represents the backbone of a song. Often, it is prominent in the groove of a song (for example, in funk music) and sometimes the bass even plays a melodic or contrapuntal line (such as Paul McCartney's bass in many of the Beatles' songs).

For the bass, it is particularly important that you make clear which role it plays in the musical arrangement.

Frequently, the bass is part of the background, merely the foundation that sits under the other instruments in the mix, but if the bass is funky and foregrounded, the other instruments should provide space for the bass, and its sound should be completely different.

A Motown-inspired bass guitar should be played with flat-wound strings and fingers, while the use of a pick emphasizes attack transients and makes it easier to make the bass come forward in a busy rock mix. To help, the bass can be supplemented by a synth bass played through an amplifier.

As with most other instruments, good sound is achieved when sound and playing style fuse together. Even the same instrument and the very same amplifier do not always sound the same when played by different musicians, because the musicians' playing styles can be very different: velocity, duration, where the string is plucked, the interaction between the instrument and amplifier, and so on.

Mic or DI?

It can be straightforward to record great bass sound simply by connecting the instrument to the mixer using a DI (direct input) box (see box 4.1). A DI performs amplitude level matching and minimizes noise and distortion. The DI adjusts the high-impedance output of the bass to a low-impedance microphone input and, at the same time, converts it to a balanced signal (usually via an XLR connector).

In most digital audio interfaces, a hi-Z input replaces the DI, and the bass can be connected directly to this. A bass with active pickups (battery) makes the DI redundant.

Compared to using a microphone, DI recording benefits from a clean and dynamic sound that is easy to shape in the mix. DI recording responds well to compression and EQ and accurately reproduces the timbre and character of the instrument. DI also provides more sub-bass than most microphone setups.

Of course, if the bass speaker is part of the required bass sound, there is no getting around using the microphone to catch it.

The setup is similar to that used for recording the electric guitar, but where the guitar speaker reproduces frequencies from 100 Hz to 5 kHz, the bass goes both lower and higher (for instance, slap bass attack transients). The bass speaker, unlike guitar speakers, is not designed to completely roll off the high frequencies; it only reduces grittiness above 6–8 kHz, while the guitar speakers typically roll off from approximately 2.5 kHz.

Both condenser and dynamic microphones can be used on the bass speaker, but as long as they provide a good reproduction of the sub-bass area, most mics work well. Microphone placement is the same as for the guitar (see p. 45), though a little more distance from the speaker front (15–40 cm) will give more fullness. In placing the mic close to the center of the speaker cone, more top and therefore definition is captured. Moving towards the outer edge, more body and fullness is captured, but also less in-your-face dynamics.

The Electro Voice RE20 mic (see figure 3.1) is widely used in front of the bass speaker. Equally, a Shure Beta 52 or Sennheiser MD421 (see the right in figure 3.2) provides a good solution, but they must be placed close to the speaker front to catch the low end, as these microphones are designed with a roll-off of the low frequencies to compensate for their proximity effect. This applies to most dynamic vocal microphones that have a cardioid characteristic.

If you happen to have a Neumann U47 microphone in the closet, good for you; generally, large diaphragm condenser microphones (LDC; see p. 123) cover the low frequencies with ease and have an open sound as well. However, if the amp is blasting away at maximum volume, condenser microphones might have difficulties dealing with the sound pressure.

Figure 3.1

Frequency response shown for Electro Voice RE20. Very unusually for a cardioid, it has virtually no proximity effect and hence reproduces linearly down to 60 Hz. © Electro-Voice

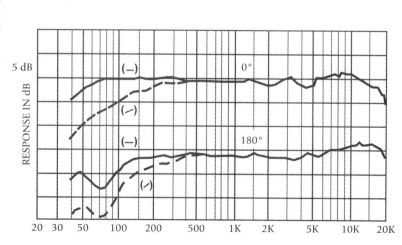

Microphones designed specifically for the bass drum are usually suitable—for example the AKG D112—but do try them out. They are nonlinear and so are prone to emphasizing a certain frequency range.

Never use the low cut of the microphone; if it is necessary to clean up the bottom end, wait until the mix, where a low cut on the bass track is often made below the microphone's cut-off frequency.

Or Both?

Often the microphone recording is combined with a DI recording. This is done by taking a line out from the bass amp or by splitting the signal between the bass amp and a preamp. In this way, the bass is recorded on two separate tracks, making it easier to achieve a rich, distinct, and dynamic bass sound. The preamp provides definition and sub-bass, while the microphone provides color and body and, often, a more dirty sound that might help to define the bass in the mix.

 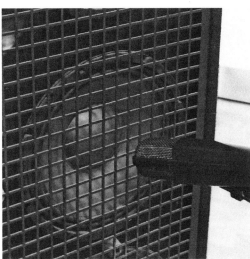

Figure 3.2
A Royer R-101 ribbon mic and a Sennheiser 421—both angled toward the outer edge of the speaker. © Royer Labs

There will be a slight delay between the DI and the microphone track depending on the distance between microphone and speaker. If the microphone is 34 cm from the speaker, the delay will be approximately 1 ms. Although this may not be enough to produce an audible effect, it causes comb filtering at certain frequencies. The solution is to move the waveform of the mic recording slightly forward in time (to the left in the DAW) so that its peaks and troughs match those of the DI waveform.

Virtual Amps

A third option is to use the digital models of (physical) bass amps and speakers. Line 6 Bass Pod, Johnson J Station, and several others are quite convincing virtual bass amps imitating the sound characteristics of real-world amps and speakers. Because they also allow you to combine different speakers, microphones, and so on, this means that it is easy to select the bass sound that suits the arrangement. Often, this ability to combine more than compensates for their shortcomings compared to the hardware they emulate.

Used as a plug-in in a DAW, the virtual amp can be fed with a DI signal so that the perfect bass amp (the right speaker, microphone, etc.) that best matches the song can be configured while mixing.

Virtual amps use a speaker simulator to mimic the high-frequency roll-off taking place in the speaker. A great simulator will remove high-frequency grittiness without killing attack transients, and this sounds more natural than EQing.

Mix Settings and Effects

Compression

The bass guitar illustrates perfectly why compression—reduction of the dynamic range— works so well in recordings:

- The bass is a very dynamic instrument.
- Uneven plucking is strongly reinforced by DI recording.
- Certain playing techniques, such as slap bass or pulling, result in individual notes being overemphasized.
- Many speaker cabinets (when mic recording) produce resonances.

Without compression, some notes would stand too forward in the mix, while others would be too weak. Compression is used to even out unwanted variations in level so that the plucking becomes more consistent. Compression also foregrounds the bass sound in the mix because it increases the average energy level in the bass track and makes it fuller without its overall level being raised.

A medium compression ratio of 3:1 is the starting point. In addition, use an attack of 20–30 ms to let the attack transients through and a short release adjusted to the tempo of the song. The release can be as high as 200–300 ms. The auto setting automatically adjusts release according to the dynamic fluctuations of the recording, and in most compressors it is excellent on most bass-playing techniques.

Sometimes it is necessary to insert a limiter right after the compressor, as attack transients might overload the signal path. The threshold of the limiter is set to just below 0 dB.

Often, the bass is compressed during recording—if you do this, do so only slightly in order to leave room to add more compression later. If the compression is postponed to the mix process, it is still appropriate to use a limiter during recording in order to protect against overdriving the input.

Box 3.1

See chapter 21, "Compressor/Limiter and Expander/Gate," for more tips on using the compressor.

When recording using a microphone, less compression is needed when mixing as speakers naturally compress dynamic fluctuations. EQ'ing may become easier too since, for example, a tube preamp often provides bass fullness and distinct overtones.

EQ

The bass often requires extensive equalizing in order to fit into the overall mix. Unlike vocals or an acoustic guitar, bass guitars and bass synths are not acoustic sounds. Therefore, we have no fixed preconceptions of how they should sound, and you are free to attenuate the wrong frequencies and boost the good ones far too much.

Many engineers prefer to let the bass guitar be the only instrument that is "on the move" from 80 Hz and down. The reason for this is that you tend to physically feel the sub-bass area, in which there are typically only two elements: the bass guitar as movement and variation and the bass drum as rhythm pattern. Therefore, the role of the bass guitar in relation to the bass drum must be clear: either above or below, so they do not fight each other in the same frequency range.

Crucial EQ areas in relation to the bass are:

- The range from 40 to 350 Hz, which includes the frequencies that define the body of the bass.
- The 150–400 Hz range, which is often of concern and where you might have to make a cut in order to avoid overlaps with other instruments and a boomy and undefined sound.
- The range from 700 Hz to 1.5 kHz, which contains attack and definition. If boosted, this will make the attack more audible (and imprecise attacks more evident too).
- Around 2.5 kHz where the buzzing from the strings can be attenuated or highlighted.

It is wise to check the raw mix on a small home system or car stereo (without subwoofer) to see if the bass sound still works. The 41.2 Hz tone from the low E string sounds impressive on big studio monitors, but it might be inaudible on small speakers. If the bass is to translate well on all systems, there must be a fair amount of energy in both the 40–80 Hz and 100–350 Hz ranges.

Distortion

Bass players often use tube amplifiers to add musically pleasant distortion at high gain levels (harmonic distortion). A bass track recorded with DI often benefits from tube emulation (i.e., a plug-in) because the (often subtle) distortion helps to make the bass stand out in the mix and adds character; place a tube plug-in before the speaker simulator (which will remove the grainy part of the distortion). Tube compressors and limiters also add character and body to the bass, but if you want to go for the sound of the Stranglers' bass, an overdrive or distortion pedal will do the job.

Effects like chorus or flanging are used with the bass as well—occasionally while recording, but usually not until the mix. Other effects, like the octave effect, are more special, and it is used to create the unique sound of Peter Gabriel's "Sledgehammer."

Reverb is rarely used with bass and only sparsely if not in a solo or as a special effect.

44

Box 3.2

Traditionally, the bass is recorded after the drums, and it is often tempting to make the bass sound massive to serve as the foundation of a rock song only to discover that when the guitars are recorded, the kick and bass are taking up all the space. This makes the guitars sound small and eventually can lead to the recording of extra guitar tracks in the mix, with the result that the instruments are competing for space. Try to avoid tinkering with the bass sound in this way during the recording process.

Most songs on the Foo Fighters *In Your Honor* were recorded in layers. Drums were recorded while playing to a rough version of the tune, and then guitars and vocals were added. Unusually, bass was laid down last in order allow the bass to adapt to the whole song, and its sound was tailored to fill the hole left between the kick drum and the guitars.

TIPS

✓ Always use new strings for a distinct and brilliant tone.

✓ Smaller spaces create standing waves (see p. 283), resulting in some notes sounding boomy. Move the speaker cabinet around the room to find the best-sounding location.

✓ The bass produces lower frequencies than most home sound systems can handle. A low cut from 30–50 Hz prevents the muddy and distorted sound that results from frequencies that the home speaker typically cannot reproduce.

✓ When the bass guitar is played through the bass amp and speakers, its highest frequency content is attenuated by the speaker. In DI recording, though, the noise from the fingers and strings may become annoying, and so a roll-off from 4–5 kHz will attenuate these higher frequencies and thus creates a tighter and fuller sound.

✓ If the bass is recorded with a microphone simultaneously with other instruments, it is important that the speaker level is reduced as much as possible in order to reduce spill into the other microphones. Low frequencies travel far and can never be completely removed using sound screens.

4

The Electric Guitar

The Instrument

The electric guitar is the central nervous system of rock music—one of the prerequisites of the music's aggressive and raw sound, used for many of its sound experiments, and thus a great part of the aesthetics of rock music.

In the mid-1950s, Chuck Berry gave the guitar a prominent role in rock 'n' roll and the Beatles and the Rolling Stones built on this sound. In the 1960s, Eric Clapton, Jeff Beck, Jimmy Page (all former Yardbirds guitarists), and Pete Townshend (the Who) gave the guitar the main role, while Jimi Hendrix made the guitar, it could be said, the soul of rock music.

While sound experiments flourished in the studio, guitarists started developing their individual sound, which was often associated with a specific amplifier and particular effects pedals, and which, along with the vocal, from the late 1960s strongly characterized the sound of a band. With digital modeling of amps, speakers, and so forth, the path mapped out by the furiously aggressive distortion pedal around 1967 has been completed, while the DAW itself presents new opportunities for editing and layering of guitar sound.

Mic Techniques

Figure 4.1
An SM57 and a Royer-101 ribbon mic angled toward the side of the speaker. Close-miking eliminates the acoustics. Alternatively, an SM57 is placed close and the R-101 at a greater distance. In both setups the Royer-101 can be replaced with a condenser mic or completely omitted (as in the picture to the right).

Figure 4.2

Pointed directly at the speaker center, the microphone picks up a bright and well-articulated sound. Angled 20–30° off-axis, it captures more fullness, and this frequency range increases with more angling toward the speaker edges.

Normally the guitar is recorded with a single dynamic mic placed close to the speaker and angled 20–30° away from the speaker center. The Shure SM57 is the most commonly used mic, but a Sennheiser 421, Audix i5, Beyer M88, or Audio Technica ATM650 will do the job just as well (although they add other nuances to the sound). Condenser mics capture not only more dynamics and a broader frequency range but also the gritty treble that then must be attenuated in the 4–6 kHz range.

Ribbon microphones provide a softer and fuller sound (often referred to as "warmer") due to their treble roll-off, removing the grittiness captured by a condenser mic. Since the ribbons always have figure-of-eight characteristics, they also capture the ambience of the room behind the microphone, and if this is unpleasant, a screen must be placed behind the mic. The closer cardioid and figure-of-eight microphones are placed to the sound source, the more proximity effect (see p. 131) there is, boosting within the 100–250 Hz range. The proximity effect often adds fullness and body to the recording, and without this guitar recordings tend to sound thin. With many guitar tracks in a song, you must pay attention to bass buildup; multiple proximity effects may be too much, muddying the bottom end and blurring the other instruments that share the low frequencies.

Ambience and Acoustics

A little ambience picked up by the microphone opens up the sound of the guitar. One ambience mic (or more) placed from 40 cm to several meters from the speaker creates depth in the recording. A distinct ambience, though, recorded at some distance from the speaker can sound cold in the mix and will blur the sound. In most rooms, the ambience recorded at a distance of 30–60 cm from the speaker sounds best.

If the room does not sound right with the guitar, then drop the ambience mics and rely on reverb units, delay, and so on. A completely dampened room does not add anything, so it would be better to use the ambience of a bathroom or a basement room.

The ideal location of the ambience mic is found by moving it around until it sounds right with the close mic. The guitar has the main part of its sound between 200 Hz and 3 kHz, and so a few centimeters may be crucial to whether there will be phase problems (phase cancelation; see p. 272) due to the distance between the two microphones. Listen to both mic signals simultaneously (on headphones) while trying out different placements for the ambience mic.

Remember that distance creates depth; moving the ambience mic further away makes it pick up more reverberation.

Placed close to the floor, the ambience mic adds extra low frequency content too.

A third mic can also be used—sometimes placed behind the cabinet for a mellower sound (reverse the phase so that the two mic diaphragms picking up the speaker signal move in phase).

For the ambience mic, a condenser is the best choice. Few have access to a Neumann U67, so choose the fullest sounding mic (avoid mics that emphasize treble) that best captures the guitar sound you hear in the room. A good starting point is 60 cm from the speaker. At distances over 25–30 cm, no proximity effect is present with the cardioid, and some might sound a little thin. An omni picks up more bottom end (and more of the acoustics) than a cardioid.

If you want to keep all options open, it is fine to record several of the above mic setups and choose the best combination later.

Box 4.1 What Is DI Recording?

Audio interfaces and preamps often have a DI input to record electric guitar or bass directly to the DAW. This is often called a hi-Z input, because it adapts the high impedance output of the guitar pickups to the line level input.

While the XLR inputs of the preamp and the mixer only work with microphones, a DI box adapts the signal from the guitar pickup to the mic level inputs. Both the hi-Z input and the DI box convert the signal to line level (which can then be used by a DAW or an amplifier). (For more on signal levels, see chapter 34, "Levels and Meters.")

A few DI boxes with a very high impedance sound great by themselves if, for example, the clear sound of a Fender Strat is to be recorded. Steve Lukather's crystal-clear guitars on some Toto songs are recorded directly through a Demeter VTDB-2b Tube Direct.

Guitar Effects and Setup

The guitar is probably the most electronically manipulated instrument in recorded music history. Guitarists always base their sound on an amplifier with a character to their liking, combined with effects like chorus, flanger, reverb, delay, pitch, and tremolo.

Often, effects pedals are too noisy in a recording, and they must be replaced by studio effects. It is important to recreate the delay, chorus, and so forth accurately in the headphone mix, because normally they are part of the guitarist's playing style (such as a rhythmically vital delay or the modulating fluctuation from chorus). The effects are rarely recorded with the guitar, though, because they can be more accurately fine-tuned during mixing.

The guitar is often doubled on a new track. Since no one plays exactly the same way twice, it will make a fuller sound (even a deviation of 2–4 ms adds fullness), especially if you pan the tracks to either side of the stereo image.

▶ Audio example 04.01a demonstrates the effect of doubling the guitar.

The hard rock and heavy metal genres are rife with two or more guitars basically playing the same riffs. This is rarely done with clean (rhythm) guitars, and so tube overdrive is an essential part of this technique. When the guitars are panned in the stereo image, each using its own EQ and effects, this creates the impression of a wall of guitars. The phase shift obtained by such multiplication is very different from the electronic phase shift that takes place with the chorus effect (see p. 214). Chorus provides width but does so in a way that is softer and less dynamic; that is, it is less aggressive and therefore more suitable in soft rock and symphonic guitar chords.

⊚ Audio example 04.01b demonstrates the effect of chorus on doubled guitars.

Virtual Stacks and Re-amping

Figure 4.3

Little Labs PCP Distro is a three-way splitter able to distribute a guitar or bass signal to three different amps at a time.

Millennia TD-1 (*right*) is a splitter, a DI box, and a mic/line preamp. In addition, the TD-1 includes a re-amp option converting the recorded line signal to the Fender or Gibson guitar output level, so that a track can be sent to a guitar amp and re-recorded. The TD-1 sports a great-sounding EQ. © Little Labs © Millennia Media

An amp simulator makes it possible to change the sound of a guitar or bass recording later.

If the recording space (i.e., its size and acoustics) is unsuitable for ambience miking, a close mic complemented by a DI recording might do the job. The DI track can be used either to feed an amp simulator (plug-in) or for re-amping.

When using an amp simulator, two guitar tracks are recorded simultaneously:

1. Duplicate the guitar signal through a splitter (or a half-normalized jack in a patchbay).
2. Signal 1 is sent to the guitar amp and is recorded to track 1 as usual using a mic.
3. Signal 2 is sent to a DI box or preamp with a hi-Z input and is recorded to track 2. Make sure that the signal is completely clean and uncolored, because distortion cannot be removed later.

When mixing, track 2 is treated with an amp simulator plug-in (Line 6, Guitar Rig, Brainworx, Softube, Amplitube, etc.) or sent (via the output of the audio interface) to an external simulator. Mix this with track 1, and also experiment by delaying track 2 a few milliseconds (3–6 ms) to add extra body and fullness to the basic track 1. This sounds even better when the tracks are panned opposite each other.

This recording technique is called layering or stacking, and the DI track can easily be copied to yet another track using a different amp simulator plug-in so that the various layers of guitar complement each other. This is clearly the way to create a wall of guitars, but an overdriven guitar with lots of sustain can also be complemented with a crunchy or completely clean amp to add definition to a solo part when mixed in at a discreet level.

The advantage of guitar simulators and amp plug-ins is that they can be utilized to test sounds and textures that would otherwise be time consuming and require a lot of equipment and that would add quite a noise in an analog system. In the virtual world, they can be combined and intertwined with and without effects and so on. Though a plug-in does not sound or feel like an analog tube amp kicking off with maximum volume gains at 13 over the top, it can, in combination with a real amplifier, create a top-dollar sound. And you do not need a Mesa Boogie, Fender, Marshall, Bogner, or Engl taking up space in your home studio.

If you want the real thing, re-amping is the alternative. Track 2 is sent to a guitar amplifier, allowing the opportunity to create the exact sound that matches the song and to select the best microphone and the best placement before it is re-recorded and mixed with the first guitar track. This requires a re-amp device that converts the line signal of the DAW back to the instrument-level signal matching the guitar amp.

Mix Settings and Effects

EQ

A low-cut filter is normally used to reduce frequency content below 80–100 Hz to separate the electric guitar from the bass and the drums. Start at 50 Hz (with a relatively steep slope—12 dB per octave) and find the setting that makes the guitar more present in the mix without making its sound too thin.

The guitar has fullness (body) around 200–350 Hz. Add punch to trebly recordings in the 100–200 Hz area, but just as often the 120–250 Hz range should be attenuated to remove muddiness, because the guitar shares frequencies with many competing instruments in this area (vocal, bass, keyboard). A cut with a wide Q may remove the "veil" that can conceal the guitar within the rhythm section.

The 800 Hz range (the "honk" area; see p. 154) often has to be reduced by a few dB, while the range around 1.5 kHz should be opened up, especially on a clean rhythm guitar.

Between 1.5 and 4 kHz the attack of the guitar is found, the distinct sound that makes it stand out in the mix. Too much 2.5 Hz content, though, makes the sound cutting and nasal, and an attenuation here makes for a more rounded and polished sound.

A 5 kHz boost sounds excellent on the acoustic guitar but on the electric guitar makes for a thin sound; in this case, reducing the high area (5–10 kHz) allocates more space to the midrange and low-mid range (complementary EQ; see p. 163). To compensate for the reduced top end, add some brightness between 10 and 15 kHz.

In recordings with multiple guitar tracks, highlighting and attenuating these differently in the 1.5–4 kHz area creates space for them all.

Box 4.2

The lowest note of the guitar is the low E string, vibrating with a fundamental frequency of 82.41 Hz. The remaining open strings are A3 (110 Hz), D3 (146.83 Hz), G3 (196 Hz), B4 (246.94 Hz), and E4 (329.63 Hz). Overlapping frequencies with the vocals, bass, piano, and drums correspond roughly to the range between the D and G strings. The lowest strings of the full-bodied rhythm guitar playing in barre style (bar chords) often sound messy in the mix.

Compression

Compression is used sparsely on high gain or overdriven guitars, as they have already been compressed by the tubes of the guitar amp. Lightly distorted and crunchy guitars, though, may be beefed up by parallel compression. Make a copy of the track (or send it to an aux) and insert a compressor with a ratio of approximately 4:1. Blend this into the mix to create fullness in balance with the original track, thereby retaining the guitar dynamics.

The undistorted guitar, though, should be compressed, because it contains large dynamic fluctuations. An attack of 5 ms and a long release of 500 ms (adjusted to the song tempo/guitar rhythm) add a singing sustain to a crystal-clear Fender guitar. Used like this—as powerful compression with high ratio and/or low threshold—the guitar must

Box 4.3

The Teletronix LA-2A and LA-UA 610 are optical compressors controlled by a photocell producing a soft-knee compression (see p. 174), that is, a "soft" attack on the transients even if the attack is set relatively short. The Universal Audio LA-2 has a fixed attack of 10 ms, but the release is more crucial to its sound. Half of the release takes place in the first 60 ms while the remaining half occurs starting at 60 ms and up to 15 s, depending on how high the signal is set on the input (i.e., relative to the threshold).

Like the LA-3A (see p. 13), these compressors are optical compressors that color the signal—but this is exactly what makes them sought after for particular purposes. © Universal Audio

be monitored in the headphones during recording, because compression will affect the guitarist's playing technique. To this end, the Teletronix LA-2 and LA-3 type optical compressors are highly suitable.

▶ Audio example 04.02a demonstrates the effects of heavy compression on doubled electric guitars that have been recorded without distortion through a DI-box while audio example 04.02b is the same recording but now with chorus added.

For a more moderate compression, a side chain filter that equalizes the signal that controls the compressor (but not the signal itself) might be better. A high-pass filter at 250–400 Hz stops the low and powerful frequencies from triggering the compression.

Panning

Start by panning dueling mono guitars to L (left) and R (right). Using delay (or reverb) and panning this opposite the guitar track makes it take up less space in the stereo image while creating width and fullness. If there are multiple guitars, distribute these between L and R to create an even wider stereo image.

Reverb and Delay

Delay works extremely well on guitars; think of it as a spatial definition of the guitar in the mix. Remember that delay is time-based and should therefore be set so that it suits the guitar's rhythm while also creating fullness.

Reverb, by contrast, tends to make the guitar sound remote and even washed out. Therefore, it works best with short reverb times (less than 1 s), and ambience and plate reverbs generally yield the best results, especially plug-in models of the EMT 140 (see figure 4.4) or EMT 250 (if you don't happen to own the analog hardware).

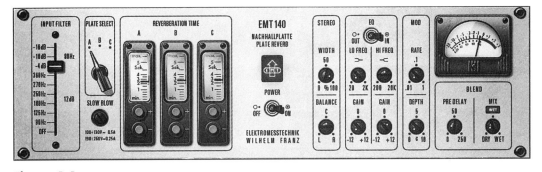

Figure 4.4
The EMT 140 plate reverb has a distinct and vibrant sound that fits perfectly with the guitar's midrange sound. Plate reverb also emphasizes vocals and the snare drum without making them seem remote. It is made as a plug-in by Universal Audio, among others. © Universal Audio

The pre-delay parameter separates the reverb effect from the guitar signal. And setting it to 10–15 ms makes the guitar seem closer. Longer pre-delays interact with the pulse of the song. At slow tempos, a pre-delay of 80–120 ms might be possible, but long pre-delays do not generally work with rhythm guitars.

Tempo-synced effects, like delay and tremolo, work well on the guitar, creating a larger width with different delay settings in L and R, respectively. The feedback of the delay is often set to zero because several repetitions can create a rhythmic mess and lack of transparency. It is all about creating an illusion of space surrounding the guitar, so often a 40–80 ms delay is enough.

High-gain guitar riffs and solos love stereo and tape delays that add a floating character, both the sustain and width being emphasized. Also, a ping-pong delay is an old-school trick to add fullness and width to a guitar; it consists of two mono delays panned L and R. With each side set, respectively, to a quarter and an eighth note (using tempo sync in the DAW or the tap function), the delay might be just what is required. Feedback, determining the number of delays repeating back and forth between the speakers at decreasing levels, should be set low.

The slap delay can be used to extend the tone and highlight the pulse of the guitar rhythm, but this is easily exaggerated and can be disturbing.

Another tool to add fullness is the stereo harmonizer, which changes the pitch slightly while adding delay to the signal. Send the guitar to an aux channel containing a harmonizer or pitch plug-in. One side is pitched 5–15 cents up (adapted to the song and to personal taste) while the other is pitched down correspondingly (one cent = 1/100 of a semitone). Next, add 10 ms delay to L and 15 ms to R. Overall, it provides a mono guitar with a beautiful spread in the stereo image.

Box 4.4

See chapter 23, "Tape Echo and Digital Delay," and chapter 24, "Ambience and Reverb," for more tips on guitar effects.

✓ Both the acoustic and the electric guitar sound better with new strings—this improves tuning as well.

✓ A rhythm guitar track panned L and R with a stereo effect leaves space in the middle for the bass and other instruments. It's almost like having two rhythm guitars.

✓ Two guitars along with a stereo keyboard often seem indistinguishable, as they share the same frequencies. Pan one guitar to C (center) and the other to L (so that the guitar takes up one side of the stereo field), and pan the keyboard to R and C (so it takes up the other side), thus creating space for the instruments to complement each other.

✓ Two (doubled) guitars playing power chords and panned L and R, complemented with a cleaner sounding guitar panned to C, fill out (along with bass and drums) the entire sound stage. Adding chorus to the C guitar would fill in even the smallest gaps.

✓ Multing of the guitar: the original track is EQed to fit the song. Make a copy of the track and boost this in the 1.5–3 kHz range along with severe compression (an LA-2 or an 1176-type compressor). When mixed in discreetly, this track adds definition and pushes the guitar forward in the mix.

✓ In the mix, the guitar does not need to have content across the frequency spectrum. Often, there is more primal energy to a bass-light, raw guitar sound. Check out the album *Led Zeppelin II* (1969) in headphones!

✓ Positioned a little further away (20–30 cm) from the speaker, the microphone captures ambience as well, often supplementing the clean guitar sound.

✓ Powerful guitar stacks do not sound as great in the recording as in the recording room, because they can choke the microphone with sheer volume. In the studio, small guitar amps at moderate strength have a better frequency response and greater detail, and they do not overload the mic. Moreover, small amps achieve their full sound without overexciting the recording space and creating (unwanted) resonances. Always try to adjust levels to the size and acoustics of the room when recording electro-acoustic instruments.

✓ A fuller sound can be obtained by placing an additional microphone behind an open back cabinet where the tone is more mellow.

✓ Be sure to highlight interesting passages and attenuate the lesser ones, thereby directing attention to the most important instruments in the mix. Automation of the levels may help to increase focus on the essence of the song. Often, a guitar part should be completely left out, making it all the more effective when it comes back in and really has something to add.

5

The Piano

The Instrument and the Acoustics

The grand piano and the upright piano (here both referred to as "the piano") can be recorded in a number of ways, and the means for shaping the piano's sound in the recording are countless, as it is an acoustic instrument with a large soundboard and various tonal areas.

The piano is designed to interact with the acoustics. Like all other acoustic instruments, it sounds best in ambient acoustics that are preferably characterized by wooden surfaces.

Classical recordings always include the acoustics, but in pop and rock the acoustics are recorded to a lesser extent, often being completely omitted because here the goal is a close-up and percussive sound that is achieved by placing the microphones near the piano hammers (where they hit the strings) and the soundboard (boosting the sound from the strings).

Because of the size of the instrument, you need at least two microphones—usually a mic for the treble range and one that covers the bass, and the spacing between them determines the width of the stereo image.

To record classical music, use a stereo setup to capture both the piano and the acoustics of the room at a distance of at least one meter, depending on the room reverberation and the sound you want.

In pop and rock recordings, the piano is normally recorded as an overdub, since the microphones on the piano would pick up too much from the drums and the electric instruments. Another option is to screen off the piano or to isolate it in an isolation booth (see p. 289), ideally using a bit of reverb in the mix.

For classical recordings, a reverberation time of up to 3–4 s is used (from the room acoustics). In pop and rock recordings, a shorter reverb time of 0.6–1.0 s is preferred, since it would otherwise be difficult to place the piano tonally and spatially with the rhythm section.

Always Use Condenser Microphones

The most frequently used microphones are condensers. In the top studios, quality mics like the DPA, Neumann, Schoeps, AKG 414, Sanken, Sennheiser, Microtech Gefell, and Audio Technica are used because they have a wide dynamic range matching the range of the piano. In classical recordings, mostly omnis are used (being linear and having great depth), while cardioids are preferred for rock's close-up sound due to the proximity effect that provides a more solid bottom end and a more focused sound. If the piano is recorded together with other instruments (i.e., in the same room), cardioids also provide a better separation.

An omni works better as an ambience mic and captures more bottom end as cardioids attenuate frequencies below 200 Hz at distances of more than 25–30 cm.

Recording Acoustic Pianos in the Studio

Five Mic Setups for the Grand Piano

Although each instrument, room, and musician is different, there are some basic principles for recording the piano, as shown in the following examples. They all use two or more condenser mics.

Example 1

Two omnis are placed inside the piano, right above the soundboard and pointing respectively at the bass and treble range. The lid is opened to full height or removed completely to avoid reflections.

Figure 5.1
Two Earthworks mics in a spaced omni setup (see p. 142). The distance between the mics determines stereo width and at the same time covers the bass and treble.

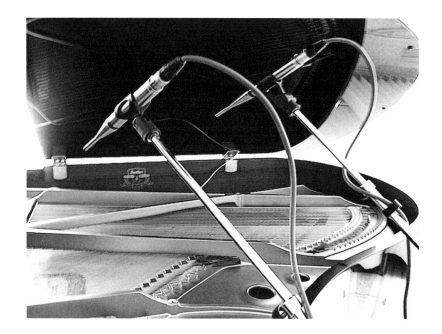

Raising the mics to 40–50 cm will capture some of the acoustics, providing a more spacious and large sound with a less distinct attack. Usually, the mic tracks are panned hard L (left) and R (right), but a narrower stereo spread can also be used.

Example 2

A stereo setup can be located slightly further away, free of the lid and at 50–80 cm distance. Point mic 1 toward the point where the first and second metal braces meet and point mic 2 toward the point where the main and bass bridges meet.

This setup captures ambience, and therefore it is great for solo piano and arrangements where the piano plays a prominent part. The further away from the edge of the piano, the less definition and attack is recorded. In return, a more spacious and homogeneous sound is captured across the entire soundboard, a sound that is enhanced by the acoustics.

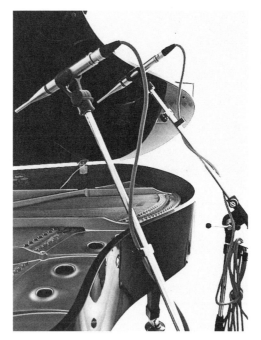

Figure 5.2
Recording with ambience. Appropriate stereo setups are X-Y, ORTF, or spaced omni (see p. 142–148).

Example 3

Remove the piano lid and place two mics 20–30 cm above the hammers: mic 1 halfway between the lowest note and middle C and mic 2 between the highest string and middle

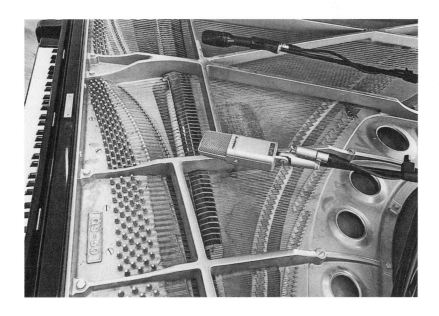

Figure 5.3
Microtech Gefell UM70s and Sony C-48 both set to cardioid characteristics. This setup is called spaced stereo.

C. This recording technique makes for a dense and distinct sound with plenty of attack from the hammers. Use for rock and pop with mics panned full L and R.

Example 4

The Blumlein setup uses two figure-of-eight mics. Located at middle C right above the hammers, this setup captures a close-up, percussive sound. The two mics are placed as close as possible and their figure-of-eight characteristics must be angled 90° to each other.

Figure 5.4
Two Royer ribbon mics in the Blumlein setup (see p. 146). Ribbon mics add fullness, and so the overtones of the piano probably have to be boosted using a high-shelf EQ. © Royer Labs

Combinations of the above setups can also be used, and often multiple stereo configurations are used and the best one chosen when mixing. Meat Loaf's *Bat Out of Hell III* (2006), in which the piano sound is extraordinarily rich for a heavy rock arrangement, was recorded with a double stereo setup: two Royer R-122 ribbons (figure-of-eight) along with a set of Neumann U-67s in cardioid configuration.

Example 5

The two bridges of the piano are key to its basic sound. On modern pianos, the main bridge runs from the highest notes to the low midrange, switching to the bass bridge around A1 and G2. From this lower area a very distinctive sound, rich in harmonics, is projected, because the sound of the strings is reinforced here. The two bridges are the optimal points of projection, and, placed here, two mics provide a fine stereo width and a particularly good representation of the harmonics.

With a microphone placed on each of the bridges, the sound is very up-front and in-your-face; this is due also to the short distance to the hammers (the proximity effect adding body and impact to the piano in a crowded mix comprising drums and electric instruments).

Figure 5.5
Place mic 1 between the hammers and the main bridge near the first and second metal brace. Place mic 2 where the main bridge and the bass bridge run in parallel for 30–40 cm. This setup is a spaced stereo pair, both mics being cardioids and placed 4–5 cm above the bridge. mic 1 captures the treble and the midrange while mic 2 captures the midrange and the bass.

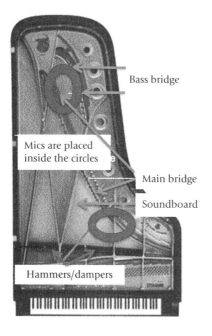

Bass bridge

Mics are placed inside the circles

Main bridge

Soundboard

Hammers/dampers

Ambience Mics

With the first four examples shown above, a pair of ambient mics is sometimes additionally used in order to capture the acoustics if this is deemed useful, placed further away from the piano to capture the reverberation and coloring of the room. In the mix, the ambient tracks are used to add spaciousness, width, and depth to the recording—a bit like coloring using artificial reverb. Consequently, the mics are panned full L and R. In classical solo piano recordings, the ambient mics constitute the basic sound of the recording.

Upright Piano

Though the upright piano does not sound that impressive in itself, it may have more impact than the grand piano in a recording because it is easier to make space for it in a mix with a rhythm section.

Remember to check the tuning! For some reason, the planet is overrun by upright pianos that are out of tune. In old movies and 78rpm phonograph recordings, they are always out of tune; in a saloon in a Western, this is part of the authentic atmosphere, but in real life this will just annoy you.

A microphone pointing down into the lid sounds quite poor because of the acoustic reflections inside the narrow space. The sound is best around the back of the piano. The soundboard of the upright piano benefits from being close to a wall (although at some distance); this enhances fullness and projects the sound into the room. The soundboard transmits both the percussive sound of the hammers and the sustain of the strings.

Move the piano at least 2 m away from the wall, so that the two microphones do not pick up strong reflections from it. Mic 1 is pointed toward the treble end of the soundboard and mic 2 toward the bass end, both at around 60 cm height and with a 10–30 cm gap between them.

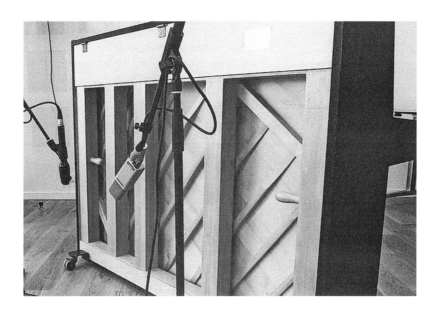

Figure 5.6
Upright piano recording with a Microtech Gefell UM70s and a Sony C-48 (spaced stereo).

Experiment with both distance and height according to the instrument. Condenser mics sound the best, but dynamic microphones can be used instead for a retro sound.

This setup may be combined with a third mic capturing the piano at head height from the front and pointing toward the hammers. Make sure mic 3 does not cause phase problems when mixed with the main stereo setup, and move it around until it adds fullness and depth.

The recorded sound is improved by:

- The lid being open.
- The front top plate being removed, making the hammers and strings visible. This provides clarity and dynamics.
- The front plate below the keyboard being removed, providing a better projection of sound.

TIPS

✓ The closer the microphones are to the hammers, the more the attack is recorded. The further away, the more the body and sustain are recorded. Start from the hammers and gradually move the mics backward until the balance between attack and sustain pleases you (grand piano).

✓ Try with a third mic at the far end where the piano sounds round and ringing. Mixed with the bass and treble mics, this adds plenty of sustain, and if a long reverb is added, this becomes a bit like a synth pad below the piano sound (grand piano).

✓ If you do not wish the sound to be reflected and reinforced by the lid, then remove it for a more open sound with less definition (grand piano).

✓ On piano tracks with a strong rhythmic element, hard compression can be used to add clarity and impact by reducing the dynamic range. If the playing is staccato, the release must be set shorter than the next attack in order to separate each individual attack. This is used on 1950s rock 'n' roll piano and also in the Beatles' "Lady Madonna."

Digital Piano

Quite a few pianos in pop and rock recordings are digital pianos, as they are simple to record through line-in and in stereo. Normally, their built-in reverb and other effects should be deactivated, as studio effects are better.

In the mix, digital pianos can work almost as well as (and sometimes better than) the grand piano, because the sound of a good digital piano is created for the particular sound of popular music. Both dynamics and the tonal spectrum are severely limited compared to the grand piano, and this is exactly what makes them easier to place in the mix.

If recorded to a tempo track via MIDI, they have the advantage of being editable in the DAW. With a dynamic range that is much smaller than that of the acoustic piano, they readily work well in a rhythmic arrangement without compression.

Live Recording

The DPA 4052 is a compact stereo kit for mounting inside the grand piano. The DPA 4052 is well suited for live recording because, when positioned inside the piano, the microphones are screened against spill from the drums, bass, and so forth.

Schoeps PZM mics are equally good for both live and studio recordings because they can be placed directly on the piano soundboard. This type of microphone is called a boundary microphone, and it does not capture reflections from other surfaces. Boundary mics have a natural and linear sound and can also be placed on the floor below the grand piano. (Likewise, they do a great job as "under head" mics on the drums: when placed on the floor in front of the drum kit, a PZM captures a very full, and relatively cymbal-free, drum sound.)

Mix Settings and Effects

In the jazz and classical genres you are trying to capture the natural sound of the grand piano, while in rock music the timbre and dynamics of the piano are altered to suit the arrangement using EQ, compression, and reverb. The rock mix rarely has the space to accommodate the wide sound spectrum and dynamics of the piano, except for a ballad where the drums and guitars take a back seat. Normally, the bottom end is reduced and the high-mid range boosted, while the dynamic range is narrowed using compression so that the piano does not drown in the overall sound. EQ is also used to attenuate the frequency ranges that overlap with the other instruments and that can blur the entire mix.

A fuller and more dynamic grand piano is found in the singer-songwriter genres and pop ballads.

EQ

The piano requires a lot of space in the mix. The fundamentals on the grand piano range from 27.5 to 4186 Hz (and on top of this are the harmonics). Along with large church organs, the piano is the instrument with the greatest frequency range. Depending on the genre and instrumentation, it is often necessary to do a bit of trimming if the piano is not to take the lead.

Bottom end and fullness are found in the 60–250 Hz range. Be careful that the "thump" of the sustain pedal does not become too evident when boosting this range.

The sound of a honky-tonk piano is best produced by boosting at 2.5 kHz with a narrow Q.

Presence is found between 2.5 and 5 kHz.

The attack is found in the range of 5–10 kHz—and this can be a piercing sound as well—while air is from 12 kHz and upward. Harmonics must sometimes be reduced with a high-shelf filter from 15 to 17 kHz to make space for other instruments.

Dynamics

Because of the striking of the hammers and the sustain of the soundboard, the piano has a huge dynamic range, and hard compression might be seen as a desecration of the piano's tonal expression. For this reason, the grand piano is never compressed in the classical genre, but in the rock genre, such desecration is seen as beneficial and is used to add impact, and when there is a rhythm section, compression is needed to make the piano cut through. Start with a gentle 1.5:1 ratio for solo piano and push it slightly higher in an arrangement with drums and bass. If the piano is to maintain its natural sound, the attack time should provide room to let the attacks pass through (min. 20 ms). Release is set to 200–350 ms so that the decay is not raised unnaturally. An attack of 17–20 ms and a release of 75–150 ms will affect the transients more.

In a powerful accompaniment, a combination of slow to medium attack and fast release will make the piano stand out clearly in the mix, but since the compressor attenuates the attacks, it is often necessary to subsequently boost EQ in the presence area.

An optical compressor (see p. 243) has a slower attack and release. It is perfect, therefore, for a less dense and lighter accompaniment without strong attacks. In a recording with percussive attacks, use an FET compressor, as it is more responsive to transients. The FET compressor affects the transients quicker (so they do not stick out that much in the mix) and releases quickly enough to let the next transient pass through unaffected.

Reverb

The piano feels comfortable with natural reverb, but an artificial hall reverb works fine too, and convolution reverbs from natural acoustics are even better.

Reverb time depends on the tempo of the song and the rhythmic pulse of the piano but generally must be kept short; only in ballads and the classical genre does reverberation exceeding one second work well. Pre-delay can be used to separate the attacks from the reverberation, preventing the piano from becoming too distant sounding.

6

The Acoustic Guitar

The Instrument

When it comes to recording, the acoustic guitar has more in common with other acoustic instruments such as violin, cello, mandolin, and saxophone than with the electric guitar. These instruments generate their sound and timbre through the soundboard and/or body, and so the interaction with the room acoustics is a part of that.

Figure 6.1
A single mic, pointing at where the neck joins the body, provides a rich and full mono recording. Here, a Lauten Atlantis mic in cardioid mode is shown.

Wood lining in the recording room supports the sound of the acoustic guitar—preferably in combination with absorbent surfaces like walls of rough, plastered bricks, which create diffusion (i.e., sound distributed in many directions and phase shifted depending on the roughness of the bricks).

Mic Setup

Use a condenser mic at a distance to record the sound of the acoustic guitar. A dynamic mic will make it sound undefined and woolly, because it does not pick up the frequency range in a linear fashion and has a more pronounced proximity effect if directional.

Figure 6.2

The Oktava MK012 cardioid aimed at the fourteenth fret and another aimed toward the bridge. If there is too much rumbling, angle the mics away from the sound hole, and vice versa if lacking fullness. This setup is a spaced stereo, the distance between the two mics determining the stereo width (see p. 142).

In the pop and rock genres, close-miking is normally used, only picking up a small portion of the acoustics and thus making it easier to control in the mix using reverb. A single mic placed close to soundboard (15–25 cm) will capture a close and dynamic sound but has no depth or width. For this reason, two mics are often used (stereo spread) as well as reverb in the mix to fashion the acoustics.

▶ Audio example 6.01 shows the acoustic guitar recorded with a single microphone, while audio example 6.02 demonstrates the use of two microphones.

Around the fourteenth fret, where the neck joins the body, the acoustic guitar has both fullness and a distinct timbre (among other sources, from the fingering on the neck), and this is a great spot to place mic 1 in a stereo setup (see figure 6.2). At the bridge, a softer and less distinct sound is found, and a mic placed here will add body and also width when the two mics are panned.

If it is the only instrument in the recording, the acoustic guitar sounds best in great-sounding acoustics. This is called ambient miking; a mic placed at a distance of 80–160 cm, pointing toward where the neck joins the body, captures articulation and definition, while another at the same distance and pointing toward the bridge of the guitar adds body. The distance determines how "close" the guitar will sound—that is, how much ambience is recorded. In the classical genre, ambient miking is always used, often with a stereo pair (see p. 141) located at a distance some meters from the guitar.

A different approach is to place mic 2 at shoulder height (at the right side of a right-handed guitarist) and pointing toward the lower end of the guitar body in order to capture the fullness as the guitarist hears it. This technique also avoids the proximity effect if using a directional mic. Alternatively, point mic 2 toward the neck of the guitar

Figure 6.3
The Earthworks QTCs are particularly good on the acoustic guitar. Even close up they capture a bit of acoustics and, at the same time, a great picture of the guitar, full of presence. Just like any other small diaphragm mic (see p. 123), they have a little more self-noise, but, close up, this is no problem.

in order to capture more attack and definition while mic 1 points toward the fourteenth fret. Check for any phase problems by summing the signals in mono, and solve any such issues by moving one of the mics slightly. The two mics are panned either partially or completely to the L (left) and R (right) side.

Box 6.1

See chapter 18, "Stereo Recording," for advice on stereo setups and their uses.

A third approach is to use MS stereo. An omni or cardioid mic is pointed toward the fourteenth fret as before and a figure-of-eight mic is placed precisely on top of this, its null directed toward the guitar and the eight pattern positioned alongside the length of the guitar. In the mix, the two signals are MS-decoded (see p. 146), and then the guitar can be placed in the mix with a variable stereo width; from mono (i.e., only the omni or cardioid mic) to gradually wider. MS stereo is a great method for controlling the width of an instrument in the mix.

When it comes to mic placement, whether it comes to ambient or close-miking, the best method is always to listen to the instrument. Listen from different angles and place the mic or mics in the exact spot where the instrument sounds best.

A safe method to achieve a great sound on the acoustic guitar is to double it. This is called "produced stereo" and requires the musician to play accurately on top of the already recorded track (via an overdub). The result is a huge density and width, when the two recordings are panned hard L and R, because even a few milliseconds' discrepancy between recordings 1 and 2 will generate width. A doubled acoustic guitar can hold its own in the existential struggle for survival against the bass and drums!

SDC versus LDC Mics

Small diaphragm condenser mics (SDC) perform best on acoustic guitar (and many other acoustic instruments).

The ideal set of mics might well be a matched stereo pair of Neumann KM184s (being open in the top end and not exaggerating bass), and this pair suits most jobs with the acoustic guitar (as well as other acoustic instruments such as percussion, brass, and woodwinds). But less will also do; the Røde M5 (also available as a matched pair) is highly suitable for acoustic guitar (and choir, as OH mics, and so forth). Oktava MK012s also deliver high-quality recordings—especially when their cost is taken into account.

Most large diaphragm condensers (LDC) do a great job. If the mic is designed as a dedicated vocal mic, then pay attention to whether it is boosting the highs or the high-mid range and making the guitar sound thin.

A ribbon mic adds body and can be helpful in reducing the metallic sound of steel strings.

TIPS

✓ New strings are important if you want the guitar to sound open. String the guitar a couple of days before, giving the strings time to settle and stay tuned. A little use will remove any excessive treble.

✓ An acoustic guitar only serving as rhythmic and tonal coloring (often together with the hi-hat) can be recorded with a single microphone and is thus easier to place in the mix.

✓ The solo acoustic guitar, forming the entire sound stage alone, loves good acoustics with regard to both width and depth. Together with the guitarist, locate the spot in the room that best enhances the sound of the instrument. Then determine the spot that gives the appropriate blend of direct sound and room reflections by experimenting and listening. This is the spot to position a stereo pair; together with one or two microphones close to the guitar, they provide the required presence, depth, and width.

✓ Plectrum thickness and the point at which the acoustic guitar is plucked are of great importance to the sound; a thick pick provides more depth and body, while a thin pick is a better option if the guitarist is playing percussive eighth-note chords. Strokes near the bridge are thin-sounding, and they become increasingly fuller toward the sound hole.

Mix Settings and Effects

An acoustic guitar as the only accompaniment below a vocal and recorded in stereo and in good acoustics need only be fine-tuned with a bit of EQ. Similarly, compression is only necessary to a small degree. Reverb is used if the recording has been made using close-miking.

EQ

In a closely packed mix with a rhythm section, quite a lot has to be done to make the acoustic guitar fit in. If full and natural sounding, the acoustic guitar takes up quite a lot of space, so it must be allocated its own place in the mix. The lower end, coming from the sound hole, is problematic yet necessary. If it masks other instrumental sound, a low-cut filter must be used. Start at 50 Hz (12 dB per octave) and move upward to examine how it affects the presence of the guitar in the mix. Setting the cutoff frequency of the low-cut filter too high makes the guitar sound thin and insubstantial, and it is better to combine a low-cut filter (with a low cutoff frequency) with a 3–4 dB attenuation in the boomy frequencies at 100–250 Hz (using a parametric EQ).

Figure 6.4
It is the transients that define acoustic instruments in the mix, and so a transient designer plug-in is good for creating clarity on acoustic instruments and percussion. It often gives better results than EQ. © spl

Around 300–500 Hz, an attenuation of 2–3 dB (with a narrow Q) may help achieve a more transparent sound. A bit further up, at 400 Hz to 1 kHz, a mellow acoustic character, often referred to as the "wood" sound, can be added.

Clarity and definition reside in the 2.5–5 kHz range, while the range of 4–8 kHz provides the presence, which risks sounding metallic and hard if overemphasized.

The air is at 12–16 kHz, but emphasizing this range can make the sound become too sibilant.

Compression

Compression is necessary to smooth out the dynamics of an acoustic guitar playing with a rhythm group. However, the more predominant the role of the acoustic guitar in the mix, the less compression is used. Neither steel nor nylon string acoustics benefit from hard compression, their transients being so noticeably a part of the guitar sound that compressing them sounds unnatural.

With soft knee compression or limiting (which is the principle of optical compressors such as the Teletronix LA2, Tube TechLCA2B, and LA-610; see p. 243), compression can be made quite musical. A ratio of 2–3:1 and a threshold set high so that only the peaks are compressed will often do the job.

As a start, set attack to 10–20 ms. It is often a compromise between the amount of attenuation and the desire to preserve the natural dynamics of the guitar (as noted above). Release is determined by the rhythm (i.e., the time span between the strokes), and normally auto will take care of that.

Reverb and Other Effects

An acoustic guitar without natural acoustics or artificial reverb sounds confined, lifeless, and weak. Room and hall reverbs highlight the guitar's natural timbre, and the fewer instruments in the mix, the longer the reverb time that can be used. In a closely packed mix, a plate reverb helps to provide definition, while in a dry mix a short ambience might be enough.

The combination of a medium plate reverb of 2–3 s with a weaker and very long cathedral reverb (4–6 s) provides rich fullness both to a solo acoustic guitar and to a guitar in a closely packed mix.

Both a spatial expander and a short stereo delay can be used to provide width to an acoustic guitar that is recorded with only one mic. The principle is one of different delay times of the signal at L and R (without modulation as occurs with the flanger and chorus).

A stereo delay with a single repetition provides both width and drive at the faster tempos.

A delay with multiple repetitions can be sent via a bus to an inserted reverb, the reverb filling out between repetitions and thus providing a great ambience.

Box 6.2

See chapter 24, "Ambience and Reverb," for more tips on using reverb.

7

The Recording of Some Less Common String Instruments

Panning Acoustic Instruments Recorded with Two Mics

Acoustic instruments are designed to interact with the acoustics, the ambience providing spaciousness and fullness, and so they are often recorded with two microphones in order to capture the sound of those acoustics. A variety of string instruments are frequently recorded in this fashion.

The two mics provide control over the space that the recorded instrument takes up in the mix. Where a mono instrument is placed at one point between L (left) and R (right), a stereo recording can be spread across L and R. It makes no sense to pan a number of instruments completely to L and R, though—normally this only works with one or two instruments.

With several stereo-recorded instruments, the panning could be like this (using, as an example, an ensemble based around two guitars, but the same is true, of course, for mandolin, banjo, piano, or whatever the instruments might be):

- The neck mic of guitar 1 is placed at C (center), while its bridge mic is panned completely to the L.
- Guitar 2's neck mic is placed similarly at C and the bridge mic to R.

Following this model, the other instruments are each panned to their own position in the stereo field while, to some degree, being anchored to C. This adds width to the mix, while a solid center image of (some of) the instruments is maintained.

Reverb is used to make the instruments blend, but the technique described above might only require reverb to a small extent, since the width is also coming from the two mics and the panning.

The Mandolin

Basically, the mandolin can be recorded with the same mics used for the acoustic guitar. Using one mic located about 15–20 cm away and pointing toward the lower part of the neck or the upper part of the body captures the full sound of the mandolin. For a more mellow and rounded tone, a ribbon mic may be used to great advantage.

Figure 7.1

An Audio Technica 4040 aimed at the f-hole and a Royer ribbon toward the lower part of the neck.

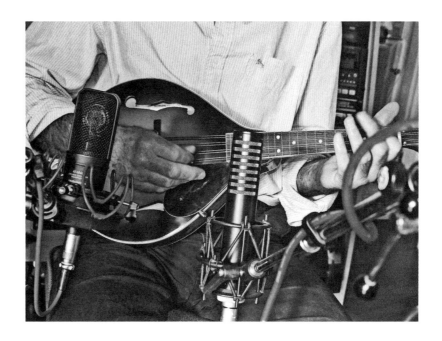

One mic can be sufficient, because the instrument is so small, yet it is common to use an additional mic pointing at one of the f-holes, where the mandolin has a little more body and a woody tone. The second mic is also placed at 15–20 cm distance, and, when panned, the two mics create width.

If the mandolin has a leading role in the track, a narrow stereo configuration at a slightly greater distance provides more spaciousness: two condenser mics, one pointing to one of the f-holes and one at the neck, at approximately 15 cm distance from each other. A fast preamp (e.g., Millennia, api, Neve) is best at capturing the fast and powerful transients of the mandolin. The mandolin cuts through easily in the mix, its bright sound keeping it from having to compete for its frequency range with the other instruments. For the same reason, you often have to attenuate the top end (high-cut) and/or boost the low-mid range, but otherwise it does not need much EQing.

Compressing with a fast attack and a fast release time (almost the same settings as for the snare drum) will smooth its dynamics and raise its sustain slightly.

The Dobro

The dobro is recorded in stereo using a pair of condenser microphones 20–40 cm above its soundboard—one pointing between the two small sound holes where the neck joins the body and one pointing toward the resonator (see figure 7.2).

Dobros, however, sound very different across types, so listen for the "sweet spot." If the sound is too metallic, then place the mics at a distance or use a ribbon mic so that the top end is attenuated. Although its sound is dominant in the midrange area, EQ can pull the dobro in different directions, allowing it to balance tonally with the other instruments. Warmth and fullness are emphasized by boosting in the range of 150–400 Hz. The metallic sound, for the large part, resides in the range between 500 Hz and 2 kHz, and this often must be attenuated. The range of 4–8 kHz provides transparency but can also make the dobro sound strident. Boosting the range of 10–12 kHz will add

Figure 7.2
The dobro can be recorded in its entirety with a spaced stereo pair at a distance of 40–60 cm in a good acoustic space that provides fullness and consistency. Shown here are a Royer ribbon and Oktava MK012.

71

pleasing air to the dobro. Compression can be discreet but can also be used to highlight the long, singing tone of the instrument. A stereo delay will likewise highlight this tone while at the same time adding a floating feel.

The Banjo

Sound-wise, the banjo is a crossover between a guitar and a snare drum. It is characterized by significant transients and a clear strike from the skin during each attack. At its middle, the banjo has fullness and a strong attack, while further out toward the edges, it sounds more open. It makes sense, therefore, to place two mics at 40–80 cm distance to capture the banjo's sound in its entirety if the acoustics allow.

However, one single condenser mic pointed slightly below the spot where the neck joins the body and placed at 20–30 cm distance also provides a good

Figure 7.3
DPA d:vote 4099V clip mic on the banjo. © DPA microphones

picture of the banjo—it only remains to filter out a bit of the harsh midrange (see figure 7.3). The mic does not have to be a Neumann U87; a Røde, Audio Technica 4033, Oktava MK012, and even a dynamic Shure SM58 will be fine, but a quick preamp is essential.

An additional mic can be placed pointing toward the center of the banjo head. Here, the sound is a little harsh, so a ribbon mic is ideal for the task. Place it 20–30 cm away from the first mic (which is placed where the neck joins the body); the two together provide both body and width when panned.

Fullness is found in the 100–300 Hz region and is essential to the banjo's definition in the mix. Clarity is found at around 3–5 kHz. Often, though, the sound must be attenuated somewhere in the 500 Hz to 5 kHz range.

Compression with a fast attack and fast release will smooth out its dynamic range and make the banjo consistent in arpeggios and fast, melodic playing.

Reverb is used to a lesser degree and is often a short plate reverb, since the banjo already has a ringing sustain.

Figure 7.4

DPA 4060 omni mic aimed at the soundboard of the harp. © DPA microphones

The Harp

An unfair but not entirely untrue musician's joke says that harp players spend half of the time tuning and the other half playing out of tune, so pay attention that not a single one of the harp's 36–47 strings is wayward.

As an overdub or solo instrument, the harp is easy to record; a quality omni mic at a distance of 30–60 cm and pointed at the height where the player plucks the strings, but aimed at the soundboard, captures most sound and is sufficient when the harp does not have to be spread out into stereo.

For recording purposes, the harp behaves like the piano, with the exception that its plucking is softer than the piano's hammer action and also that there are no reflections from a lid. Therefore, two mics in a stereo setup, where the instrument is either solo or being recorded as an overdub, can be placed to pick up the bottom and the top end, providing more depth and width.

As part of the orchestra, the harp is difficult to record, because its playing volume is so weak that a great part of what a mic captures is the spill from the other instruments. The solution is either comprehensive screening or the use of the harp's sound hole

Figure 7.5
Recording Trio Rococo with DPA 4011 omnis. The harp is recorded in stereo; the distance of the two mics from the harp means strong spill from the clarinet and the cello.
Since the clarinet is louder, the mic directed toward its valves picks up relatively less spill. The cello mic can be placed as close as 15 cm from one of the f-holes to reduce spill. As all the mics are omnis, some experimentation with mic placement could eliminate phase problems, and in good acoustics the spill will give depth and width to the recording. © DPA microphones

as the source. The back of the soundboard has sound holes, and a mic in the middle sound hole, optionally with screening, provides a cleaner signal. Alternatively, the mic can be wrapped in a piece of cloth and attached to the sound hole, the cloth dampening mechanical vibrations. The sound picked up from the soundboard is fairly natural and should be opened up with just a little EQ and reverb.

8

Percussion

This chapter describes the recording and mixing of the most common percussion instruments and an explanation of some of their idiosyncrasies.

Basically, percussion instruments should be treated like the various drums in the drum kit. The principles of microphone placement are the same and the use of EQ and dynamic processors is similar, as are the use of reverb and effects to a certain extent. The drum kit chapter (p. 19), therefore, is a complement to this chapter, so check there for further details. Percussion instruments, though, are simpler to record, because you only have to deal with one drum type at a time.

Congas and Bongos

As with the toms of the drum kit, dynamic mics like the Shure SM57 and Shure Beta, Sennheiser 421, Audix D2 or D4, and Audio Technica ATM25 are used for close-miking. When recording with other instruments in particular, dynamic mics are best suited to the task of close-miking, as they pick up less spill.

The placement of microphones is 5–10 cm above the heads—either one on each (in which case they should be panned in the mix) or one between the two drums. This captures plenty of the attacks as well as fullness because of the proximity effect.

If you need a little air and ambience, a condenser is the best choice (everything from sE Electronics to a Røde, an Audio Technica, or a Neumann) at 30–70 cm distance and pointing down at the drums (see figure 8.1). The sound pressure of the bongos, though, is so weak that they do not really activate the acoustics, and so reverb added later works better than an ambience mic.

To record the deep end of the congas, an additional mic is placed on the biggest of the two (the tumba). This requires that the congas are in the rack, so that the mic can

Figure 8.1

Stereo recording with two AKG 414s at 40 cm distance. As always, the AKG 414 captures a rich and open sound with lots of dynamics.

be aimed diagonally up toward the sound hole. When congas are the only rhythm instrument, this provides added fullness, but in a large arrangement, this can cause muddiness in the 100–250 Hz range.

Compression

Fast attack settings will destroy the attacks (in particular when using slap technique), so set it to 10–20 ms. Release should be short to cancel the compression before the next strike.

EQ

Use EQ to ensure that the congas maintain their natural sound. Normally you have to add presence in the 4–5 kHz range and air above 12 kHz.

Congas and bongos must also be attenuated in the 200 Hz region to enhance clarity and remove rumble. In turn, boosting slightly higher at 300–400 Hz can be used to add fullness.

The Transient Designer plug-in (see p. 67) generally does a good job of adding transparency to percussion instruments (as well as most other acoustic instruments).

Reverb

Reverb is needed to make the congas blend in the mix if close-miked, and the bright sound of a plate reverb will highlight the attacks.

Cajon

At one and the same time a cajon works a bit like a bass drum, a tom, and a snare. Two microphones are therefore usually used. An AKG D12/112, Sennheiser 421, Audix D6, Shure SM58, or similar will capture the bottom end. As the sound box acts similarly to that on an acoustic guitar, the mic should be angled diagonally toward the rear sound

Figure 8.2
An ADK A-48 tube mic at the back and an Oktava MK012 on the front. Remember to phase-reverse one of the mics. If you find you lack the snare effect, guitar strings or metal wires can be taped on the inside of the front to provide extra snare.

opening from a distance of 10–30 cm (see figure 8.2). Placed perpendicular toward the center, it will usually pick up too much rumble.

The mic located at the rear (i.e., the sound hole) captures both the bottom and the attack, but if you want independent control over the sound of these, another mic placed 15–30 cm from the front is needed. Small diaphragm condensers like the AKG C451, Neumann KM184, Røde NT5, or Oktava MK012 are the ideal choice for this. But when used live or together with other instruments in the studio, dynamic mics like the Sennheiser MD421 and Shure SM58 will capture less spill and work just fine. Remember to reverse the phase of one mic; otherwise there will be a loss of bass and an audible phasing in the midrange frequencies because the two mic diaphragms are moving out of phase with each other.

The bass end of the cajon makes placement of the instrument critical; keep it away from corners and walls if the objective is not to amplify its bottom end (each boundary surface can boost the sound by about 6 dB; see p. 281). If bass resonances are noted at the recording position, then move the cajon around until they cannot be heard. A wooden floor highlights the cajon's sound, while blankets absorb it.

Compression

Compression works well on the rear sound-hole mic, but should be used only gently on the front mic if you are using one. As a fast compressor attack will ruin the cajon's attacks, use at least a 10–20 ms setting. Release should be kept short in order to cancel compression before the next stroke.

EQ

Use a minimalist approach only, highlighting the natural sound of the cajon and separating the two tracks (if used) by EQing toward a snare and bass drum sound. Often, the rear mic ("bass drum") is attenuated at 150–250 Hz to enhance clarity, while the Transient Designer plug-in provides clarity on the front mic ("snare drum"). A high shelf is useful in raising the high end at around 4–5 kHz in order to add definition and brighten up the "snare" and the in-between strokes.

Reverb

Using two mics will also capture some ambience, and so reverb is required to a lesser extent on the snare track. If desired, use a short and distinct reverb; for example, a slap or a plate reverb.

Claves

Claves are recorded at a distance, up to 2–3 m, the acoustics thus softening their sound. Experiment with various mic placements, both on- and off-axis, to accommodate the acoustics. Recording close to the claves requires a mic able to handle high sound pressures and to capture high gain transients.

Claves must be attenuated in the 3–5 kHz range. Reverb (perhaps carefully blended with the recorded room acoustics) is used to soften the claves and make them blend in the mix.

Djembe and Bodhrán

A djembe acts as a bass drum, tom, and snare drum combined, and so two mics are normally used. An AKG D12/112, Sennheiser 421, Audix D6, or large diaphragm condenser below the sound hole captures the bottom end. If angled diagonally toward the sound hole at a distance of 40–80 cm, the mic captures both the bottom end as well as the attacks. Keep the instrument away from the corners and walls, and pay attention to bass resonances.

To control the sound of the attacks, the second mic is placed 10–20 cm above the drum head, although, placed further away, it will also capture the ambience and add air. If indeed using two mics, one must be phase-reversed.

The bodhrán is similar to the djembe with respect to mic placement, as a mic pointing at the drum head captures most attacks, while, placed at the back, the mic picks up a little less attack and more fullness. A single good condenser mic on the reverse side will pick up the entire sound of the bodhrán, but experiment with the placement for a good balance between fullness and attack.

Compression

Use an attack setting of at least 10–20 ms. Release should be kept short to ensure the compression releases before the next stroke.

EQ

If the djembe or the bodhrán is playing with other drums, you need to make space for it in the mix; the bottom end acquires punch below and around 100 Hz and definition in the 3–5 kHz area. The djembe sounds great in the sub-bass range, and this can be boosted with a parametric EQ at around 40–50 Hz.

Reverb

Only a slight reverb is required—use a short and distinct reverb like a slap or a plate reverb.

Tambourine and Shakers

A condenser mic with an attenuated treble response is placed at least 30 cm from the tambourine. If the sound is too bright or hard, try at a greater distance and off-axis, that is, diagonally from the side. Ribbon mics are often used because of their roll-off in the top end. The same approach applies to shakers and the cabasa; they can, however, be placed closer to the mic.

Never use a second mic to capture the ambience, as this will cause an audible comb filter effect.

In the mix, both the tambourine and shakers should be attenuated in the 4–6 kHz range if they are thin sounding, while a little fullness can be found between 200 and 500 Hz.

Compression should be avoided (playing with a consistent touch is better), because this quickly makes it sound like a special effect, reducing the attacks and raising the decay unnaturally while also making the pulse imprecise.

Timbales

Anything from dynamic mics like the Shure SM57 and Sennheiser 421 to expensive condenser mics will work. Either a mic is placed on each drum (panned in the mix) or one single mic is used between the two drums at 10–20 cm distance.

The mics can also be placed underneath the timbales and should be aimed toward the edge of the drums. Both locations provide plenty of attack, but there is more when they are placed above the drums. When placed above, the mics will also pick up lots of the cowbell (if present), which would be more suppressed if recording from underneath the timbales.

If you need some air and ambience, a condenser mic is best at a distance of 50–100 cm pointing down or up toward the drums.

Figure 8.3
On top, the Sony C-48 between the drums, while below is the Microtech Gefell (both set to cardioid). Remember to reverse the phase on one of the mics.

Compression

Since the timbales have a long decay, compression is best avoided or should be used with extreme caution. A fast attack will destroy the timbales' attacks, and the compressor's release must occur before the next strike.

EQ

EQ is used to highlight the natural sound of the timbales and mostly to compensate for any shortcomings in the recording; for example, an attenuation at 150–250 Hz if the proximity effect (cardioid or figure-of-eight) results in a boomy low end. Often a little presence in the 4–5 kHz range opens the timbales up, and some air over 12 kHz works well.

Reverb

The timbales are resonant and ringing; thus reverb is less important and will usually only clutter the mix.

Xylophone, Marimba, Vibraphone, and Glockenspiel

Xylophone, marimba, and vibraphone are all recorded in stereo in the same way as the piano (see p. 55) using two mics to cover their large pitch range. The bass and treble mics are normally panned completely to L (left) and R (right) in the mix.

Use two condenser mics pointing down toward the keys from a height of 40–60 cm. A distance of 10–50 cm between them (spaced omni; see p. 142) determines their width in the stereo image. An X-Y stereo setup (see p. 145) also works well, and both configurations provide an open sound with lots of attack and great fullness from the low keys.

The xylophone and marimba have rosewood keys that provide a round, mellow sound, while the vibraphone and glockenspiel have metal keys that produce a hard, metallic sound. The attacks also depend very much on the type of mallets that are used.

A single mic is enough to capture the small glockenspiel from a height of 15–30 cm above the keyboard. The glockenspiel has plenty of attack, so use rubber or plastic mallets to reduce this, and then its fullness will come forth.

The Double Bass and the Cello

The following applies to recording both the double bass and the cello, as they share many common acoustical properties, but attention is also drawn to where specific techniques are required for each instrument.

The Instrument and the Acoustics

Recording the double bass is an entirely different matter from recording the electric bass.

First of all, acoustic instruments achieve a large part of their timbre in interaction with the acoustic environment. Second, the double bass is a large instrument, and different areas of its soundboard radiate diverse tones (see figure 9.1).

Figure 9.1
A single mic pointed at one of the overlayed circles by the f-holes provides a rich and distinct image of the bass and cello. The distance may be varied from 15 cm up to 1 m in good acoustics.

As a start, try to find the sweet spot in the recording space. Often the musician's choice of location, which comes from knowing the instrument and being used to taking advantage of the available acoustics, is the right place. If the acoustics are necessary to add volume and air to the instrument, the room should not be completely dampened. From 0.5 to 1.2 seconds of reverberation, as in a small concert room, is adequate, and the space should ideally be one with wooden cladding.

If recorded together with other instruments, the double bass (and the cello) should be isolated in a separate room or screened to reduce spill into its mic, as the double bass is not a particularly powerful instrument. Conversely, its lowest notes are unstoppable, easily finding their way as spill into the other mics.

Mic Setup

Condenser mics are the best choice for the double bass and cello. Both large diaphragm condensers (LDC) and small diaphragm (SDC) mics will capture their fullness and woody midrange.

The fundamentals of the double bass reach 41.2 Hz, and so using a mic with a linear and accurate bass response is important—for example, a Neumann U87, Microtech Gefell UMT 70S, or AKG 414—but most less pricey LDC mics such as the Røde and sE Electronics mics also produce good results. The SDC mics also have great bass response (e.g., the Sennheiser MKH series, DPA 2011, Microtech Gefells M-series, and Schoeps). If possible (that is, if it does not cause problems with spill from other instruments), use two mics, each set to an omni pattern.

Place a LDC mic 15–30 cm from the body of the instrument, pointing to the spot between the bridge and f-hole (see figure 9.2). If the mic picks up too much rumble or

Figure 9.2

DPA d:vote 4099C clip mic for the double bass. The DPA d:vote is available in different configurations for most acoustic instruments and is designed to be placed close to the soundboard, making it possible to record the double bass when there are other instruments in the same room. As these mics reduce spill significantly, the setup is suitable for live recording. © DPA microphones.

air pressure from the f-hole, then move it a little. Further up (toward the fingerboard), there is a brighter and denser sound.

Additionally, an SDC mic can be placed 30 cm from the lower part of the fingerboard, pointing at 90° toward the player's plucking hand to catch some of the attacks (or the cello bowing) and definition. If the mic is closer and pointed directly toward where the strings are plucked, an even more articulated sound combined with the abrasion from string friction against the fingerboard is picked up.

It is important to find the sweet spot when recording acoustic instruments. Use closed headphones and move the mic around until the sound of the instrument is right. Even a few centimeters can make a huge difference. When the two mics are added together, do check for phase problems, but usually phase is not a problem because of the size of the instrument (also, the two mics are panned in the mix, thus reducing phase cancelation).

A slightly different setup, which provides a precise and more woody sound, is a mic 40–50 cm from, and at the height of, the bridge to catch fullness and bottom end and a second mic, pointing toward the left shoulder of the bass, that picks up the dry, percussive, and distinct "plunk" from there.

As the wavelengths from the lower range of bass instruments are very long (8.33 m for the E string of the double bass), you often get the best recording by placing a (third) omni mic at some distance away, and this also picks up the ambience to complement the mics placed close by that capture the dry sound. Again, it is very important to find the sweet spot, and this setup is only practicable if the double bass or cello is the only instrument in the recording room. In the mix, the ambience mic should be used to the extent that it improves the overall sound of the instrument.

Often, players already have a pickup installed on the bridge, and the best designs are well suited for recording. In general, the pickup provides a slightly clinical sound with much clarity and definition but less warm fullness than mics placed at a distance. By combining it with a mic recording, though, it is often easy to make the right blend of both worlds. Remember to check the phase between the two (e.g., by zooming in on the waveforms of the two tracks and by comparing the placement of the attacks). If the mic is more than 10–20 cm from the bass, shifting the track ahead in time (i.e., to the left in the recording window) might improve clarity.

Stereo Setups

These setups serve as both mono (both mics panned to C [center]) and panned full L (left) and R (right).

If the objective is recording the double bass or cello as a solo instrument, a proper stereo setup is a better solution, because this provides a more natural image of the instrument interacting with the acoustics. Use the X-Y stereo (see p. 145) to capture the sound radiating from the large soundboard in all directions. The distance of the stereo mics (about one meter) is determined by the acoustics, that is, the balance between the direct sound and reverberation. Point both mics toward the area above the bridge.

Mix Settings and Effects

EQ

When it comes to EQing, the cello and double bass are quite different, the cello being a very defined instrument with lots of presence, whereas the double bass has to be controlled in the low end in order to remain defined. The double bass goes down to E at 41.2 Hz, and the cello stops at C at 65.41 Hz.

With acoustic instruments, we have relatively firm expectations of how they should sound—otherwise we find them unnatural sounding—unlike the electric instruments, where there is a broader scope for what can done using EQ, compression, modulation, reverb, delays, and so forth.

Recorded in good acoustics and with quality microphones, neither the cello nor the double bass should be equalized much—only minor adjustments are needed, highlighting their natural sound and addressing any shortcomings in the recording.

Both instruments are rich in overtones—especially the cello—and, as a result, even changes of a few dB in the mid and high frequencies are very audible.

The low end is found in the 40–120 Hz area.

The frequencies defining the body of the double bass and the cello are found between 120 and 300 Hz.

A nasal and even sharp timbre is between 600 Hz and 2 kHz, and often the cello has to be attenuated here.

Presence and articulation is between 2 and 5 kHz and is often boosted on the double bass track.

Air, or an open timbre, is in the 12–16 kHz range.

Reverb

Bass instruments are usually not allocated reverb; only if playing melody lines or improvising in the higher register is reverb is used. But for either instrument, a little natural ambience is often required when it is part of an ensemble.

When the cello plays melodic lines, reverb sounds beautiful, and for this hall reverb seems just right, the decay being determined by the pulse of the music. In some genres, delay also provides a great tonal enhancement.

Compression

When the double bass is used in rock music (like rockabilly), rather hard compression is used, making it cut through the wall of drums and electric guitar. However, in acoustic music, dynamic variations are important. This applies to the folk, jazz, and classical genres, and in these musicians are more trained in overall dynamic adaptation. Therefore, the double bass is compressed only gently, while the cello is hardly ever compressed because it typically plays long notes.

Compress discreetly only if you are having trouble with too much dynamic variation. No more than a 2:1 ratio and both attack and release set to auto. A better option might be gain riding (see p. 10) like in the good old days of analog mixing consoles. This requires that you know the music completely, being ready and able to perform level adjustments along the way to make the instrument sit in the mix.

TIPS

✓ If the double bass requires a lot of definition (e.g., in rockabilly), then place the mic close to the striking hand. Generally speaking, a mic placed near to where the tones are struck or bowed provides clarity and definition.

✓ Be careful when close-miking with cardioids, as the proximity effect may boost the low end significantly and strengthen resonances.

✓ Because they have higher energy, the lower notes of the double bass are reflected by the floor and walls (especially by corners). Such frequencies can be omnipresent in the room, so be wary of spill in other instruments' mics.

✓ The stand at the base of the double bass and cello transmits vibrations very efficiently to the floor. If it is a light wood floor, it may act as a resonator and create a significant bass boost. Place the stand on vibration-absorbing material—for example, a piece of wood on top of a soft fabric, or a rubber mat.

✓ Cellists often knock their headphones against the tuning pegs. As usual, it always happens in the middle of the dream take, so cover those pegs closest to the headphones with foam.

✓ Remember to check the tuning of the instrument both during recording and on the recorded tracks as well. This applies to all instruments, but especially to freely intonating instruments (those where there is no fixed pitch for each written note due to the instrument's design). Most musicians become pitch deaf during demanding recordings (the problem being worsened by the use of headphones), and it is too late to correct mistakes the day after.

85

The Violin and the Viola

The Instrument and the Acoustics

Most acoustic instruments are complex in their sound radiation pattern. When the microphone is placed close by, some aspects of their tone (or frequency content) are emphasized, while others are dampened. Therefore, it is important to listen to the instrument; where is the fullness and body? Where does it seem bright or thin? Where is it strident? And from what location does it sound as if there is a blanket over the instrument?

The alternative to placing your ears in every (im)possible place around the instrument is to use headphones while placing the mic at different angles and at varying distances from the instrument.

The sweet spot is not just one single place, so choose the one that best suits the recording—or place multiple mics and choose between them later.

The violin is difficult to record for a number of reasons (what follows pertains to the viola too):

- It interacts with the room and may sound thin and strident in poor acoustics.
- It changes greatly in tone from the low to the high register.
- It has strong harmonics, and in the high register these easily become too sharp if not softened by the acoustics.

An acoustically dampened studio only works when the mic is placed very close (close-miking), and this requires placing the violin in the mix using artificial reverb. But in a live ambience, the violin has many more shades to its sound. Together with the differences in playing technique associated with various genres of music, this means that recording techniques for the violin vary in many important aspects.

In the rock and contemporary folk genres, you should go for an aggressive and close-up sound. Consequently, the recording normally takes place in dead acoustics and with the mic close to the strings to get the raw sound of the bowing. Place a cardioid mic at 15–20 cm from the strings. For more fullness and depth from the soundboard, the mic can be moved to a distance of 20–30 cm, still pointing at where the bow strikes the strings and slightly tilted toward the bridge (see the left in figure 10.1). The further the mic is moved away, the more of the entire soundboard is picked up, as well as more of the ambience.

 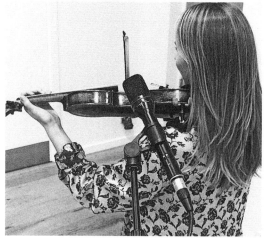

Figure 10.1

Close-miking and ambience setup using a Micro Gefell UM70s, which is based on the original Neumann M7 capsule. Shown at the left is close-miking with cardioid.

By gradually moving the mic more than 30 cm from the strings, more ambience is recorded. The location behind the shoulder reduces the direct sound from the bow and strings and provides a more full and rounded sound. Moreover, the polar pattern can be switched to omni to pick up more of the acoustics.

Both small and large diaphragm cardioids like Neumann, Studio Projects LSD2, Microtech Gefell, Røde, and similar do an excellent job. What is most important is that the mic does not boost the treble, thus making the recording sound thin.

For added fullness, use an AKG C-12 (or, if possible, the C-24 stereo version) or an Electro Voice RE20, as both are designed to highlight the bottom end, while a tube mic might provide excellent color and a ribbon reduces the top end. The close-up mic may be combined with a mic at a slightly greater distance to achieve width and depth. The balance between the ambient and direct mic depends on the acoustics, so try it out.

Close-miking technique picks up a lot of raw sound from the bowing of the strings, which, together with the proximity effect, creates an aggressive sound. This is not the natural sound of the violin and is far from appreciated in all genres. The placing of a cardioid or an omni 40–50 cm above and slightly behind the violinist's left shoulder, pointing to the low end of the violin, provides a more coherent and organic sound, because the violin radiates a lot of energy from its back and sides (see the right in figure 10.1). This—or a mic placed at a greater distance (above 80 cm, capturing a fair bit of ambience)—is the natural violin sound suited to the classical and traditional folk genres.

A mic placed below the violin provides a very round and full sound without much of the bowing. This location can also be used as a supplement to add fullness to the aforementioned setups.

A spaced-stereo recording (e.g., using two small–diaphragm mics like the Neumann KM54, KM84, KM64, or their cheaper competitor Oktava MK012) (see p. 142) provides more width and depth to the violin. They are panned to 11 and 1 o'clock or more and adapted to the mix so that they do not take up space from other instruments while still sounding natural.

Stereo recording will always be the best option when recording a solo violin, but this requires good acoustics (this applies to stereo recording of acoustic instruments in general). A stereo setup provides the greatest width and depth, and from a greater distance the mics pick up the fullness from the room reflections, and the sound is more delicate and softer than the raw and rich close-up sound preferred in the rock and folk genres.

The viola is easier to record than the violin due to its natural fullness. Since it is tuned one fifth below the violin, you are not as likely to end up with a thin and light-weight recording as with the violin. Apart from this, the same recording techniques apply as for the violin—and, as with all other acoustic instruments, listen and find the sweet spot.

Box 10.1

See chapter 33, "The Recording Room," for specific tips on using and adjusting the acoustics of the recording room.

Mix Settings and Effects

EQ

EQ is only used for the fine-tuning of the recording, because the violin and viola respond strongly even with minor EQ changes. The effective EQ ranges are almost the same as for the vocal:

- Fullness is between 200 and 500 Hz.
- Between 800 Hz to 2 kHz, use attenuation to eliminate sharpness.
- Presence and articulation are in the 2–5 kHz range. Here, the violin can be made impactful in the mix, but be careful, as the sound easily becomes strident with too much emphasis.
- Between 5 and 10 kHz clarity is found, but also scraping and scratching from the bow.
- Air—that is, the range above 12 kHz—opens up string instruments.

Instead of using EQ, a dark reverb can be used to boost the fullness or a bright one to make the violin come forward in the mix.

Reverb

Close-miking picks up no ambience, so only when using ambient mics does the violin survive without reverb. With close-miking, reverb is therefore added in the mix to open up the violin and make it blend with the other instruments, and both violin and viola feel at home with the chamber and hall reverb types. Convolution reverbs, based on actual existing acoustics, are even better, such as the Vienna MIR, whose variable parameters include microphone and instrument placement in a variety of acoustics. Among others, these acoustics include sampled concert halls like the Concertgebouw (Amsterdam), Musikverein (Vienna), and Wood Hall (London), along with many great acoustics from small churches.

Both the violin and viola love long decay times (up to 4–5 s), but the reverberation should not be too bright. On digital reverbs, attenuation with a parametric EQ is often used between 4 and 10 kHz or a roll-off combined with the high shelf.

Compression

In the classical genres, compression is never used on strings. It is not necessary because the musicians adapt dynamically to each other while the ambience also smooths out variations in level.

In the folk and rock genres, compression is used, because close-miking highlights differences in playing strength and movements in relation to the mic placement, and this results in unintended level differences. To control the dynamic range, compression is required, but merely a 2.5:1 ratio and with auto controlling the attack and release. Fairchild and most optical compressors (also their digital versions) are great with strings. The alternative is to ride the faders—that is, reducing levels with strong bowing and boosting during light.

TIPS

✓ If a string section is tracked by recording one individual violin and viola repeatedly to make them sound like a full string ensemble, it's best to record from different angles and distances, creating the small variations that are naturally found in an ensemble. At more than 30 cm, a mic will pick up some ambience from the room. This may be combined with variations in the playing, such as the same line played on a lower string (and then seven positions higher). The individual tracks are panned.

✓ Synthesized strings add life and realism through a few overdubs with live strings.

✓ DPA d:vote 4099 condenser mics, with a supercardioid characteristic, are suitable for violins both live and in the studio. They reduce spill, and at the same time they have a good off-axis response and can be attached to the violin, thus following the movements of the violinist.

✓ If you have trouble recording the sound as the musician thinks it should be, then place the mic above and slightly behind the musician's left shoulder, where the sound that the player hears is found.

Brass and Wind Instruments

The Instrument and the Acoustics

Brass and wind instruments (typically in the pop and rock genres the alto or tenor saxophone, trumpet, and sometimes the trombone or baritone sax) are acoustic instruments whose sound is shaped in interaction with the acoustics. Ambience is essential both to their sustain and to the feel of the musicians, and a recording room with a combination of wooden and absorbing surfaces—that is, a short, controlled reverberation—is highly suitable.

When recording a single saxophone or trumpet, two microphones are often used to capture both the direct sound and the ambience. In the case of a full horn section, it is rarely advisable to record one instrument at a time; in order to maintain the density and interaction of the ensemble, the entire horn section is best recorded simultaneously.

The headphone mix is particularly important, because it must feel natural to the musicians and be supportive of their playing. A short ambient reverb is often used to provide a live feel if the acoustics do not provide this. When recording multiple musicians at a time, it is important to agree on the communication used if a musician plays a wrong note, as their patience should not be tested by having to play through the entire take if it has to be re-recorded anyway.

Mic Setup

In practice, despite their acoustic properties, the brass and the wind instruments (the horns) are normally close-miked, because the recording room acoustics are inappropriate, or the horns are part of an ensemble, or because of the need to achieve an in-your-face recording. Instead, a short reverb or delay is added in the mix to restore some acoustics to the instruments.

This close-miking requires both quality condenser mics (being able to handle a high SPL) and preamps with good transient handling because of the powerful dynamics of the horns.

A widely used mic is the AKG 414, as it provides a realistic picture of both the ambience and the timbral richness of horns. Quality mics like the Neumann U87, Schoeps CMC5U, or Sennheiser MKH40 are often used, as well as tube mics, because they highlight the harmonics and fullness by adding a slight harmonic distortion. A dynamic mic may be used if you want to color the sound in a certain way or if the mics are placed

Figure 11.1

A Royer R-122 ribbon on the trumpet and angled slightly to the side at 40 cm distance. Ribbon mics soften the high-mids of the brass instruments. © Royer Labs

Figure 11.2

DPA d:vote 4099 fastened to the bell. Works great in live situations and is ideal when recording a horn section in the same room, as it reduces spill. © DPA Microphones

very close to each instrument in a horn section in order to minimize spill and the acoustics. Again, some less expensive condensers can do the job. Marshall's MXL u69 might outperform others that are more than ten times as expensive when it comes to recording a saxophone. Ribbon mics are also well suited because they round off the thinness and sharpness of the brass instruments; the sE Electronics X1R ribbon is an affordable alternative on brass, electric guitar, voice-over, and so forth.

Generally, the mic is placed 30–60 cm from and a little to the side of the bell (off-axis; see p. 135) in order to capture both the bell sound and the direct sound from the valves or keys. Use the cardioid characteristic to reduce pickup of the acoustics and omni to capture more of it. Remember that the cardioid gradually loses fullness at more than 30 cm distance, so in good acoustics an omni probably does the job better.

The close-up mic is often supplemented with a second condenser mic at a greater distance so as to capture the ambience of the recording space. In the mix, pan the two mics to provide width and depth.

The Horn Section

When it comes to the entire horn section, set up the instruments in a straight line in front of the mic following the 3:1 rule (see p. 275), balancing their levels afterwards. The 3:1 rule reduces spill and thus phase cancelation (the comb filter effect; see p. 272). It is also important that the layout is done in tonal order (e.g., first trumpet, second trumpet, tenor sax, and trombone), because there will be spill between the mics. If, in the mix, you want to brighten trumpet 1 using EQ, this setup provides more control, because the EQ will only af-

Figure 11.3

Recording the tenor sax using an AKG C314 and a Microtech Gefell UM 70. The two condenser mics are placed slightly above the bell pointing toward the valves below the left-hand playing position where the sound is rich and full. The distance may be 30–60 cm depending on the acoustics. In good acoustics, one mic may be moved further away and set to omni for use as an ambience mic. Use trial and error to find the exact location.
This setup is called spaced stereo and can also be used on the alto sax, the trumpet, and the clarinet. In the mix, pan the two tracks and use level to control their blend.

fect the spill from trumpet 2 (being the closest instrument), and since they are tonally close, this will cause fewer difficulties. If the entire horn section is placed in a circle around a single omni mic, their relative playing levels should be precisely adjusted, as there are then minimal opportunities to balance this in the mix (without a disciplined section, this arrangement might be viewed as foolhardy, as it is often said that brass players have a dynamic range comprising on and off).

The double-tracking of the horn section may well be a matter of genre, but it is also a controversial topic. In blues, smaller jazz ensembles, and old school genres, doubling is avoided like the plague, as it produces too neat a sound. In the funk genres, the trumpet and the sax are often doubled to add fullness and a larger sound. By contrast, the baritone sax (if used) is rarely doubled, because this provides too large a bottom end, thus reducing the "funk factor."

The countless tracks of the DAW encourage multiple takes, for example, of solos. Most DAWs have some kind of cycle recording mode, which groups multiple takes, making it easy to cut the final solo together.

Figure 11.4
Acoustic panels (or ISO panels; see p. 291) are used to reduce spill between the individual instruments when recording a full horn section.

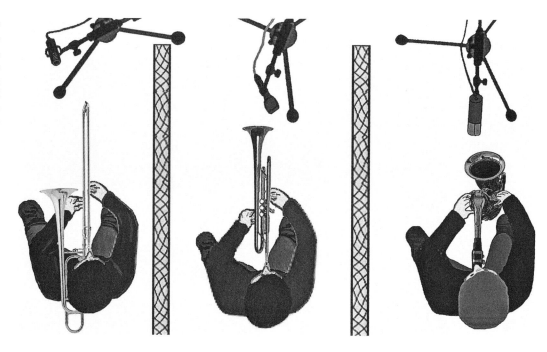

Mix Settings and Effects

EQ

While it is quite easy to make a horn sound clear and defined in the mix, it is not that easy to maintain its body and fullness. Instead, try to capture the entire tone of the horn while recording. Experienced engineers avoid EQ'ing the horns during recording and use only very little EQ in the mix, because it is difficult to make anything but a minimal EQ sound right on horns. Even a few dB gain in the highs makes the horns thin or sharp sounding, and boosting low frequencies tends to put a blanket over their tone.

On the horn section, it is often better to add a deeper or a higher transposition of a melody line rather than trusting to low- or high-end EQ. If the recording does not already include a baritone sax or a trombone, one of these can be added to provide bottom end. Trumpets are easily doubled to create fullness in the midrange and/or a distinctive top end.

The small doses of EQ used for minor repairs can be found in almost the same areas as for the vocal. Density and fullness is between 120 and 240 Hz, while between 800 Hz and 2 kHz you often have to attenuate to remove a nasal and tinny tone. Presence and articulation are between 2 and 5 kHz, and it is here that the impact of the horns in the mix is to be found, though too much makes them sharp and strident.

Any shrillness can be reduced by cutting between 5 and 8 kHz. The air, as usual, is above 12 kHz.

Reverb

Since the horn section in the pop and rock genres often performs rhythmically distinct riffs and fill-ins, only very short reverbs, slap back reverbs, or short delays are used.

A short, dark reverb emphasizes the section's fullness, and a short light reverb makes it stand out in the mix. For the solos, of course, longer reverbs or delays are used to make them sound bigger. A sax solo in the rock genre loves the floating character produced by a stereo or tape echo that highlights both its sustain and fullness.

Maintaining Dynamics

Compressing the trumpet is almost never done, as this will strangle the transients, making it seem as if there is a blanket over the sound. By contrast, it works fine on the sax and the trombone with a moderate compression, providing tightness to their bottom end. Also, a trumpet left uncompressed at the top of the horn section has the added benefit of making the remaining horns seem virtually uncompressed.

Use a ratio of 2–3:1 and gain reduction of 2–4 dB to smooth out the horns' levels in the mix.

Likewise, a sax solo tolerates a light compression; not much is usually needed, since the playing technique itself compresses the tone of playing in the range from medium to powerful.

TIPS

✓ The players in a well-functioning horn section instinctively control their dynamics. In less experienced sections, it may be necessary to use a medium compression to make them sound tight. Compress most in the lower horns.

✓ To achieve a gritty, raw rock 'n' roll or blues tone on a sax solo, a dynamic vocal mic such as a Shure SM58 will most often do the job. Also, add a delay of short or medium length (adapted to the tempo of the song).

✓ If the horn section is doubled—preferably using alternating inversions—the effect of twice the number of horns is achieved.

✓ In pop recordings, synthesized brass instruments are often used, as they are easily arranged and recorded. When these synthesized brass instruments are mixed with a single, real-world horn—normally a trumpet—they will seem quite authentic while being tight and aggressive, as on Peter Gabriel's "Sledgehammer" (1986).

✓ Too many instruments in the headphone mix might confuse the players' sense of pitch. Since the horns are wind instruments reliant on their human players for their tuning, try limiting the mix to the rhythm section and a basic chord instrument if the horns are having difficulties with intonation.

12

Synthesizers and Electronic Keyboards

The Instrument

As music lovers, we are used to instruments with complex waveform envelopes; for example, dynamically variable percussive strikes and bowed sounds develop and change their timbre over time, with each harmonic having a different ADSR envelope (see p. 175). However, compared to both acoustic and electric instruments, sample-based and synthesized sounds are still fairly static in their compound ADSR envelopes.

In concert and gig situations, however, most synthesizer presets immediately work because of the modulation, reverb, delays, and other spatial effects that are used by the manufacturer as an integral part of their sound. But even though sample-based keyboards are increasingly attaining the characteristics and parameters of natural instruments and have larger memory and so forth, there is still a little work to be done with modulation and spatial effects to make them come to life and blend in the mix.

Synthetic sounds based on waveform or FM synthesis, for example, often have a more complex and adjustable ADSR envelope than a sampled waveform and, in any case, are typically not subject to our expectations regarding natural instruments; they are easier, therefore, to blend in the mix.

DI, Mics, or MIDI?

The electronic keyboard and the synthesizer are simple to record because they can be connected directly to the line-in of the audio interface (or mixer).

Basically, their built-in reverb and delay effects should be deactivated and replaced by a studio reverb that makes them blend with the other instruments in the recording. As they are of better quality, the studio effects can also be customized and fine-tuned during the mix. Only effects that are completely integral to a synth patch should be kept.

Sometimes, an extra track is used to record the synth played through a speaker (recorded with a mic) to add a bit of ambience and harmonic distortion. Fender Twin amplifiers and the like are suitable because of their clean sound, and new amp types like the Line 6 DT25 also do a great job here because they can change their topology (that is, the digital modeling of different amps) across the range from clean to distorted.

Figure 12.1

Most synth patches are mono, and only their effects (chorus, reverb, etc.) add stereo width; the effects should be deactivated and only the mono output recorded, because studio effects are added in the mix. However, the Nord piano, among others, provides true stereo samples and so can be recorded with or without effects according to taste. © Clavia Digital Musical Instruments

There are major benefits to recording the synth and other MIDI instruments to the DAW sequencer as MIDI tracks that are then editable. In the MIDI track, chord changes (such as inversions) can be made, imperfections corrected, note lengths and velocities adjusted, and so on. If the track is recorded to tempo (click track), even entire sections, like a chorus, can be copy-pasted, and tricky or speedy figures can be edited and quantized to 100% perfection. In the electronic genres, the advantage of the synth (and MIDI

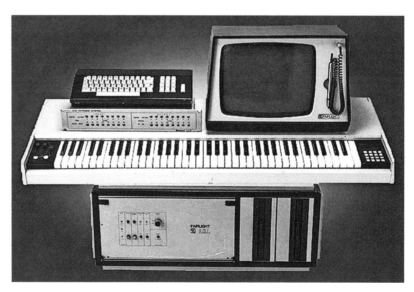

Figure 12.2

The Fairlight CMI sampler, designed in 1979, sported 16 kHz sampling, 8-bit resolution, 16 kb of memory for each of its eight polyphonic voices, and, in addition, two 8″ floppy disk drives. The loops and samples produced on the Fairlight CMI were used innovatively and creatively by Peter Gabriel in 1982 on his fourth album. The largest model, CMI Series III (1985), cost £60,000 (at the time, triple the price of an average house in the United Kingdom). It boasted 16-bit sampling and a built-in memory of 14 mb. Together with its sampling feature, the built-in sequencer revolutionized the way music was produced, and a new production aesthetics took over the studio.

Yes's "Owner of a Lonely Heart" (1983) was the first release to use samples as a breakbeat, and the song also used MIDI editing in its fast, percussive synth figures. The producer on the album was Trevor Horn, and his Fairlight programming came to influence the sound of the 1980s. His exploration of the creative possibilities of programming became an important inspiration for later electronic genres (techno, dance, etc.) that used the studio mainly for programming and only to a lesser degree for recording. © Peter Vogel Instruments

instrument plugins) is that creative editing on the sequencer facilitates fills and runs that are unplayable by musicians, as it likewise facilitates music production by non-musicians.

Mix Settings and Effects

Synth and sampling instruments span a vast variety of sounds, making it impossible to give guidelines other than that they generally should not have too much bottom end or they will blur the bass, kick drum, guitar, and vocals in the boomy range of 100–250 Hz. Synths may be equalized fairly freely. A Yamaha DX7 piano, for example, may be EQed to extremes without sounding unnatural. Samples of acoustic instruments, though, are subject to a great extent to the requirements of natural tones compared to synthetic sounds that are freed from these expectations if they are not too sharp, strident, boomy, and so forth.

Just like with any other instrument, the space around the synths and electronic instruments is crucial for their blending in the mix. Delay and chorus can be used in larger quantities than with acoustic instruments. Always remember to check the time-based effects in relation to the song's pulse and tempo.

A synth sound that does not blend tonally with the remaining tracks might benefit from being recorded via both line-in and to a sequencer MIDI track so that it can then be tried out with a variety of patches, perhaps being layered with one or more of these to make it fit into the space of the mix not already taken up by other instruments.

99

TIPS

✓ Editing the synth patches (using the built-in filters) is often more effective than using EQ when making them adapt to the rest of the mix. Using inversions of the chords to make them heavier or lighter also works better than EQ.

✓ If there are gaps in a song's overall sound, a synth pad might be the glue that binds the entire mix together when added discreetly in the background, only being felt and first noted as a lack in the mix if it is muted.

13

The Leslie Speaker

The Instrument

The Leslie speaker is almost always associated with the sound of the Hammond organ. Made up of a rotary horn at the top, reproducing the midrange and high range, and a bass speaker at the bottom, which has its own rotor (and speed), it is basically an amplifier with a two-way loudspeaker. It is the rotating speakers that make the Leslie sound special, the variations ranging from slow to fast rotation. In addition, the sound of stopping the rotors creates a special effect, the brake effect.

The electric guitar and the Leslie speaker are also a perfect match, and on the voice it can be used to add a dreamy and evocative effect.

The Leslie effect is due to the Doppler effect (see figure 13.2) and there is also a tremolo effect produced at fast rotation. Though the Leslie effect is difficult to mimic perfectly because of the two speakers and the use of distortion from the overdriven amp, it has been quite successfully digitally modeled, and this makes it a lot easier to carry around with you.

Mic Setup

To pick up the full Doppler effect, the Leslie is recorded in stereo with three microphones. Theoretically, the bottom mic and a pair of top mics should be placed at the same distance to the speakers, thus reducing phase issues. In practice, though, the bottom mic often ends up closer, so it does not capture the sound of the top horn.

Pointing at or slightly below the upper rotary horn, a stereo pair is placed at a distance of about one meter, being spaced 1–3 m apart (the distance determining the stereo width). One set of Neumann U67 mics does a great job, but more accessible mics, like sE Electronics, Oktava, and Røde will also do an excellent job. Dynamic mics, like the Shure SM58 and Sennheiser 421, also do a decent job here. As a general rule, the mics should merely not boost the top end.

A mic with a good bass response is used on the low rotary speaker, like the Shure Beta 52, AKG D-112, or Electro Voice RE27 (which are also suitable as kick drum mics). It is placed up to 10–15 cm from the speaker and used to balance the fullness of the sound relative to the top mics. Pay attention: the mic might pick up wind noise from the rotor; if necessary, use a windshield.

Figure 13.1
Two AKG 414 mics spaced slightly more than 1 m apart capture the top end while a Neumann TLM 103 captures the bottom end.

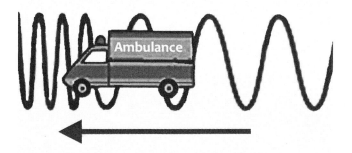

Figure 13.2
The Doppler effect explains why a sound moving toward the listener will have higher frequencies and lower frequencies while moving away. In this way, we can hear the differences in speed being reinforced by the modulation of the amplitude via the Leslie rotors.
The effect is even more apparent when it comes to an emergency vehicle racing by; the frequency of the siren is increased when approaching, suddenly becoming much lower as it passes. The variation in pitch is determined by the ratio between the speed of the vehicle and the speed of sound (which is roughly 344 meters per second, or 1,238 kilometers per hour).

As with the guitar, dynamic mics will pick up a solid sound, while condensers have more subtlety and a greater frequency range. Vocal mics might have a high-mid boost, making the Leslie/Hammond combination sound thin and grainy.

Another approach to the top stereo pair is the MS stereo setup. An omni or cardioid mic is pointed directly at or slightly below the upper horn, and a figure-of-eight mic is placed on top of this (as coincident as possible), its null being directed toward the horn and the figure-of-eight pattern covering the rotor movements. In the mix, the two MS signals are decoded (see p. 146), taking advantage of the variable stereo width—from mono to gradually wider and full L (left) and R (right). This arrangement solves the problem of two mics thinning out the rotor action of the Leslie (while a single mic would not pick up any movement at all).

Mix Settings and Effects

The Leslie provides a vast amount of spatial information, depth and width included. Pan the top mics to L and R while keeping the bottom mic centered. The Leslie/Hammond setup is an obvious choice with which to emphasize the width of a recording; perhaps it should develop from a narrow mono in the verse to a full L and R spread in the chorus.

EQ is required only to a small extent and often only to make space for other instruments competing in the same frequency range. Often the high or high-mids should be dampened slightly to reduce the grittiness of distortion, but apart from this, EQ easily makes the Leslie/Hammond thin or dull sounding.

Compression is not needed, since both the distortion from the amplifier (in the Leslie) and the Hammond deliver a powerful, natural-sounding compression.

A little reverb may be used to make it blend in the mix, but due to the long, sustained notes and the full sound, it should be kept light and short; use something like an ambience or plate reverb.

14

Live in the Studio

Isolation Booths and Screens

In some genres, especially acoustic ones, the musicians prefer to record "live," as an ensemble, so that they hear and see each other playing much like onstage. The objective is a live feeling with organic ensemble playing.

With a complete drum kit and electrically amplified instruments, the blues- and guitar-based genres are typically recorded live in the studio. Here, it is necessary to isolate the most powerful instruments (or alternatively the weakest) each in their separate isolation booth to avoid spill. Larger studios, therefore, have recording spaces with variable acoustics and booths to isolate the individual instruments.

Often, though, the multiple instruments are recorded simultaneously in the same space. This requires a large studio with enough distance between the walls and to the ceiling to minimize the early reflections, while the instruments are isolated from each other by means of acoustic screens. The vocal is normally a cue vocal (not the final recording), and acoustic guitars, solos, and so on are also recorded later as overdubs.

When recording multiple instruments in this manner, separation becomes essential. The guitar, with its own track in the recording and with no spill from the other instruments, allows for overdubs later and for EQing and so on without affecting the sound of these instruments. This also means that you have to compromise on the rule of recording music in the acoustics to suit the instruments and genre.

Separation is improved by:

- Placing the mic as close as possible to the speakers or instruments.
- The use of directional microphones (cardioid, supercardioid).
- The use of isolation booths for the weakest or the most powerful instruments.
- The use of acoustic screens (also called baffles or gobos).

If the acoustics are good and controlled, then that is enough to reduce spill to some degree. Omni mics can therefore be used, their advantage being that they have less off-axis coloration than cardioids, and they also provide more depth and ambience to the recording.

With only acoustic instruments in the recording room, there is a near perfect solution for "live in the studio" while also meeting the engineer's desire for isolation

Figure 14.1

Live in the studio using acoustic screening of the instruments. Guitar, bass, mandolin, cajon, and saxophone work well in this lineup. Flute, violin, trumpet, and tambourine are a bit harder, as their piercing tones tend to spread all over the room.

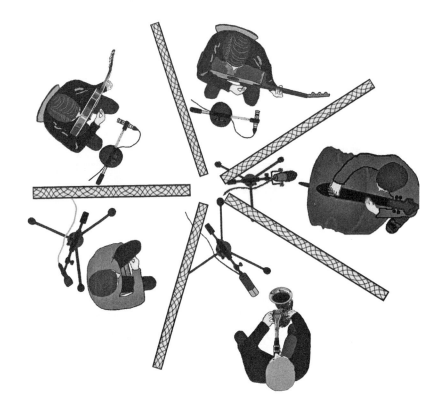

of individual instruments on separate tracks with minimal spill. To this end, acoustic screens are set up so that they radiate from the center like the spokes of a wheel. In the enclosures, the musicians are placed facing the center of the circle so that they can see each other. Directional mics are placed pointing away from the center toward each instrument, picking up the other instruments only minimally due to their cardioid characteristics and the screens. Equally, there will be no significant pickup of the room's acoustics. In the case of evident reverberation, this should be reduced by putting up blankets, carpets, and the like in the corners and on the hard surfaces of the recording room. When recording multiple instruments like this, we need to reduce the ambience, as each microphone would also record the spill from the other instruments. (There is more about general mic placement below and specific mic placement to account for the quirks of individual instruments in the chapters on those instruments.)

Box 14.1 Spill

Spill, also called leakage or spillover, occurs when using several mics to record multiple instruments in the same room. The various instruments are each recorded to their own tracks in order to control and shape their sound in the mix, but each mic picks up the sound of other instruments to a greater or lesser extent. Spill therefore is an issue that makes it impractical to use EQ, compression, and so on on a single instrument without instruments spilling onto that track also being processed.

The drum kit is a great example, because it is usually recorded with several mics. In rock music, the snare is an important element in the overall sound, and so its sound is shaped extensively by the use of EQ and effects. A noticeable spill from the hi-hat (and the other drums) to the snare track will be colored by the effects added to the snare.

In many cases, it is not the spill in itself but a poor-sounding spill that is the problem. Dynamic cardioid mics, traditionally used for the snare drum, have a fairly poor off-axis response, and the hi-hat always sounds nasty through a Shure SM57 that is used on the snare.

The quality of the spill is much better with omni mics, because they pick up as linearly at the front as from the sides and the rear, often making the spill useful in creating fullness and depth of sound even on the drum kit (see p. 19).

The greatest benefit of ensemble playing in the studio is that it is not ruined by the separate recording of each instrument as an overdub. The focus on the sound and performance of each individual instrument is replaced by the focus on the whole sound and ensemble playing, ideally making the end result better.

In this situation, first takes often are the best, because they have the alert and buzzing energy of the present moment. In most genres, the feelings are the fuel that gives energy to the musicians' mastery of their instruments. A tune sung with a strong emotional impact always beats one that has lost its spontaneity and freshness over the span of multiple takes recorded in the pursuit of perfection.

Except for the electronic genres that are programmed and have a machine-based expression as a structural aesthetic element, it is the human factor that constitutes the essence of music. Neither the studio nor its machines can rival the importance of the performance.

Box 14.2 The Basic Rules of Microphone Placement

The following rules apply to both acoustic and electric instruments, whether you are recording a solo instrument, overdubbing, or undertaking an ensemble recording. In the latter case, you might be somewhat limited in the placement of microphones regarding distance from source, but the basic concepts still hold true. And always use headphones to protect against the sound pressure from drums and guitar speakers and to monitor how the mics themselves pick up the sound.

1. Use your ears! Find the spot in the room where the instrument sounds the best, and listen from different angles and distances. Utilize your experience of where the various tonal nuances of the instrument radiate from: the cabinet, the soundboard, the valves of wind instruments, and so on.

   If you are not familiar with the instrument, the best way is to move yourself around it until you find the sweet spot: the place where it sounds full, defined, and natural. This is especially true for acoustic instruments, because we associate these largely with how they sound in their acoustic surroundings. Experienced musicians clearly sense when the room is responding to their playing, so listen to their judgment as well.

2. Select the best microphone for the purpose. This requires you to be familiar with the available mics—if you are not, try them out.

3. Place the microphone where the instrument sounds best in the room. Listen in quality (i.e., neutral) headphones while making small adjustments. A few centimeters or a different angle might make the difference. Are the attacks or the fullness missing? Is it too bright or dark? Even acoustically challenged spaces may have sweet spots, so try out different mic positions.

4. The more distant the microphone is from the sound source, the more of the room acoustics is captured. An acoustic instrument will have a richer sound when recorded in interaction with the acoustics. As a fundamental principle, it is always best to use a space with proper acoustics and an omni mic (as ambient mic) to capture the mix of direct and reflected signals—just as the ears do.

   In acoustically challenged spaces when ensemble recording, it is the better to use close-miking techniques and then replace the acoustics with reverb and spatial effects in the mix.

5. Check the recording in the control room monitors and continue until the sound is right. Replace the mic with one picking up the instrument as you hear it in the room or with one highlighting the sound you are after. If necessary, change the instrument, or even the musician.

6. Only after that is it time to EQ, compress, and otherwise manipulate the recording so that the tracks contribute to the mix. Though it is always possible to correct shortcomings in the recording with EQ, this is often at the expense of something else.

7. *Great raw material provides the best mix. This is obvious, really—and it works!*

Ghost Notes

In practice, not all instruments of an ensemble are recorded simultaneously when using multitracking. (For recording entire ensembles such as choirs all at once, see the next chapter.) In the initial tracks, usually the melody instruments and solos are left out, allowing them to receive particular attention during the recording and mixing.

This is especially important because fixes (e.g., overdubs) are only possible to a limited extent on the individual tracks of a live recording, since there will be ghost notes from the previous recording; these are the remains of the original recording of the instrument that are still on other instruments' tracks in the form of spill. For this reason, the vocal (or the melody instrument) is recorded later, because noticeable leftovers from such prominent tracks are unacceptable. The violin, the timbales, and the like also tend to be everywhere, so they should preferably be recorded as overdubs or isolated in a booth when recording.

Rather than using overdubs to make fixes, sometimes two or more takes are spliced together—those having the best ensemble playing—and only after that are the vocal, melody instruments, and solos overdubbed above the spliced basic tracks. A similar method is used for orchestral recordings of classical music, in which, for example, a recording of a late Romantic symphony (i.e., with a large orchestra and long movements) is often composed of several hundred takes. While there might be just a few recordings of the whole piece, difficult sections or a couple of bars might be recorded several times before being deemed acceptable with the final version being spliced into the whole. There is no shame in music performers of any genre taking advantage of studio techniques to creatively shape and perfect their performances; the pianist Glenn Gould, the renowned Bach interpreter, would spend hours splicing tapes of his performances together in the hunt for perfection.

TIPS

✓ Check out each mic for spill before recording. If spill is a concern, then swap the positions of the instruments involved. If the djembe leaks its rumble onto the upright bass's mic, this will be hard to eliminate in the mix, since the two share a lot of their lower frequencies. In contrast, the same rumble on the mandolin track is relatively easily dampened by EQ without ruining the sound of the instrument.

✓ Place instruments that have the same function in the mix next to each other—for instance, the guitar and mandolin if they both play chords or the same melody line. Thereafter, EQ and compression will probably do a good job of reducing any spill.

✓ Or place instruments that are timbrally far apart next to one another. Low frequency content from the upright bass that has leaked to the guitar or banjo track can, in most cases, be attenuated without issues.

✓ Acoustic instruments change with temperature and humidity. Some may sound better in dry and warm air, others in damp or cold temperatures. For the same reason, recordings made at different times sound vastly different, making the splicing of takes and overdubbing impossible.

Box 14.3 The Headphone Mix

The sound in the headphones should excite the musician already while recording. Musicians always "play on the sound," and if this is not in the headphones, it will not inspire the best take. The fix-in-the-mix approach is rarely a good one; taking the time to set up the right sound makes the raw material better.

Also, remember that it is always important to make the musicians feel at home in the studio. Create a comfortable zone with a relaxed atmosphere, or use a disarming joke if the atmosphere becomes too tense. Many musicians create their best work (perhaps even their best solo) if they think that the technician is still struggling with the sound of the microphone (so keep the tape running even while the musicians think they are not yet being recorded).

When setting up the headphone mix for an entire rhythm section or an acoustic band, you will often find that however much you twist the controls and faders, move around the mics, and so forth, the mix does not really fall into place; in the monitors and headphones, the mix does not sound like the music will ever become a whole. But then—all of a sudden—it is there.

Perhaps it is due to the sum of the slight changes, but it is equally likely that the musicians' playing has changed. The musicians, having become accustomed to the space and the unfamiliar situation of using headphones, are finally listening to each other and playing together.

Therefore, it is important to do everything possible to facilitate this process and to make the routine of setting up the headphone mix (or mixes) comfortable for the musicians.

This also explains the no-headphones approach preferred by some engineers. If you place good musicians in a space where they have good eye contact and where they can hear each other clearly, they will adapt their levels and play together a lot better. When this approach is successful, the recording is likely to mix itself in terms of levels.

15

Recording Choirs and Small Acoustic Ensembles

Choral music and small acoustic ensembles are recorded live and usually in acoustics suiting the genre and the size of the ensemble. With these ensembles, therefore, the focus is shifted from close-miking and overdubs in the studio to capturing the entirety of the ensemble and the acoustics. The technical setup is fairly simple, but the ideal conditions—the proper acoustics and a setup working optimally both for the musicians and the recording—are more difficult to establish.

In the following, a choral recording is used as an example, but the same approach applies to small classical ensembles (e.g., a string quartet or a wind quintet) and to acoustic ensembles with instruments having comparable sounds and strengths. The principles also apply to larger acoustic ensembles, though these are complicated by the use of a larger number of microphones, the placing of the instrument groups, and the interaction between the acoustics and the larger ensemble sound.

The Acoustics

Choirs are not recorded by overdubs, because this would cause problems with changes in tempo, dynamics, choral texture, and intonation—in short, overdubbing would work against many of the qualities that a choir works hard to perfect.

Thus, the acoustics are crucial to the recording, and the stereo mics, placed in front of the choir, become the main mics. Only a few studios have the space for these kinds of recordings. A choir's phrasing and articulation are affected by the acoustics of the space and so it can be difficult to find the appropriate room; the reverberation time and the coloration of the room are therefore essential both to the performance of the choir and the sound of the recording.

The reverberation time should fit the genre and size of the choir and, for smaller choirs, it can be relatively short like 1.5–2 s. Also, high ceilings are important, at least 4 m, to reduce the early reflections that create comb filter effects (see p. 272). The echo-like reverberations (called flutter echoes) being thrown back and forth between corners and parallel walls are likewise highly destructive, even when present to a lesser extent, and must be dampened, such as by using a heavy stage curtain.

Figure 15.1
A long-tested tradition has led to the establishment of various types of concert halls adapted to the genres and sizes of orchestras and ensembles.
Aarhus Concert Hall in Denmark was originally a multifunction space, with the result that the concert hall was not very good for either classical or popular music. The building was refurbished in 2007, and the Symphonic Hall was given a reverberation time of 2.5 s, while the new Rhythmic Hall had a reverberation time of 1.0 s. The Symphonic Hall features mobile shutters on top of treble-absorbing surfaces, enabling the reverberation time to be reduced to 2.2 s.
© Musikhuset Aarhus

Assembly halls or auditoriums, with a combination of wooden surfaces and absorbing materials, are sometimes adequate, though it may be easier to find a church with a smooth decay, since churches are built to distribute sound and to add reverberation to singing. In the church, the sound spreads out from the high space of the nave across columns, rows of seats, and aisles—all of it distributing the sound evenly without causing problematic early reflections. Equally, the many different distances and spaces found in the best churches distribute the reverberation evenly across most frequency ranges.

The reverberation time for a large choir should be 2–3 s—however, for sacred music it can be up to 4–6 s—and this requires a church of a certain size. Odense Cathedral in Denmark, for example, completed in 1499 in the Gothic architectural style, has a pleasant, smooth reverb at just over 5 s that is suitable for classical music if the stereo mic set is placed relatively close to the choir (that is, at 4–7 m); a popular music choir, though, would be washed out in such acoustics. Placing the stereo mics further away provides a reverberation more suitable for cantatas and other sacred choral music.

Sports halls are usually unsuitable, as they always have uncontrolled acoustics due to their shoebox form, and they have a long decay in combination with echo-like reflections from the corners. In addition, the reverberation in this kind of space is uneven, with different reverb times for different frequency ranges (the reverb time is the time it takes for a sound signal to drop by 60 dB after the source ceases to sound. The cladding, carpets, curtains, and so forth determine by how much different frequencies are absorbed). There is a more detailed discussion of acoustics in chapters 32 and 33.

Gospel choirs and popular music choirs are special cases when it comes to the acoustics of the recording space. When they are accompanied by a rhythm section, they can be recorded live in churches. However, due to problems with the rhythm section leaking into choir mics, such ensembles are frequently recorded in the studio: the instruments are isolated, the choir uses headphones, and artificial reverb is added during the mix.

Mic Placement

For recording the choir, only quality condenser mics are used (linear frequency response and low self-noise), and these are generally small diaphragm (SDC) omnis. In principle, the recording can be made with only two mics set up for stereo recording (see p. 141). The stereo set is placed in the ideal listening position in front of the choir. Depending on the reverberation of the space and the size of the choir, this is 2–5 m or more from the choir. The exact position can be found by using those old-fashioned analog listening devices that are placed on either side of the human central processing unit. In a spaced omni setup, the distance between the mics is determined by the ensemble size—and by listening. For a small choir or ensemble, a distance of 30–40 cm is appropriate, whereas for a larger choir or the symphony orchestra, 40–60 cm is better. As mentioned, the distance to the sound source is also dependent on the acoustics and the size of the ensemble; a general rule would be right behind the conductor and 2.5–4 m above the floor.

Use headphones to find the right blend of the direct sound and reverberation. Fine-tune this by changing the placement of the microphones—even 50 cm can make a huge difference.

A variation of this stereo setup is the Decca tree (see p. 143). This is a spaced omni setup with an extra mic that fills out the hole in the middle of the stereo image (this hole is sometimes an issue with spaced omnis). If there is poor reverberation in the room, move the Decca tree closer to the choir; the mics still capture the overall image but less of the reverberation. Reverberation cannot be removed from a recording; in contrast, you can compensate by adding reverb in the editing process (the mix), and the better devices actually have hall and cathedral reverbs that blend well with natural reverb. In particular, convolution reverbs (see p. 207) provide excellent reverb that is sampled from natural acoustics.

Spot Mics

Normally, extra microphones are added covering each voice group or section in order to subsequently adjust the balance between them. A soloist will also have a separate mic. These mics are called spot microphones, and they are set, according to the recording space, either to the omni characteristic, capturing some of the other voices, or cardioid, which is directional with off-axis coloration (see p. 135).

Figure 15.2

A mic array with spot mics. In order to separate the recording of the choral parts, the voice groups are positioned next to each other, each being captured by a separate mic. An MS stereo setup is placed behind the conductor and a wide, spaced stereo setup at the sides.

It is essential to check for phase problems between the voice group mics. These can be discovered by matching levels of the various mics and then muting them one by one to check whether any of them result in audible phase cancelation. If necessary, switch to mono to enable comb filter effects to be clearly heard.

TIPS

✓ To separate the recording of the choral parts, the voice groups can be placed in a row rather than in the traditional setup with sopranos and altos in front. However, pay attention that this does not affect the singers' abilities with respect to texture, rhythm, and intonation. In any case, doing this will position the voice groups a little untraditionally in the stereo image, since the spot mics must be panned consistently with the setup of the choir (and thus the stereo mics).

✓ When recording straight to stereo, it is advisable to make a trial recording and assess it in a familiar listening environment prior to the actual recording taking place. In this way, you have the opportunity to change the position of the spot mics in relation to the voice groups, but in particular you can make adjustments to the vital placement of the stereo set.

✓ Listen for noises coming from outside of church during recording. Many churches can resonate with low frequencies from outside engines and so on, and they are not very well isolated against aircrafts and birdsong.

Choirs with Accompaniment

Choirs with accompaniment recorded simultaneously can be quite complicated to record. Quiet acoustic instruments are manageable as long as they are screened, but a rhythm section with drums, piano, and bass or trumpet is asking for trouble.

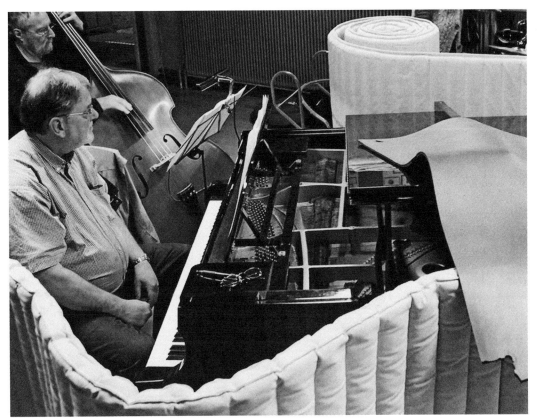

Figure 15.3
The grand piano and the upright bass screened from the choir using roller mats from a gym.

The only way is to isolate those instruments behind acoustic panels, rollup mats, and the like to reduce the sound picked up by the choir mics. An unscreened drum kit both becomes too powerful and results in a phased sound on the drums due to the delay in the drum spill captured by the spot mics on the choir.

The instruments are recorded using close-miking (cardioid setting), though the electric bass is better recorded by splitting the signal into a direct signal to the audio interface and one to the bass amp (which is then only used as a monitor at the lowest possible level and facing away from the choir mics). In an ideal world, the rhythm section would be isolated in a separate room, but then the choir would have to hear the accompaniment through headphones, and this would ruin the performance of most choirs. Only a few gospel and rock choirs are able to do this.

To reduce the spill from the instruments, the spot mics on the vocal parts can be set to (hyper) cardioid. A stereo set for the overall sound can only be used in particularly good acoustics and when the instruments are heard at only a very low level in front of the choir.

Mixing and Editing

When you record like this, there is no chance to correct mistakes by overdubbing. You need to record a virtually perfect performance and, if there are any mistakes, retake a few measures or entire sections that can then be spliced together in the editing phase.

In reality, (at least) two full run-throughs are made of each song to produce the raw material for fixes. While it is fairly easy to splice together various recordings of choirs and classical ensemble music, it is a little harder if there is also a rhythm section, because the pulse must match precisely.

The stereo mic set capturing the entirety of the choir mixed with the acoustics provides the width and depth in the recording when the mics are panned to the L (left) and R (right). In ideal situations, the stereo mics capture a perfect balance of the voices and the acoustics; usually, though, it is necessary to use the spot mics to balance the levels of the individual parts in the mix.

The mix is built up around the stereo tracks, and the individual spot mics are brought in to provide clarity and presence. If the stereo mics have captured too much of the acoustics, blurring the voices, then the level of the spot mics should be raised and the stereo tracks should then be used as the reverberation tracks, providing breadth and fullness. The spot mics are panned so that they are consistent with the actual voice groups' position in space. Also, listen carefully to the individual voice groups to make sure they are localized in accordance with their placement as recorded with the stereo mics (the panning of a spot mic track should not fight against the stereo mic placement of those musicians).

A recording made in good acoustics with good condenser mics rarely needs much EQing, because the ideal is a natural tone that has hopefully been established with the selected acoustics and mics. EQ is used primarily to compensate for any lack of clarity in the recording and to tighten or remove an ill-defined bottom end.

It is only when the recording space or the mics have colored the recording that more extensive EQing might be needed in some frequency ranges. Likewise, sharp and shrill sopranos must be compensated for with an attenuation around 4–7 kHz, while thin basses may need boosting in the 80–150 Hz range. To do this, it is best to use the parametric EQ (p. 158) and select the frequencies to be boosted or attenuated very precisely. The EQ's Q must also be set so that only the problem frequencies are affected.

Reverb is used only to compensate for an imperfect ambience captured by the stereo mics, and normally reverb is only added to the tracks captured by the spot mics in order to make them blend. For this, a convolution reverb providing impulse responses from sampled acoustic spaces similar to the recording room is particularly suitable (see p. 207).

Compression is rarely used on choirs, and then only sparsely on specifically gospel and popular music choirs. Of course, an accompanying rhythm section recorded using close-miking is treated with EQ, compression, and reverb as described under the respective instruments in the previous chapters.

PART II
Microphone Techniques

16

Microphones
Types and Specifications

Microphones all sound different from each other, and no single mic is perfect for all purposes. Mics for classical recordings must be neutral in their frequency response and exhibit low self-noise and low total harmonic distortion while the rock genre often demands a certain coloring. Manufacturers design mics to solve various tasks—often based on the audio ideals of a specific recording approach. Quite a few vocal mics are designed to highlight the 4–8 kHz range, while others are intended to be all-around mics; only a few succeed, among them the AKG 414, which performs most tasks in the studio excellently.

For live use, in order to eliminate feedback, separation and a narrow polar pattern are important. In the studio, clarity and transparency are the main criteria, while noise and distortion are unacceptable. Professional recording studios have a large selection of mics, each being suitable for a particular purpose—perhaps even a specific instrument. Conversely, versatility and price are the key criteria in the home studio, and this means compromises in quality.

A great starting point for choosing a mic is understanding what makes them different. The main features that characterize a mic are:

- **The transducer type:** Most often the dynamic, condenser, or ribbon type is used. Other types are electret, carbon, piezoelectric, and fiber optic, which are almost never used for sound recording.
- **The polar pattern:** the directional characteristics for capturing sound.
- **The frequency response:** the mic's ability to reproduce the audible frequency range.
- **Small diaphragm and large diaphragm (SDC and LDC)**: forms of condenser mics.
- **The dynamic range**: the limits on the weakest and strongest audio signal the mic is able to pick up without ruining the signal with self-noise or distortion.

The mic specifications are a rough guide both for choosing the right mic and for taking full advantage of its features. However, these technical specifications do not tell you everything about how a mic actually sounds; there is no substitute for experience. Make an effort to notice how different mics reproduce and color an instrument. Sharpen your ability to distinguish shades by putting different mics on the same sound source and describing the differences in sound reproduction.

While all features listed above are discussed in this chapter, polar patterns, although introduced here, are important enough to be dealt with in greater detail in the next chapter.

The Transducer Types

Sound waves and electrical signals have some basic properties in common that the early inventors took advantage of from the development of Alexander Graham Bell's telephone (1876) to the first condenser mic in 1915.

Figure 16.1
In 1931, RCA developed their RCA 44 ribbon (*left*). Like Shure's Unidyne Model 55 (*right*) from 1939, the RCA 44 became one of the most iconic mics, appearing with such celebrities as Elvis, John F. Kennedy, and Bing Crosby. The Unidyne Model 55 was the first directional cardioid mic with a single dynamic element.
© RCA © Shure

The mic converts acoustic sound waves into electrical signals via transduction in the dynamic, condenser, or ribbon elements.

The Dynamic Mic

The dynamic mic works just like a reversed loudspeaker, and as a loudspeaker can be used as a (poor) dynamic mic, the reverse is also true (but this will destroy the mic).

The dynamic mic generates electrical signals when its membrane is exposed to the pressure of sound waves and thus moves in phase with them. Sitting on the membrane, a coil surrounding a magnet produces an alternating voltage when the membrane moves. In this way, the sound waves are transformed into alternating electrical voltage that is in turn transduced back into sound waves when it sets the diaphragm of a speaker in motion.

The membrane of the dynamic mic is both thicker and heavier than that of the condenser mic; as the coil is mounted on the diaphragm, this increased weight increases the inertia of the diaphragm. In particular, the higher frequencies do not have sufficient power to make the membrane move, meaning that the frequency range of 8–20 kHz is not reproduced naturally (that is, linearly) by the dynamic mic.

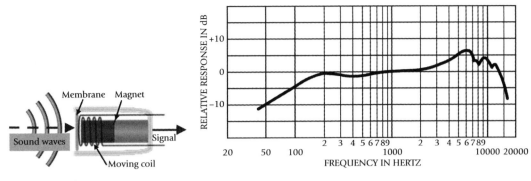

Figure 16.2
Sound waves set the membrane in motion. The magnet produces an electrical signal in the moving coil.
To the right is the frequency response of the Shure SM57. To compensate for the dynamic mic's poor treble
response, the SM57 is designed to boost the 3–12 kHz range by a considerable 2–6 dB. © Shure

General properties of the dynamic mic:

- Robust.
- Less sensitive than condenser mics and therefore more resistant to feedback.
- withstands high sound pressure levels (SPL) and is therefore not suitable for weak sound sources.
- Reproduces the low and high frequency range nonlinearly.
- Tolerates phantom power, but, since it makes some mics generate noise, phantom power should be switched off.

The Condenser Mic

The condenser mic comprises two capacitors (it is also called a capacitor mic): one fixed and the other moving with the membrane. To this end, phantom power is required to generate an electric field between the two capacitors. When the diaphragm is moved by the pressure of sound waves, the distance between the capacitors varies; thus, the stored electric charge in the capacitors varies, producing an electrical signal that is subsequently amplified in the built-in preamp. The diaphragm can be made extremely thin, which makes it very sensitive and quite accurate in its motion in relation to the sound waves. This creates a signal of high quality that may come very close to being linear, that is, identical to the original sound waves.

The quality of the diaphragm and the built-in preamp is directly proportional to the price of a condenser mic.

General properties of the condenser mic:

- Requires phantom power at 48 volts (a few requiring a higher voltage).
- Reproduces the low and high frequency range better than dynamic mics.
- Can have a close to linear frequency response.
- Generates a higher output level, but can be overdriven (its preamp and its diaphragm knocking against the back plate) compared to the dynamic mic.
- Not typically resistant to shocks or moisture, but as condensers are being made more robust, they are used increasingly live.

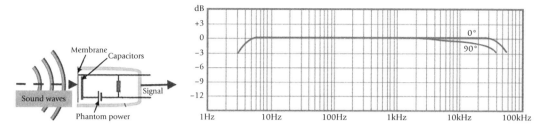

Figure 16.3

Sound waves make the diaphragm vibrate, and, via the two capacitors, these vibrations are converted into an electric signal.

On the right side, the frequency response of the Earthworks QTC40 omni. An omni mic can be made quite linear in frequency response. For the QTC40, the high range is boosted very slightly in order to compensate for the fact that air resistance attenuates high frequencies more than low frequencies. © Earthworks

The Ribbon Mic

The ribbon mic is similar to the dynamic mic in that both make use of magnetic induction, but its capsule is more sophisticated. A very thin metal sheet (the ribbon element), usually made of aluminum, is suspended in a magnetic field, and when it is moved by the sound waves, its vibrations generate a small voltage in the magnetic field corresponding to the amplitude of the wave.

Since the ribbon element is very thin, it will respond well to fast transients. Ribbon mics also have a wide dynamic range, making them particularly suited for horns (trumpet, trombone, etc.) and percussion.

The high sensitivity of the ribbons also makes them fragile; in particular, the vintage models may be destroyed by powerful air blasts or mechanical shocks. The ribbon mic, having roughly the same output as a dynamic mic but a higher impedance, is very demanding on preamps and requires a low noise and a high gain in excess of 65 dB that is only provided by the better preamps.

The ribbon element responds to sound from both the front and back but virtually nothing from the sides (called a "null"). This inherent bidirectional pattern—known as a figure-eight pattern—makes them ideal for recordings using stereo setups (see p. 141) and in situations where you want to eliminate sound (noise or spill) from the sides.

The classic ribbon mics do not tolerate phantom power, but newer models usually survive being exposed to it.

General properties of the ribbon mic:

- Brilliant reproduction of transients.
- Has a built-in treble roll-off, providing ribbons with a fuller and more "analog sound"; however, the quality of their treble response is great, even after being heavily boosted in the highs.
- Produces a low output signal.
- Dislikes shocks and humidity.

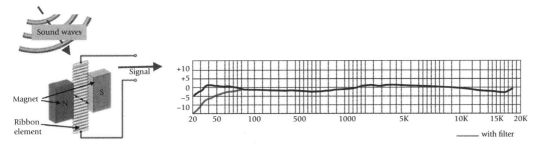

Figure 16.4

Sound waves make the ribbon vibrate, and the two magnets convert the movement to an electrical signal. To the right is the frequency response of a Royer R-122 ribbon mic. The older, classic ribbons capture very little frequency content beyond 15 kHz, while the treble response of modern designs has improved significantly.
© Royer Labs

Small Diaphragm Condenser versus Large Diaphragm Condenser Mics

Small diaphragm (SDC)	Large diaphragm (LDC)
Better off-axis response means less coloring.	Poor off-axis response imparts coloring.
The diaphragm, weighing less, makes the SDC response faster than that of the LDC. Reproduces the high frequencies and transients better; that is, the acoustic guitar, percussion, etc.	Provides a comparatively fuller sound, as the proximity effect of a directional LDC is more powerful than that of the SDC. This is one of the reasons for the extensive use of the LDC for vocals in the studio.
With a stiffer diaphragm, the SDC handles high sound pressure levels without distorting.	Has a more flexible diaphragm, and so it is more sensitive to pops, wind, and air currents.
Being less sensitive than the LDC, it requires more gain. The SDC therefore has a higher self-noise than the LDC.	Has a stronger output signal and better signal to noise ratio.
With its diaphragm placed at the front of the cylindrical housing and behind a smaller grille than the LDC, it produces almost no internal resonance.	With its diaphragm sitting inside a larger housing and behind a larger grille than the SDC, it produces reflections and resonances coloring the frequency response.
Has a better off-axis response than LDC: the small diaphragm produces fewer phase shifts in the high frequencies that come from the sides, and that can end up time-shifted on the LDC.	Imparts a psychological advantage. Looking more cool, the big LDCs make a singer feel important.

SDC and LDC mics have different properties, even though they are both condensers operating on the same transducer principle. The SDC has a diaphragm of about 1 cm, and the LDC usually has a diaphragm of 2.5 cm.

The diaphragm of the SDC is slightly stiffer but easier to set in motion.

Both on-axis and off-axis, the SDC is more linear than the LDC throughout the frequency range; this is particularly the case with the off-axis response, and so this difference is even more pronounced with the cardioid pattern. Moreover, the cardioid pattern of the LDC is more directional than that of the SDC in the on-axis direction and the farther from the sound source the mic is.

In practical terms, this means that the SDC is better for recordings where sound is picked up from the sides, at greater distances, and when a linear frequency response is required. That the LDC is virtually always used to record vocals is due to the fact that the most common mic technique of the recording studio is close-miking, and thus the off-axis issues of the LDC are of lesser importance. Moreover, vocal mics are typically manufactured to boost the high-mids and high range.

SDCs in the studio are mostly used to record acoustic instruments and as OH mics for drums—both in omni and cardioid mode. One of the myths about LDCs is that they reproduce the bottom end better, but this is more due to the fact that the LDC does not reproduce the high end linearly and thus sounds relatively fuller. SDC omnis, like Schoeps, DPA and Earthworks, have more sub-bass than LDCs, a frequency range lower than those frequencies boosted by the cardioid's proximity effect.

Reading Mic Specifications

While the previous section dealt with various mic types, this one is meant to provide an explanatory overview of other mic specifications that will allow a comparison of mic properties. These mic specifications are measured by exposing the mics to various signals in an anechoic chamber (see p. 195). However, the performance relative to a measuring apparatus will never give a complete picture of how the mic sounds; rather, it is an indication of how it might sound.

For example, the frequency response only displays how faithfully a mic reproduces pure sine waves for the four to six critical frequencies measured. This does not indicate how detailed and transparent the mic will be in reproducing the harmonics of a musical instrument. Moreover, the measurement methods of manufacturers differ considerably.

Frequency Response/Range

The frequency response shows how precisely the mic reproduces a frequency range that is typically from 20 Hz to 20 kHz. The graph shows the discrepancies (measured in dB) relative to certain sine wave frequencies emitted in an anechoic chamber.

If the plot is completely smooth at 0 dB, the reproduction is said to be linear, while peaks and dips mean coloring of the recorded audio. The coloring can be seen as a kind

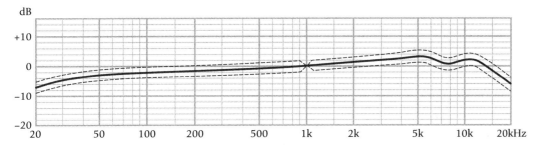

Figure 16.5
The Neumann TLM49 is regarded as one of the better mics for vocals and voice-overs. This is due to its characteristic boost in the 2–7 kHz range. Note the bass roll-off starting gradually at 400 Hz; this is typical for cardioids at more than 25–30 cm distance from the sound source. © Neumann

of built-in EQ (and so is displayed in dBs), and this may reflect a lack of accuracy or a deliberate shaping of the mic sound.

Frequency response usually refers to on-axis pick up, the source being right in front of the mic (= 0°). However, off-axis response is also important, since a mic always picks up sound from the sides as well, the cardioid specifications normally being given at 90° and 180° off-axis (the sides and the back side).

Always be critical of the vertical scale to the left. The number of dBs represented by each unit of measurement will vary somewhat between manufacturers. If the plotted distance between larger dB values on the scale is small compared to the plots used for other mics, then the curve will appear more linear in comparison.

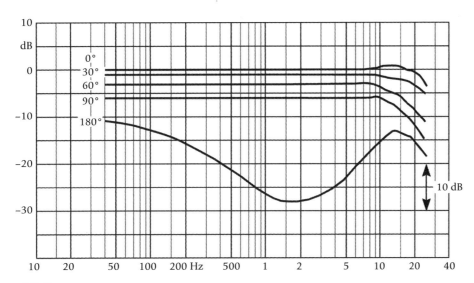

Figure 16.6
The DPA 4011 cardioid measured at 30 cm distance at 0°, 30°, 60°, 90°, and 180°. The objective of the Neumann TLM49 is a specific coloring of the voice, while that of the DPA 4011A is a linear response, making it suitable for acoustic instruments, OH mics, choirs, and classical ensembles in good acoustics. © DPA microphones

Whether a mic should be linear or have coloration depends on the task. Linear mics can be used on a variety of sound sources, while a mic that is tailored to recording the vocal has a fairly limited application. This is particularly true of mics with a boost in the 4–6 kHz range (the presence area); a quality mic like the Neumann TLM49 sounds great on vocals but mediocre on an acoustic guitar.

Polar Diagram (Polar Response)

A polar diagram displays the sensitivity of a mic for a number of selected frequencies all around the entire mic. Also called a polar response, a rough or distorted circle represents the sensitivity in pickup of a particular frequency. Its deviation from the perfect pickup is measured in dB all the way round. The color-coded or dashed lines represent different frequencies.

The more regular the circles, the more linearly the mic will represent the entirety of its surroundings. The polar response constitutes the fundamental difference between omni, cardioid, and figure-of-eight mics.

Cardioid mics reject sounds from the rear, while figure-of-eight mics reject sounds coming from the sides (on the latter type, the areas of rejection are known as nulls). The side effect is that both, having a directional polar response, display a nonlinear off-axis pickup pattern. The less it picks up from the back, the better the directional polar pattern of the cardioid (thus rejecting distant sound sources), but this should always be evaluated in the context of the polar response curves: How smooth are these at 0°, 90°, and 180°, and how does this affect the sound of the mic?

For an omni mic, the polar diagram should always be very close to a perfect circle for all the measured frequencies.

Self-Noise

Self-noise, or equivalent noise level, is the signal produced by the mic itself even when no sound source is present.

Low self-noise is important when you are recording weak sound sources or recording at a distance, since the mic's own noise will become more apparent. The self-noise sets the lower limit of the mic's dynamic range, so the lower it is, the better.

The self-noise must be less than 15 dB(A) for a quality mic. Small-diaphragm mics have a higher self-noise, 12–20 dB(A), than large-diaphragm mics at 5–10 dB(A). Tube mics (condenser mics with preamps powered by vacuum tubes) have the greatest residual noise, vintage models often having more than 30 dB(A).

Sensitivity

Sensitivity indicates how well the mic transduces acoustic energy (sound waves) into an electrical signal. The higher the sensitivity, the better, because this reduces the gain needed in the built-in preamp and hence reduces the imperfections caused by the preamp.

Max SPL (Sound Pressure Level)

Max SPL shows the sound pressure level (in dB) that the mic can withstand before clipping (limiting the tops of the transients) and distorting (caused by its diaphragm knocking against the back plate or the built-in preamp being overdriven). The higher the max SPL, the better.

Total Harmonic Distortion (THD)

THD is the distortion added to the signal by the mic. The stronger the signal, the higher the distortion. THD usually ranges from 0.5% to 1%, but as manufacturers measure the THD at different sound pressure levels, it can be difficult to interpret and compare the readings. A good condenser mic should have approximately 0.5% THD at 130 dB and not more than 1% at its max SPL (which, in quality microphones, can be considerably higher than 130 dB). In withstanding a higher max SPL, one mic might actually have less distortion than another if the THD of the first is measured at 130 dB.

Figure 16.7
The DPA 4004 omni has the following specifications: max SPL of 168 dB SPL; total harmonic distortion at 142 dB SPL (<0.5% THD) and at 148 dB SPL (<1% THD). The figures demonstrate that the DPA 4004 produces a clean and undistorted audio signal. © DPA microphones

Dynamic Range

The dynamic range is the distance between self-noise and the max SPL that the mic can handle. The higher the dynamic range, the better.

The signal-to-noise ratio, as the distance between the self-noise and the peak of a recorded signal, is a somewhat similar measurement.

127

Comparing Mics

Understanding the specifications is helpful in choosing the right mic. However, it should be complemented with listening and the practical use of the mic. Only by trying a specific mic on various sound sources or testing different mics on the instrument to be recorded can you determine which mic is the best for the task.

The choice can be a subjective one. Regardless of the specifications, does the mic sound appropriate for the instrument to be recorded? If its tonal characteristics are to your liking, then most certainly you can use it with musical results.

Only experienced technicians can assess a mic purely from its specifications and without practically comparing it to another. If you are still learning your craft, the best method might be to compare two (or more) mics by recording the same source and then going back and forth between the two recordings (called A/B testing)—preferably together with a friend so the test can be made without the one person knowing which mic is open. A good starting point for the comparison is to include a mic that you are familiar with.

Compare the on-axis pickup at different distances (5–40 cm) to get an impression of the mic's frequency response, proximity effect, and dynamic range. Go around it while singing (using headphones) to get an impression of its directional characteristics and the quality of its off-axis sound. Try it with the instruments or vocals it is intended be used with.

Poor mics are revealed by exposing them to demanding tasks like the triangle (a bunch of keys can act as a stand in), the tin whistle, the grand piano, or the acoustic guitar.

They all have complex harmonics and strong transients that are difficult to record. Great mics can handle them, while the lesser ones distort, filter out the transients, have an excessive coloring, and do not work in the mix.

Some of the many tests displayed on YouTube might add to your experience in learning about a mic that is not yet in your collection. Search for the mic brand, instrument, and "microphone test," or, for example, "comparing ribbon microphones recording the trumpet."

Microphones
Polar Pattern

The polar pattern (or polar response) is a schematic of the field around the mic capsule indicating the directions in which the mic is most sensitive to sound.

There are three types of basic polar pattern:

- **Cardioid** is a directional pattern capturing sound mostly in front of the mic. It also comes in two variants: supercardioid and hypercardioid.
- **Omni** picks up sound all the way around the mic and so is a spherical pattern.
- **Figure-of-eight** is a bidirectional pattern capturing sound from the front and the back of the mic. Its shape is similar to the figure eight and it is the pattern that captures the least from the sides (these less sensitive zones being called nulls).

OMNIDIRECTIONAL	CARDIOID	SUPERCARDIOID	HYPERCARDIOID	BIDIRECTIONAL

Figure 17.1
The polar patterns of omni, cardioid, and figure-of-eight in addition to supercardioid and hypercardioid patterns. A few studio mics feature multiple, selectable patterns. © Shure

Cardioid

The cardioid pattern (also called unidirectional) is not a perfect directional pattern. Mostly capturing sound from the front, it also captures quite a lot from the sides and a little from the back (180°) as well.

Cardioid is the most commonly used polar pattern in the studio and is normally used for close-miking to capture a single sound source. This facilitates the adding of EQ and effects in the mix to one single instrument without affecting the other instruments. Cardioid also reduces feedback and is therefore the most commonly used pattern in live situations too.

Supercardioid and hypercardioid are variants of the cardioid mic with a narrower polar pattern; that is, they are more directional, in that they pick up less from the sides

Figure 17.2

The cardioid polar pattern. © Shure

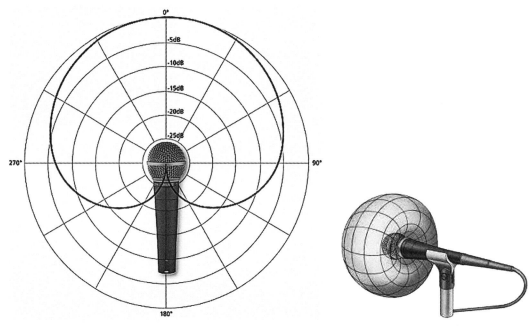

compared to a standard cardioid mic, while at the same time they pick up a little more from the rear.

As a polar pattern, cardioid is somewhat imperfect. One of its weaknesses is the proximity effect. When placed close to the sound source, this results in a bass frequency boost in the 100–250 Hz range. Another significant shortcoming is that it does not pick up all frequencies linearly from the sides (off-axis), resulting in a coloring of the sound source.

Applications and Usage

- Cardioid is useful if the ambience of the space should not be recorded.
- The sound captured from the sides (off-axis) is nonlinear with regard to frequency; that is, it colors the sound of an instrument. With several sound sources, screening is therefore essential.
- Placed closer than 30 cm to the source, the cardioid can become bass heavy because of the proximity effect. At greater distances, the cardioid can become thin sounding.
- Cardioid is very sensitive to wind and pop noises.
- Supercardioids and hypercardioids reduce feedback. They are also used to capture the soloist in larger bands when recording live or the hi-hat in a drum kit, as their polar patterns reduce spill from nearby sound sources.

⊙ Audio example 17.01 demonstrates the cardioid polar pattern.

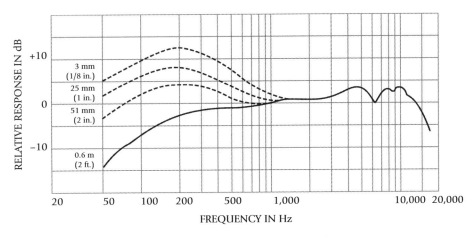

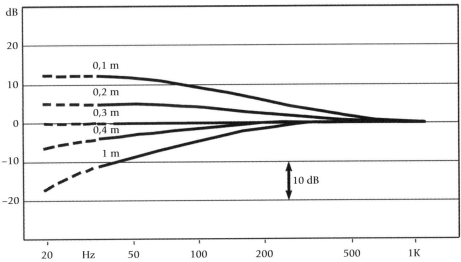

Figure 17.3

The proximity effects for a Shure Beta 57A (dynamic) and a DPA 4011A (condenser) (both cardioids). For the Beta 57A, the effect is shown at some very close distances (0.3 cm, 2.5 cm, 5.1 cm) as well as 60 cm because handheld vocal mics are used close up. The DPA 4011A is displayed at 10 cm, 20 cm, 30 cm, and 40 cm, plus 1 m and 10 m. The Beta 57A displays a distinctive bump between 80 and 400 Hz, while the DPA 4011A extends more smoothly into the sub-bass range. The bass in both microphones is rolled off at distances greater than 30 cm. © Shure © DPA microphones

Box 17.1 The Proximity Effect

Used close up, directional mics (cardioid types and figure-of-eight) exhibit a bass boost in the 100–250 Hz range; at 10 cm and closer, this can be as much as 10–15 dB. Moving closer to the source can shift the upper limit of the boosted frequency range to 400–500 Hz (depending on the distance and the mic); see the proximity responses in figure 17.3. As a 10 dB boost is significant, most manufacturers recommend using cardioids at 20–25 cm distance. Likewise, several cardioid mics placed close up in a recording session cause bass buildup in the mix, requiring a bass cut on some of the tracks, if not all.

However, the proximity effect can be used to great effect, creating an in-your-face fullness both on vocals and on some instruments, in particular the electric guitar and the snare, making them stand out in the mix and providing the ideal sound for most popular music genres.

The proximity effect decreases with distance, and at 30 cm the cardioid is almost linear. At greater distances, a bass reduction takes place; cardioids and figure-of-eight mics gradually become thinner sounding at a distance from the sound source of more than 35–40 cm.

The polar patterns also vary with frequency; the cardioid approaches the omni pattern at low frequencies, while the omni becomes more directional in the higher frequencies.

The proximity effect can be attenuated using the parametric EQ with a low Q setting (about 0.5), though the amount of bass boost might vary from mic to mic.

Omni

The omni pattern captures sound with the same sensitivity from all directions, so in principle the omni provides the most natural and linear reproduction of a sound source ("natural" relates to human hearing, which itself is almost omnidirectional in its characteristics). Omni should therefore be the first choice when an instrument is to be reproduced naturally and when natural reverberation is an essential part of the recording. Omnis are also used for sound sources spread over a larger area and for recordings of classical music.

The boundary mic, a special application of the omni, is designed to be placed on an even surface (the floor or wall) that provides a boundary at 180°. It thus has a polar pattern that is half that of the omni (think of an orange cut in half) and eliminates phase

Figure 17.4

The omni polar pattern. © Shure

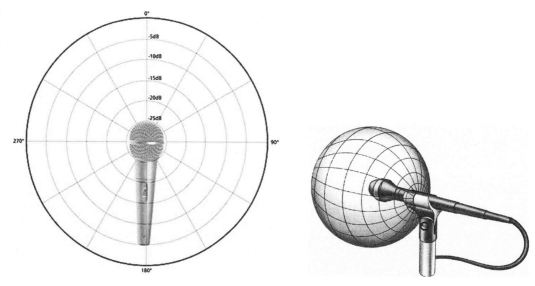

issues between direct and reflected sound, resulting in a flatter frequency response than that of a stand-mounted mic close to the same position. It is often used below grand pianos and to record ensembles in good ambient acoustics.

Applications and Usage

- Omni is the only polar pattern capturing the entire frequency range linearly from any direction.
- Omnis are great for recording drums, acoustic guitar, saxophone, and double bass—instruments that all create their sound in interaction with the acoustics.
- Its construction principle is simpler than that of a cardioid, and so omni is therefore easier to make more dynamic (capturing fast transients) and linear in the reproduction of a complex sound source.
- Omnis captures fullness better than the cardioid at distances of more than 30 cm.
- Omnis can be placed close to the sound source without adding proximity effect.
- Omnis capture sound from all directions and so, being sensitive to feedback, are unsuitable for live applications.
- Omnis are less sensitive to wind and pop noises.

▶ Audio example 17.02 demonstrates the omni polar pattern.

Figure-of-Eight

The figure-of-eight pattern (bidirectional) picks up the sound from both the front and rear and next to nothing from the sides. Like all directional mics, it adds some proximity effect, though this is less pronounced than the cardioid. The pickup from the sides is colored, but as the figure-of-eight captures only a little from the sides (the nulls), this is also less pronounced than the cardioid.

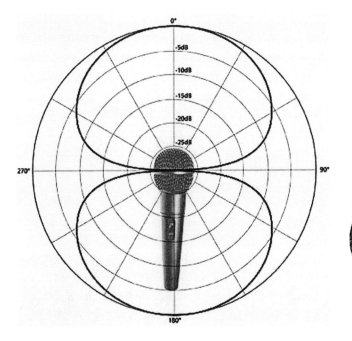 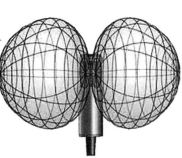

Figure 17.5
The figure-of-eight polar pattern.
© Shure

Figure-of-eights are used in recordings that have two sound sources and when eliminating the sound from the sides is essential.

Ribbon mics have an inherent figure-of-eight response due to the construction of the ribbon element, which always captures sound from the rear as well as from the front. Some manufactures such as Royer construct their ribbon mics to be brighter sounding at the rear, and when the mic is reversed, it can provide a more open-sounding recording.

Applications and Usage

- Two singers can be placed on each side of the mic and recorded to one track.
- Placed inside a kick drum, the figure-of-eight captures both the impact from the pedal and the reverberation inside the body.
- At distances of more than 30 cm, the figure-of-eight captures increasingly less low end and can become thin sounding.
- Figure-of-eights are used as part of the Blumlein and MS stereo setups (see p. 146).

⊙ Audio example 17.03 demonstrates the figure-of-eight polar pattern.

Multi-pattern Microphones

Mics combining cardioid, omni, and figure-of-eight always have built-in compromises. Set to omni, the multi-pattern has some of the weaknesses of cardioid-like sensitivity to wind and pop noises and a less linear off-axis sound. Yet they are widely used, since it is cheaper to acquire a three-in-one mic than to buy three separate ones, and it is also useful to be able to experiment with the pattern while recording. Several manufacturers make fine sounding three-in-one solutions; for example, the AKG 414, Sony C38, Audio Technica 4050, and the costly Telefunken ELA M 250/251.

Shotgun Microphones

The shotgun mic features an extended hypercardioid polar pattern. Its long tube has certain acoustic properties that make it particularly directional with respect to the midrange and high frequencies. This is achieved with the narrow openings in the tube, which are located so that certain frequencies arrive with a specific time delay, thereby boosting or canceling each other out (phase reinforcement/cancelation, see p. 272). The openings should always face away from the closest reflecting surfaces—preferably upward relative to the sound source. The shotgun is (almost) never used in the recording studio, as its frequency response and dynamics are nonlinear.

Mic Techniques

Various techniques are used when recording with mics, and each has its advantages and disadvantages. The decisive factor is the distance to the sound source. Changing the distance to the sound source alters the sense of remoteness or closeness due to the balance between the direct sound and the reverberant sound picked up by the mic.

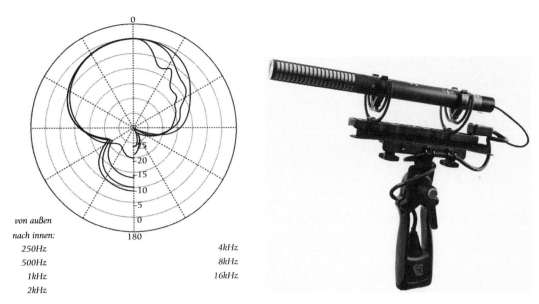

Figure 17.6

The shotgun mic is mainly used to capture dialogue for movies and TV. Its distance from the sound source is important, its directionality gradually becoming more diffuse at distances greater than 1 m. The shotgun, therefore, is used close up and mounted on a boom pole that keeps it out of the picture frame. Mounting it on the camera is a bad approach not only because the mic is sensitive to mechanical noise but also because the hypercardioid characteristic captures quite a lot sound from the rear.

Displayed here is the Schoeps mounted in a shock-absorbing grip. The polar pattern to the left describes the sensitivity of the microphone at different frequencies from 250 Hz at the outer ring to 16 kHz at the inner ring. © Schoeps

When selecting the mic's polar pattern, some degree of control over the sound coloration is achieved, along with control over the amount of spill from other sources and the impression of the size of the instrument and the space around it.

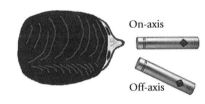

Figure 17.7

A directional mic placed at right angles to the source is said to be on-axis as opposed to being off-axis.

Close-Miking

Close-miking is a recording technique in which the mic is placed close to the sound source so the recording room acoustics are captured to a lesser degree. It also reduces the spill from distant sources. Close-miking gives a high level of presence and dynamics to an instrument.

A large proportion of the recordings of popular music uses close-miking, while in the classical tradition this technique is used only for the spot mics—mics placed on individual instrument groups used to adjust the balance between instruments while stereo mics capture the whole.

Ambient Miking

Ambient miking is a recording technique in which the mics are placed at some distance from the sound source, thus capturing more of the room acoustics. Ambient miking does not provide as much presence and dynamics for an instrument as close-miking. In return, though, it gives depth and width to the sound stage. Moreover, ambient miking reproduces the whole of an orchestra with the natural-sounding timbre of the instruments.

For the same reason, ambient miking is used in part on the drum kit in the form of the overhead (OH) mics that are located 40–100 cm above the drums and that capture the depth and entirety of the set. In studio recordings, which often have a very up-front sound, this is a means to create space for the many instruments sharing the limited space of the stereo field. Thus, if you wish to maximize space in your recordings, use ambient mics on drums and any instrument that creates its sound in interaction with the acoustics.

▶ Audio example 17.04 demonstrates differences between close-miking and ambient miking.

Omni versus Cardioid: Choosing the Right Polar Pattern

Generally, a cardioid located at 17 cm distance picks up the same proportion of direct sound and reverberant sound as an omni located at 10 cm distance from the same sound source. Also, an omni can be placed closer to the source without adding proximity effect; in other words, more or less the same separation that cardioids provide can be achieved when there are multiple instruments in the same room. Since the omni mic does not color off-axis (like the cardioid does), the omni can again be used to advantage particularly when recording several acoustic instruments in the same space.

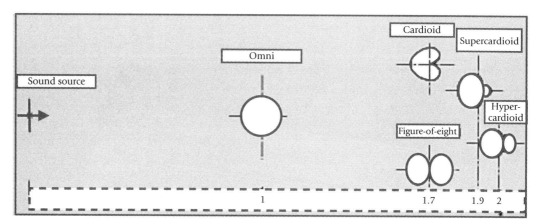

Figure 17.8

The relative distances between the source and the mic if the polar pattern indicates the mic should capture a balance between direct and reverberant sound. Cardioid, being directional, must be 1.7 times as far from the sound source as an omni to have this balance. Hypercardioids reject sounds from the side even better than cardioids and so should be placed twice as far away for the same result. © DPA microphones

Conventionally, though, omnis are placed at a certain distance from the sound source (and this requires good acoustics), while cardioids are primarily used for close-miking (thus eliminating most of the acoustics).

For the same reason, omnis are associated with a natural sound—spaciousness and depth being the aesthetic normally associated with acoustic instruments. Traditionally, omnis are used for classical music, which is recorded in the acoustics that suit the genre and ensemble size, and, to a large extent, for folk music and acoustic jazz.

In the studio, the cardioid is almost chosen by instinct (except for acoustic guitar, OH mics, and the grand piano), since cardioids are associated with close-miking and

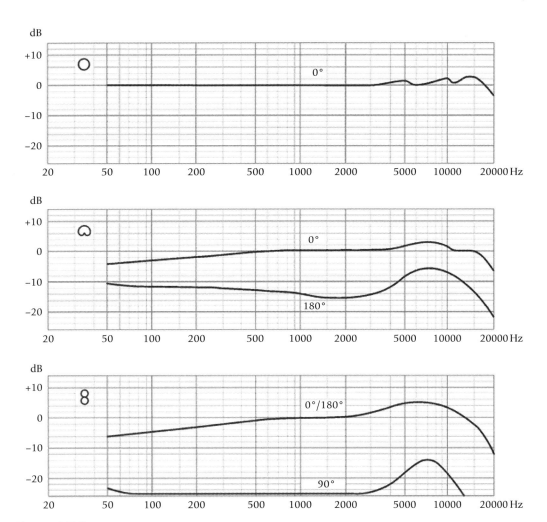

Figure 17.9

The frequency response of a Microtech Gefell UMT 70S with omni, cardioid, and figure-of-eight characteristics. The measurement is made at 30 cm distance (no proximity effect). Cardioid and figure-of-eight boost in the presence area (4–6 kHz) and roll off below 400 Hz, whereas the omni response is completely linear. The bottom graph shows the cardioid pickup from the rear (180°) where there is a poor frequency response. For the figure-of-eight, the bottom graph displays the pickup from the sides (90° or the null), only capturing the narrow frequency range 4–12 kHz. Microtech Gefell is the old East German equivalent of Neumann. Both originated from the same company, which was divided between East and West Germany at the end of World War II. The Gefell mics still bear many similarities to the Neumanns; for example, the UM92 series is based on the original Neumann M7 capsule. © Microtech Gefell

in-your-face aesthetics. The cardioid has become part of that recording studio approach that uses overdubs, compression, reverb, and so forth—an approach that, historically, developed within the popular music genres.

Furthermore, omnis apply no coloring to the sound coming from the side (off-axis sound). This results in a better reproduction of the highest frequencies (air), and it can also be used to advantage when multiple (especially acoustic) instruments are recorded in the same room. The spill picked up from other instruments, in fact, will be less of a problem than that imparted by the cardioid's off-axis pickup.

Also, with the new types of miniature mics, such as the DPA and Schoeps, omnis have become the obvious choice—both in the studio and in live situations—as they can be attached directly to most acoustic instruments.

Since cardioids normally roll off in the low end, omnis also provide more low-end to work with in the mix. However, the often great-sounding boost added to instruments' transients by cardioids must often be recreated on omni recordings by using EQ to increase the presence range (3–5 kHz).

Omnis generally are also less susceptible to distortion than cardioids. In recent years, omnis withstanding increasing sound pressure levels have been developed; while not yet on a par with cardioids, most omnis comfortably manage 130 dB and hence the high SPLs from the drum kit.

Recording with Omnis

The objective of what follows is not meant to emphasize the omni as the ideal solution to any recording but merely to point out some useful properties of the omni pattern in applications where a cardioid might otherwise be automatically selected. Remember, though, when the proximity effect (of cardioids and figure-of-eights) is a part of the desired sound, the cardioid should not be replaced by an omni; the classic choice of Shure SM57 and Sennheiser 421 (cardioid mics) still sounds stunning on the snare, the toms, and guitar speakers, as the coloring of these mics is great for these instruments. But the omni is an alternative that in some cases achieves better results in terms of fullness and depth in the recording, while in other cases it solves particular practical issues.

Recording the Drum Kit with Omnis

The following is an optional setup using omnis on the entire drum kit.

The kick drum

A good omni picks up linearly from 20 Hz to 20 kHz, in contrast to the roll-off on cardioids, which starts somewhere in the 80–300 Hz range. Omnis thus pick up more sub-bass from a kick drum. With no proximity effect, the omni is less boomy in the 100–250 Hz range (when placed closer than 25–30 cm), and so the kick drum can be easily separated from the bass guitar.

The snare

Close-miking is needed so that the sound of the snare can be isolated in the mix and thus easily edited. However, the placement of the mic demands compromises for the sake of the drummer's freedom of movement and the spill inevitably leaking from the hi-hat. The omni may be placed very close to the drum without proximity effect, and, even more importantly, the spill from the rest of the kit is uncolored and might be useful in the mix.

The same applies to the toms, in that the spill from cymbals, snare, and so on is not colored as much as with a cardioid; it instead provides more space and depth in the mix.

OH mics

Omnis are already used to some extent (though not as often as cardioids), as they provide more air and a natural texture to the kit. Spill is not a problem with OH mics, as their purpose is to capture the entire kit. Here too, omnis capture slightly more sub-bass below 60 Hz from the kick drum and the toms.

Figure 17.10
Two DPA 4011s in a spaced omni setup as OH mics. © DPA microphones

The Voice and Some Other Instruments

In a recording space with a balanced sound, an omni will solve the problem of singers moving too much in relation to the mic. With a cardioid, even small changes in distance are audible, as this can change the proximity effect on a single phrase. Moreover, variations in the proximity effect cannot be repaired completely by compressing but only by a smoothing of volume-level differences.

▶ Audio example 17.05 demonstrates the proximity effect.

Miniature mics (often omnis) can be attached to most acoustic instruments; even very close to the sound source, they are still quite natural sounding; they are most useful on acoustic guitar, trumpet, upright bass, and so forth.

18

Stereo Recording

The human auditory system evolved to decode location and moving sounds in the landscape quite precisely, which was useful in the struggle for survival if, for example, this skill helped to locate and avoid a hungry sabertooth tiger just a few seconds before the beast was right in front of you.

Our auditory system has also developed the ability to decode distance based on differences in sound intensity and, to a lesser extent, the filtering effects of air; the sound pressure is approximately halved each time the distance to the sound source doubles (equivalent to just over a 6 dB decrease in the sound pressure level). Sound direction is decoded through a combination of intensity difference and time of arrival of the sound wave at each ear and, to some degree, the filtering effects of our ears' pinnae.

This sound-based perception of space, of depth and width, is more or less reproduced with the technology of stereo audio. As an analogy to our ears, two microphones placed in the correct spots can pick up spatial information, and this can be more or less reproduced by stereo loudspeakers or headphones when played back.

A stereo recording, then, closely reproduces the depth and width of the sound sources, and in the recording of music stereo is mainly used to record single instruments or even orchestras, those musical sound sources that create their sound in interaction with the acoustics.

Box 18.1 Acoustic or Artificially Produced Stereo

There are two basic approaches to creating width and depth.

Acoustic stereo derives from a recording with a minimum of two mics. Time and intensity differences in the arrival of the same sound waves at the two mics reflect the relative position of the sound sources in the acoustic space. The mixture of the direct sound and the reflections (more reverberation perceptually equates to more distance) provides a picture of the size the room along with its width, depth, and wall materials. The space between the two mics provides the perception of stereo.

Artificially produced stereo is also recorded with multiple mics and is often a mixture of basic tracks and overdubs. However, if the recording is made using cardioids and by close-miking, reverb, modulation effects, delay, and panning are needed to recreate an acoustic space for the instruments (mostly mono tracks) in the mix. Artificially produced stereo is thus used to bring width and depth to the studio-based recording that mainly uses close-miking, omitting (most of) the acoustics.

When recording in stereo, only the best available condenser mics should be used (e.g. DPA, Schoeps, Sanken, AKG, Sennheiser, and Neumann), the quality criteria being a linear frequency response without coloration or distortion. Often SDC Mics (see p. 123) are used, preferably a matched pair.

There are a number of configurations for stereo recording providing quite different results. This chapter shows how to create depth and width in the recording using these stereo techniques.

Spaced Omni

The spaced omni setup (also known as A-B stereo) is based on time and therefore phase differences in the sound arriving at the two omni mics. (This setup can be done using cardioids or figure-of-eights as well but will result in a reduced bass response at distances of more than 30 cm.)

Two omni mics are placed in the same horizontal plane pointing toward the sound source, spaced at 20–70 cm, depending on the separation/width of the sound source (or multiple sound sources), the distance from it, and the acoustics. The distance between the

Figure 18.1

Two DPA 4006 omnis in a spaced omni setup. © DPA microphones

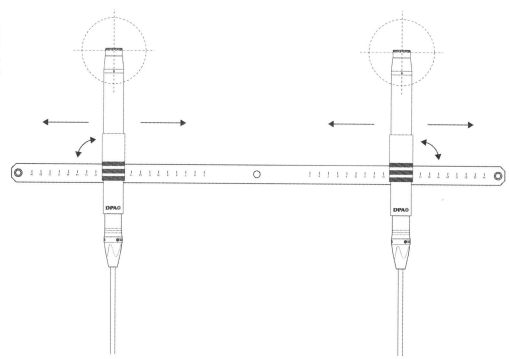

two mics determines the width of the stereo image and consequently must be adjusted to the size of the sound source—from 17 cm (that is, the distance between your ears) when recording a single instrument (the acoustic guitar, congas, or entire drum kit), to 25–40 cm for small ensembles (string quartets or folk ensembles), to 40–60 cm for the symphony orchestra. The distance to the sound source determines the blend of the direct signal and the reverberant signal; this is best decided by testing with headphones. When recording classical ensembles, the mics are often placed on a bar just behind and slightly above the conductor's head.

The spaced omni provides natural reproduction due to the properties of the omni pattern. Although theoretically the two signals generate comb filter effects when summed (see p. 272) due to time differences in the arrival of the signal at the two mics, this stereo technique is widely used. Practically, such effects are rarely a problem when reproduced in stereo (only when summed to mono can they be heard). In turn, spaced omni provides a great perception of the stereo width compared to coincident stereo.

Too great a distance between the mics is liable to create a hole in the middle of the stereo image, which is why a third mic is sometimes placed in the middle (in particular if there is a solo piano or vocal) in order to fill in the hole. This mic is panned to the center (C), while the stereo mics are panned L (left) and R (right). The C mic is attenuated 4–6 dB in the mix.

Applications

- Brings great stereo width to the recording.
- Picks up the location of sound sources well, though not as accurately as X-Y and Blumlein stereo.
- Generates no phantom image: the experience of a particular instrument being located at a specific point between the two loudspeakers is replaced by the experience of width.
- Unsuitable for mono playback. If mono compatibility is required, check for any phase issues by listening in mono to long and bright sounds such as cymbals. Phase cancelation sounds swirling and chorus-like in mono.

The Decca Tree

The Decca tree is a refinement of the spaced omni setup and was developed in London by Decca for the recording of classical ensembles. Three omni mics are set up, forming a triangle that is typically placed half a meter behind and 1–3 meters above the conductor's head. The setup is raised or lowered to capture the best acoustics possible.

The Decca tree provides a greater perception of presence than spaced omni, since the C mic is

143

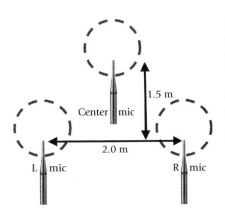

Figure 18.2

The Decca tree. The distance between the left and right mics is 1.5–2 m, and the center mic is placed approximately 1.5 m in front to form an equilateral triangle.

closer to the orchestra. Moreover, the hole in the middle is filled out by the C mic. In mixing, the three mics are panned L, C, and R.

It can be used for any other ensembles and instruments that should have width yet also need a well-defined middle. It is therefore particularly well suited to situations where there is a soloist with the ensemble.

Baffled Stereo

Baffled stereo is also a variation of the spaced omni using an acoustically absorbent screen (a baffle) to improve the separation between the spaced omnis.

Figure 18.3

Two DPA 4006 omnis in a baffled stereo setup. © DPA Microphones

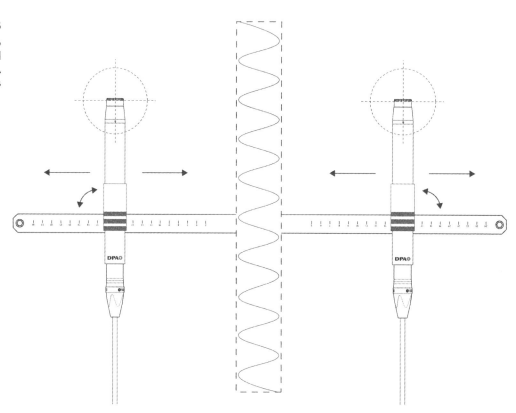

A well-known baffled stereo setup is the Jecklin disk. The distance between the mics is 17–20 cm (equivalent to the distance between your ears), and the screen, at some 35 cm high, should be made of acoustically absorbent material to avoid reflections. The baffled stereo setup reduces comb filter effects and sounds excellent for stereo recordings close to the sound source. Use it for instruments such as percussion, acoustic guitar, or a string quartet.

Coincident Stereo

Coincident stereo implies that the setup is constructed so that the sound waves reach the two mics simultaneously because they are placed next to each other. Coincident stereo is the concept behind both the X-Y stereo setup and the Blumlein setup (invented by Alan Blumlein in 1934).

X-Y Stereo

The X-Y is a dual cardioid mic array with the diaphragms placed at the same point. In practical terms, the two mics are placed one above the other and as close as possible. As the sound in principle arrives simultaneously at both mic diaphragms, there is no phase shift between the two mics. The two mics must be placed equidistant about the center axis and then they are angled 90° to each other (this is adjustable according to the required width of the sound source).

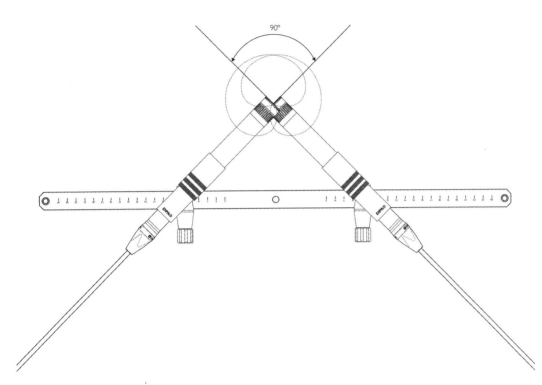

Figure 18.4

Two DPA 4011 cardioids in an X-Y setup. © DPA microphones

145

The stereo image of coincident stereo is created by intensity level differences, whereas the spaced omni also uses time differences in sound arrival at the two mics. Therefore, the X-Y array does not create as large a stereo width, but this can be widened by increasing the angle between the microphones to some 120–130°.

Bidirectional (figure-of-eight) mics and supercardioids may also be used for X-Y stereo.

X-Y recordings can be converted to mono with no added coloration (that is, no comb filtering), which is why they were particularly used for radio and TV recording before stereo reproduction became commonplace.

Because the sound waves impinge on the mics from the sides, and as the off-axis frequency response of most cardioids and figure-of-eights is quite poor, there will be some coloring of the sound. The X-Y setup is often used quite close to the sound source to accentuate the low end by means of the proximity effect.

Applications

- Provides a stable directionality and picks up the depth position of the sound source in the room well.
- Does not reproduce much width.

- Reduces the bottom end and the fullness at distances of more than 30 cm.
- Does not quite precisely reproduce the sound field in the middle.
- Perfect mono compatibility.
- Using hypercardioids, produces a stereo image approaching that of the Blumlein setup (which is more directional at the front) but does not capture quite as much from the rear (ambience).

Blumlein Stereo

Figure 18.5
Two figure-of-eights in the Blumlein setup.

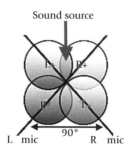

Sound source

90°

L mic   R mic

The Blumlein setup is made up of two figure-of-eights placed in a cross on top of each other (that is, at the same point and forming an angle of 90°), and it provides a smooth and consistent stereo image of direct and reflected sound without having a hole in the middle.

This setup displays many similarities to the X-Y setup, the essential difference being that the Blumlein setup captures the ambience from the rear—that is, more of the acoustics—because of the figure-of-eight characteristics. For the same reason, it should not be placed too far from the sound source, not only because this can make it capture too much reverberation but also because the figure-of-eight mics will attenuate the low-end frequencies with increasing distance from the sound source.

Applications

- Provides a strong center image.
- Ideal in rooms with good acoustics, whereas the X-Y setup with cardioids performs better in rooms with poor acoustics.
- Since this setup is coincident (thus relying on amplitude differences as opposed to phase differences), mono compatibility is quite good.

MS Stereo

MS stereo is short for mid and side stereo and has traditionally been used for TV and film sound but is now increasingly used to record instruments.

The two mics are positioned as vertically coincident as possible—that is, one above the other at the same point (coincident stereo) forming an angle of 90°. The mid mic is usually a cardioid directed toward the sound source (an omni may be chosen and will provide an increase in width from 90° to 180°). The mid mic picks up the direct sound and depth. For the side mic, a figure-of-eight is used in order to pick up sound from the sides and thus provide (more) width. The recording levels should be the same for both mics.

An MS signal cannot readily be played back in stereo, as it requires decoding of the mid and the side into a common L and R signal. An MS matrix decodes the signals as $L = M + S$ and $R = M - S$ while applying a phase reversal between the two signals and panning them equally to L and R.

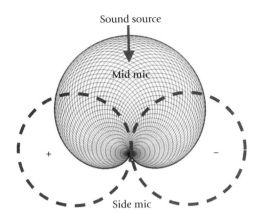

147

If you do not have an MS matrix, the MS signal can be decoded into L and R stereo by using three channels on the mixer:

a. The cardioid signal (mid) is sent to mixer channel 1 panned to C.

b. The figure-of-eight signal (side) is sent to mixer channel 2 (also panned to C), where it is split (using a send) onto a third channel. Note that the send should be set to pre-fader or else it will vary with the level changes of mixer channel 2.

c. Mixer channel 3 is panned to C and phase-reversed as well. Then, the levels of the three channels should be matched:

   i. Mixer channel 1 (the cardioid) is muted.

   ii. Mixer channels 2 and 3 are level-adjusted until they cancel each other out completely (phase cancelation).

d. Mixer channel 1 is unmuted, and the overall result is now mono.

e. Mixer channel 2 (side) is panned hard L, and mixer channel 3 (the phase reversed side) is panned hard R.

After this, a stereo image of varying width can be generated, from 0° (mono) to 90°, by changing the strength of the side signal in relation to the mid signal. Boosting the level of the side expands the stereo image, and vice versa.

MS stereo provides a stable center image and a great sensation of direction and depth in the recording. It is increasingly used in the studio, as it provides the opportunity to vary the stereo width of an instrument when mixing.

In film and TV sound, MS stereo is particularly suited to ambient soundtracks that also require intelligible dialogue and voice-overs; in the mix, the level of the ambient sounds (side) can be adjusted. Even when the side is made relatively strong, a "hole in the middle" can be created to be filled by the dialogue (mid) or the voice-over.

Similarly, the MS stereo can be used to record, for example, an acoustic guitar that can be adapted in the mix to the other instruments—from mono to full stereo width.

Applications

- Provides a strong center image; that is, a precise location of the sound source.
- Provides a variable stereo width.
- Mono-compatible, as it is fundamentally a coincident stereo setup.

More Stereo Setups: ORTF, NOS Stereo, and Binaural

A couple of stereo setups combine the spaced omni (time differences between the mics provides width) and the X-Y stereo (intensity differences cause fewer phase issues but less width). This is achieved by placing the two mics at a distance equal to the spacing between our ears. Thus, the sound arrives at the mics with the same time offset as for the ears, and here the brain is an expert at decoding this as information regarding the location of the sound source.

Figure 18.7

An ORTF setup consisting of two DPA 4011A cardioids. © DPA microphones

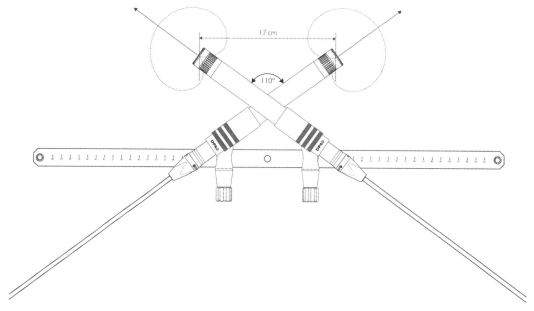

ORTF comprises a crossed set of cardioids spaced 17 cm between the two mic diaphragms at an angle of 110°.

The setup mimics the placing of the human ears, and it is therefore considered to offer one of the most realistic stereo reproductions. The ORTF provides a wider stereo image than the X-Y setup, though it potentially has more phase issues. Likewise, its low-end pickup is attenuated with increasing distance from the sound source.

NOS stereo is a variation of the ORTF that extends the spacing of the two cardioids to 30 cm and reduces the angle to 90°.

Binaural recording uses a dummy head featuring two omnis located inside the ears. It thus mimics the human ears and especially reproduces their method of detecting the distance and direction to the sound source; this is further improved by the dummy head practically eliminating spill between the two mics.

In practice, the setup can be made with two small omnis fitted into a mannequin head.

Binaural stereo must be played back on headphones to provide the full benefits, but in return it provides an experience of being in the middle of the sound stage—a virtually spherical soundscape providing width, depth, and a sense of being above and below the sound source.

Binaural stereo is mainly used to record ambiences and atmospheric sounds in computer games and virtual reality applications.

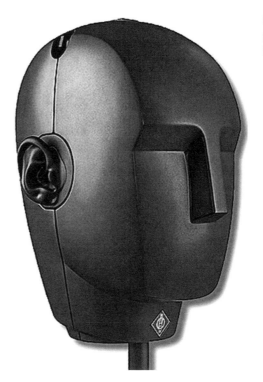

Figure 18.8
Neumann Binaural Head. © Neumann

149

Applications

- Ideal for stereo recordings at closer distances of instruments such as piano and smaller ensembles.
- Precise localization of the sound source and improved reproduction of the ambience.

Of course, there is neither a correct nor a perfect method to reproduce stereo from the natural sound field. The fact that there are so many variations in setup is due to each having been developed for various uses; every setup has its strengths and weaknesses. Moreover, the perception of what sounds good differs from listener to listener.

Therefore, choose the setup that suits the purpose best and test alternatives until the result is as desired. Always beware of hollow-sounding and flanger-like coloring. When using two (or more) mics, there will always be a risk of comb filter effects in the upper frequency ranges. They can never be completely avoided, but a way to avoid the effects' destructive tendencies is to listen alternately in stereo and mono while experimenting with the mic placement. When switching to mono, you should ideally only hear the stereo image collapsing, with no obvious fluttering from the phase cancelation.

PART III

Processors and Effects

19

EQ and Instruments

The sound of rock music was created in the studio as an artificial sound using effects and EQ. Even the genres insisting on an "authentic" live sound (folk, blues, jazz) use EQ to color the sound of the instruments. Classical music is the only genre using EQ exclusively to fine-tune the natural ambience of the concert hall. In rock music, EQ is used to place the instruments in the frequency layers of the mix, and it can be used not only to repair inadequate recorded sound but also to create new sounds.

In figure 19.1, the voice and the instruments are shown schematically represented by the frequencies they span, and the chart, originally compiled by a group of independent producers, forms the basis of the division of the frequency areas and the terminology used in this chapter. In the midrange and high-mids, however, an extra division, low-mid, has been added in order to adapt the table to EQ practices that are widespread in the recording studio.

Sub-bass (20–60 Hz)

The Instruments

In this frequency range, notes of the string bass instruments, the tuba, the piano, the organ, the bass drum, and the timpani are found. Reaching down to 27.50 Hz at A0, the concert piano (together with the organ) has the lowest pitch, while the electric and double bass only extend to 41.20 Hz on the low E1.

Sound and Timbre

The sub-bass area contains a lot of energy, and the sound is more physically felt than heard—for example, the thump of the bass drum in the chest or bass notes penetrating the walls, floors, and ceilings of a building. Most other instruments have no frequency content in this area, and therefore it is better to cut it away (low-cut or low shelf) to avoid rumbling in the mix.

Bass (60–250 Hz)

The Instruments

Most instruments' deepest notes have frequency content in this area: guitar, vocals, cello, viola, toms, snare, tenor and alto sax, clarinet, and synths. The male voice goes down

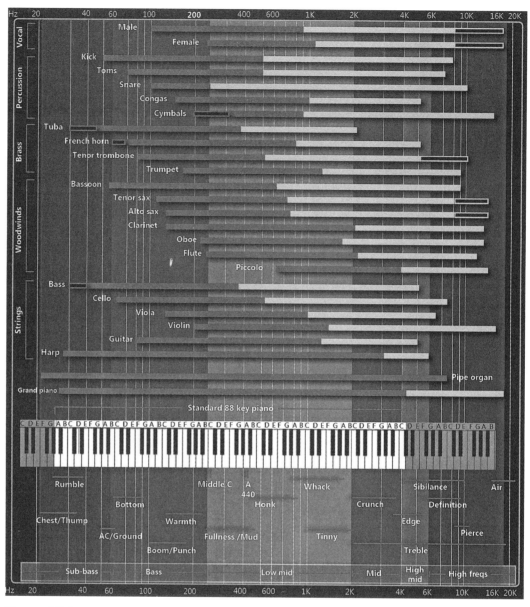

Figure 19.1

For each horizontal bar showing the instrument's frequency range, the left part (red on the companion website) represents the fundamentals, the middle part (yellow on the companion website) the overtones, and the right part (black on the companion website), at the upper frequency range, indicates extended techniques such as overblowing or overtone singing. The harmonics determine the timbre of an instrument and reach far above the fundamental (see p. 167). The frequencies are displayed on the horizontal scale, and the subjective qualities of the frequency ranges are shown just below the keyboard. The standard 88-key piano extends down to A0; the fundamental of the lowest key is 27.5 Hz, while that of the highest key is 4186.01 Hz. The piano and the church organ are the instruments spanning the broadest frequency range. (Modeled after the frequency chart by Independent Recording Network, http://www.independentrecording.net/irn/resources/freqchart/main_display.htm.)

to about E2 at 82.41 Hz and the female voice to approximately E3 at 164.82 Hz. The lowest note on the guitar is the E string at 82.41 Hz.

Sound and Timbre

The bass frequencies are of great importance for the instrument's fullness. The basic bottom of the rhythm section is located here, as is the mysterious "warm analog sound."

However, if all instruments are allocated fullness in the bass, the mix will sound boomy and muddy, blurring or obscuring the midrange and high frequencies of the mix.

Low-Mid (250 Hz to 2 kHz)

The Instruments

The flute and piccolo flute have their lowest fundamentals here, while, conversely, quite a few instruments have their highest fundamental here.

Sound and Timbre

The low-mid contains a lot of energy, which controls the impact of an instrument in the mix. In the lower parts of the range, attenuation might be needed to reduce boominess and might also be needed in the upper parts to suppress a honking and tinny sound.

Midrange (2–4 kHz)

The Instruments

All the instruments have frequency content here because of harmonics, but only the whistle, the church organ, and the piano have fundamentals reaching that high. Therefore, EQing above 2 kHz only affects the harmonics on most instruments.

Sound and Timbre

The midrange area highlights the striking of the instruments (drums and percussion, piano, guitar, etc.) in the mix, and too much midrange content produces a sharp and metallic sound.

High-Mid (4–6 kHz)

The Instruments

Almost all instruments except the bass instruments have frequency content here because of their audible harmonics.

Sound and Timbre

The high-mids provide definition, presence, and openness, and boosting the high-mids brings clarity to the mix. Sibilance (from vocals) is also found here and should be attenuated.

High (6–20 kHz)

The Instruments

No instruments have their fundamentals here except for the highest pitches of the largest church organs, but many have audible harmonics in this area.

Sound and Timbre

The high range also defines definition and clarity (6–10 kHz) on most instruments, but if this range is exaggerated, the sound might become thin and sharp. Air is heard in the 12–16 kHz range, but above 16 kHz it is only felt rather than heard due to the limitations of the human auditory system. A delicious, silky top end can be achieved by discretely boosting with a high-shelf filter from approximately 12 kHz. This requires a good EQ design.

The Components of the EQ

Equalizers are available in many forms. The standard stereo amplifier typically found in homes only provides bass and treble controls. The small live mixers have a few more options but still considerably fewer compared to the options of the expanded EQ of studio consoles and the almost unlimited EQ bands of the DAW's plug-ins.

The EQ is divided into frequency bands, having at least a gain control that boosts or cuts (attenuates) 12–18 dB on the analog EQ and up to 30 dB on the digital plug-in. Moreover, it might have a frequency control and a bandwidth pot called Q. If it contains all three, it is a full parametric EQ.

Choices of EQ settings on the studio console are often restricted; while this limits the possible settings, it often makes such EQ designs sound "musical," as this restriction to a few fixed frequencies is aimed at processing certain essential frequency ranges of the instruments and the voice in relation to the mix. There may also be limited options for Q—for example, fixed narrow and wide settings. This applies to classic designs such as Pultec, Neve, SSL, and Trident, all of which are famous for their particular musical qualities.

Common Types of EQ

In this section, in which the five most common types of EQ are examined, both the EQ of the analog studio console and the EQ plug-ins of the DAW are referenced.

The Low-Cut Filter

This filter gradually cuts below the selected frequency (the cut-off frequency, which is normally from 80–120 Hz on the console). It is also known as the high-pass filter (HPF) because it only allows frequencies above the set frequency to pass through.

The steepness of the curve, or slope, can vary. For example, a 24 dB/octave filter applies a reduction of 24 dB per octave (this defines the steepness of the curve: the higher the dBs, the steeper the gradient of the cut); if the selected frequency is 80 Hz, the input signal is reduced by 24 dB for any content at 40 Hz (which is the octave below 80 Hz). On the low-cut filter, Q determines how much the frequencies immediately above the selected frequency are affected; a high Q compensates for the low cut by raising the

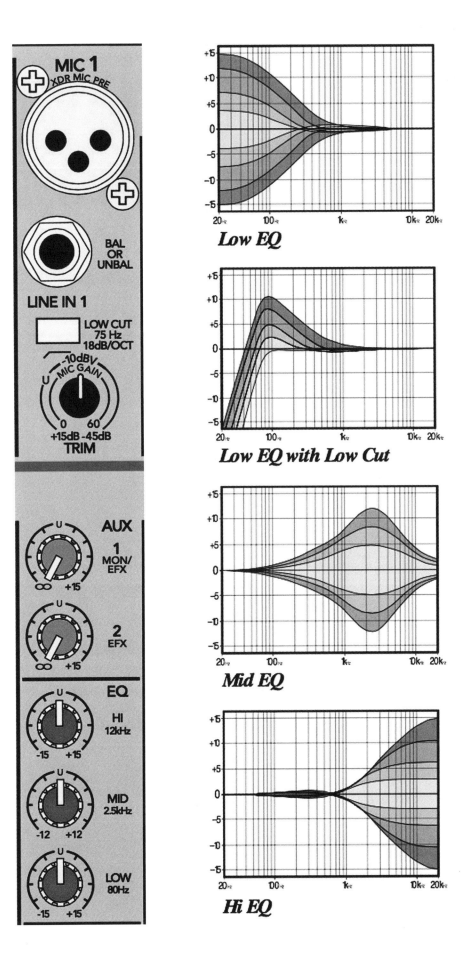

Figure 19.2
A simple EQ section with a fixed high filter (12 kHz), a mid filter (2.5 kHz), and a low-shelf filter (80 Hz). The low cut (75 Hz) is located at the input section.
© Mackie

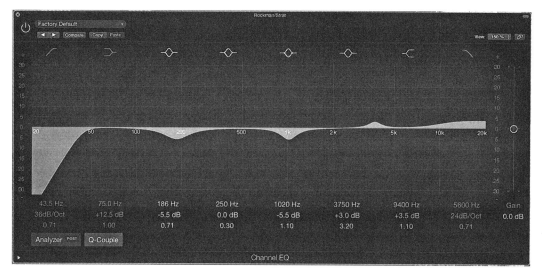

Figure 19.3

Logic's EQ with (*left to right*) low-cut filter, low-shelf filter, four parametric EQs, high-shelf filter, and high-cut filter. The top row shows the typical symbols used for the EQ types. These EQ settings are used for a Fender Stratocaster recorded through a Rockman preamp.

The selected frequencies, gain, and Q are at the bottom. A Q of 0.71 is the default setting in the Logic EQ. When Q is increased, the affected EQ range narrows, and vice versa: the lower the Q, the wider the affected range becomes.

frequencies just above the selected frequency in order to restore some of the fullness removed below.

▶ Audio example 19.01 demonstrates the effects of the high–pass filter.

The Low-Shelf Filter

The low-shelf filter boosts or cuts the frequencies below the selected frequency, and its symbol looks like a shelf, hence the name. Usually the low-shelf frequency is variable, but smaller mixing consoles often have a fixed frequency, typically 80 Hz, with a gain of +/−12–15 dB. The area above the selected frequency is also affected, but to a lesser extent. On this filter, Q determines how steep the transition is from shelf EQ to no effect.

The low-shelf filter sounds more natural than the low-cut filter, as it preserves some of the lowest frequencies. In addition, ringing or resonance is less pronounced within the frequency ranges on either side of the selected frequency.

Combining a boost on the low-shelf filter (fullness) with a low-cut filter (for example at 40 Hz to reduce rumbling) often provides musical-sounding results.

The Parametric EQ

On the parametric EQ, up to 18 dB (analog EQ) or 30 dB (digital EQ) of boost or attenuation can be achieved at the selected frequency (with the neighboring frequencies also affected but to a lesser extent). Q determines the bandwidth, that is, how wide the affected frequency range will be. A narrow Q (that is, a high Q value) can be used to cut out problematic frequencies from the recording. As an example, a resonant frequency (from the recording space or an instrument) can be located by making a frequency sweep

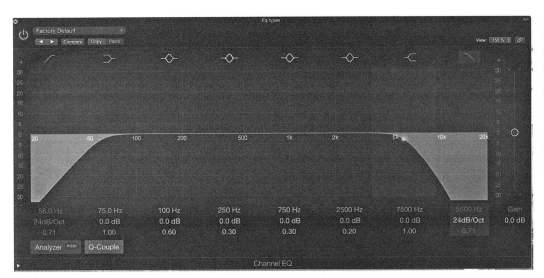

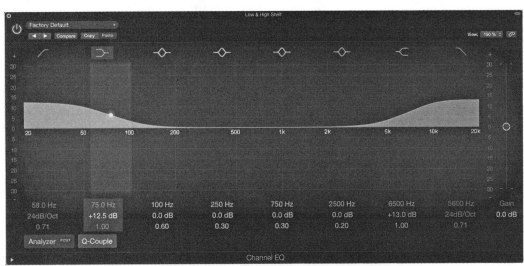

Figure 19.4
The five EQ types: the top image shows low and high-cut filters, the middle the low and the high-shelf filters, and, at the bottom, the parametric EQ. The shelving EQs and the parametric have variable frequencies.

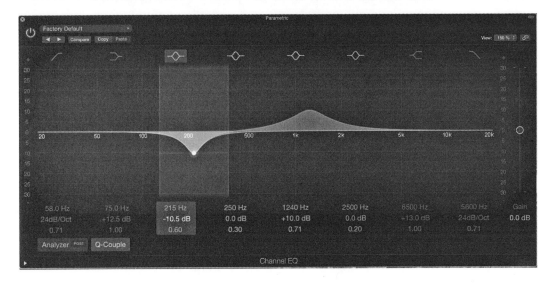

Box 19.1

EQ has a varying degree of adverse effect around the selected frequencies, particularly when boosting. The higher the Q (i.e., the narrower the main frequency range boosted is), the higher the resonance (ringing) of the boosted frequencies. This can sound unnatural and often is unwanted, which is why high Qs are typically only used when attenuating or cutting specific frequency ranges, such as to reduce noise. When boosting, it is better to use low Q values (i.e., a wide frequency range) in order to make the transition between boosted and non-boosted sound more natural and less unexpected.

---

through the problematic area. Then choose the narrowest Q possible and attenuate by quite a few dBs.

Wide EQ values (Q of 0.6 to 0.8) sound more natural than a narrow Q (2.0 or more), because wide Q settings affect the bordering frequencies to a lesser extent. The narrow Qs, as noted above, are mostly used to surgically remove noise or resonance in specific areas.

The parametric EQ, also called a bell EQ due to the shape of the curve, is the most common EQ used because it allows for precise EQing of specific frequencies. Plug-ins allow for an unlimited number of filters, since adding a few parametric bands does not considerably raise costs.

▶ Audio examples 19.02a–19.02c demonstrate various uses of the parametric EQ: boosting a frequency band, cutting a frequency band, and the effects of Q on the bandwidth of the filter.

The High-Shelf Filter

This boosts or cuts all the frequencies above the selected frequency. On the analog mixer, it is usually set at a fixed frequency that is typically 12 kHz, thus affecting all frequencies on the shelf above 12 kHz equally. On the mixer, gain is +/−12–15 dB, while plug-ins usually have the range +/−20 dB. The area just below the selected frequency is also affected, but less so, and Q determines how steep the transition from shelving to no effect is.

The High-Cut Filter

This type of filter is also called a low-pass filter (LPF). It only allows frequency content below the selected frequency to pass through; above the high-cut setting (normally between 5–15 kHz), the frequency content gradually becomes more attenuated.

As with the low-cut filter, the steepness of the cut is indicated as dB/octave. Q determines how the frequencies around the high-cut setting are affected; high Q values

Figure 19.5

The Neve 1073N EQ appeared in 1970. Integrated into a preamp, the 1073N is a very simple EQ sporting high-shelf, high-mid, low-shelf, and low-cut filters. Despite its simplicity, this EQ adds magic to most audio sources, providing openness, definition, and warmth to vocals, guitars, and most instruments. Always musical sounding, the 1073N has been emulated in many plug-ins. © Universal Audio

compensate for the low-cut effect by boosting the area just below the selected high-cut frequency to preserve treble content.

A typical use of the high-cut filter is to make an instrument darker and warmer sounding.

EQing Different Instruments: Use Your Ears—and Your Imagination!

With more than a few instruments in the recording, each instrument might exhibit a broad range of frequencies, and when that many instruments are mixed, they will overlap and steal space from each other. Therefore, their frequency scope must be made narrower and the instruments given space in the frequency layers of the musical arrangement that suits their timbral characteristics. For this reason, an artistic use of the EQ requires a good knowledge of the musical genre.

The chapters on the recording and mixing of instruments (pp. 5–116) have specific instructions for equalizing individual instruments in the "Mix Settings and Effects" sections. These instructions are based on the frequency ranges that characterize the instrument, and they will always be helpful when mixing. But these instructions are no excuse for not making a better-sounding EQ by using your ears and having a feel for the genre. And remember, some genres have specific requirements for natural-sounding instruments, while in other genres instruments can be shaped freely by your imagination.

The Technique of EQing

The basic EQ can already be applied to the recording when capturing the sound of an instrument:

- Moving the microphone a few centimeters might make the difference between a merely good sound and a truly excellent sound.
- Choosing the right microphone might make an instrument stand out in the mix.
- Improving the sound source (EQing the bass amp, tuning the snare drum, or replacing the acoustic guitar) is a miracle cure that is often overlooked.

When the basic levels are set in the mix, continue with EQing, primarily by removing ugly and troublesome frequencies in each instrument.

161

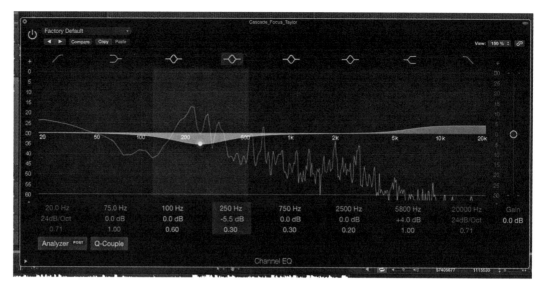

Figure 19.6

EQ plug-ins often have a spectrum analyzer displaying the frequency content of the track. Use it to get an overview of, or feel for, which frequencies contain more or less energy. The spectrum analyzer provides a visual cue of where to cut, if an instrument sounds boomy, and where to boost when an instrument does not cut through the mix. This example shows boosts and cuts based on the frequency spectrum of an acoustic guitar.

Only then are you free to use EQ as the creative tool that makes the individual tracks fit into the mix—perhaps even to creatively sculpt the frequency of a particular track to make it the centerpiece of the song.

Cut Away!—Additive and Subtractive EQ

Unfortunately, EQ does not only have positive effects as a repair and creative tool; it can be quite destructive too if used without care. Most EQ designs reduce the dynamics of the music by adding resonances in the bordering frequencies around the selected frequency when using additive EQ (boosting). Subtractive EQ (cutting or attenuating), however, is less destructive to the dynamics.

In reality, EQing corresponds to turning the volume of a limited frequency range up or down. This is why inexperienced engineers prefer boosting to cutting; an instrument immediately sounds better when boosted, but the benefits of sheer volume get lost when turning the instrument down to make it balance in the mix.

Therefore, wherever possible, subtractive EQ is the recommended method. A cut in the midrange (with a wide Q) often accomplishes the same as a boost on the low- and the high-shelf EQs. Also, a cut in the bass range accomplishes the same result as a boost in the high-mids—with a more natural and dynamic performance as a result.

Presence and clarity are created not only by boosting the high-mid frequencies—often an attenuation in the bass and low-mid (2–3 dB around 200–300 Hz) is enough to clear up an instrument in a crowded mix, removing muddiness and bringing transparency to the overall mix. Reducing the nasty frequencies always works better, resulting in a relative boost of the good-sounding frequencies, and sparse EQing always maintains transparency and dynamics.

Box 19.2 EQ procedure

A method to determine which frequencies should be boosted or cut is to make a strong boost (6–10 dB) on the parametric EQ. Working initially in solo mode and with a broad range of frequencies (that is, a low Q of 0.5–0.7) makes it easier to hear which frequencies should be processed. Determine the frequencies that highlight the sound of the instrument (these must be boosted) and those that degrade it (these must be attenuated) by sweeping through the frequency range.

Then, having determined the approximate range, narrow the Q (while fine-tuning the selected frequency) until the relevant frequencies are captured and defined as accurately as possible. Finally, fine-tune the cut/boost of the selected frequency. Test if it works both in solo mode and in the overall mix.

If you start by making a big and full sound on each instrument, you often end up with a mix that sounds messy and undefined. All the instruments with a full frequency spectrum will then overlap and fight each other in one or more frequency ranges, a typical problem area being 100–250 Hz. Many rich-sounding instruments with this type of spectrum, unless EQed, will provide an undefined and muddy sound that blurs the overall mix.

If the bass sounds undefined, the solution is not necessarily to equalize it. If it is due to other instruments overlapping, it is better to thin out the guitar, the bass drum, or the piano in the 100–250 Hz range.

In the digital domain, a lot of information is also recorded in the sub-bass area (where analog tape gradually rolls off). Therefore, low-cut or low-shelf attenuation has become increasingly necessary on almost any instrument but deep drums and bass instruments. The low-cut filters, sitting on mixers and preamps, often sound a little rough and ragged. Wait until the mix to determine how much to cut away.

Many engineers use a high-pass filter (HPF) on all instruments at 45–50 Hz to prevent the lows from overloading the signal chain, amplifiers, and speakers, and in any case, sub-bass below 40 Hz cannot be heard on most playback media. Also, be careful with sub-bass plug-ins, because much of what they do is not revealed by the studio's nearfield monitors.

Similarly, too clear and bright a top end on all the tracks can result in a thin mix. When these frequency areas are reduced on some of the tracks, the instruments are then given their own space in the tonal layers of the mix; without too many overlapping instruments, the mix sounds both clearer and fuller.

Complementary EQ and Contrasting Frequency Ranges

Some frequency ranges interact even though they are at the opposite ends of the frequency spectrum, and processing one can produce a complementary effect in the other, in that an attenuation of the low frequencies perceptually corresponds to a boost in the high range, and vice versa.

Some examples of this complementarity:

- A slight reduction of 1–2 dB in the 150–250 Hz region can have the same effect as a boost in the presence range (5–6 kHz), because the bass frequencies blur the higher frequencies. Attenuating the bass is perceived as boosting the top end, and, in relative terms, this is in fact the case. Often, the result is as if a blanket over the instruments has been removed.
- Attenuating a vocal at 1 kHz often provides a more full-bodied sound, equivalent to boosting the 200–350 Hz range.
- A harsh and metallic-sounding brass section can be softened by boosting at 250 Hz or by lowering at 6–7 kHz, both processes resulting in a more rounded and warmer sound. Then, if necessary, as little as 0.5 dB of boosting in the 15–20 kHz range will add air.
- Adding sub-bass is sometimes perceived as providing more air to a mix, such as when turning on the subwoofer. This is probably due to the extended range from the low to the top end.

The complementary frequency ranges suggested above are neither fixed nor precise, if only for the reason that musical arrangements are vastly different. But testing which of the two complementary EQ ranges should be boosted or cut is a good means of making a mix fall into place. An instrument that becomes thin or sharp when boosting the high-mids will probably be improved by cutting the low-mids. Equally, the reverse is true—an instrument lacking fullness might sound better by reducing the mids or highs, because boosting the bass often makes it sound boomy.

Figure 19.7

The Pultec EQP-1A combines ATTEN (attenuation) at the lows with a boost just above the selected frequency to compensate for the loss of fullness. The Pultec EQP-1A was produced between 1951 and 1980, and today digital models of the original are made by Manley, Universal Audio, and Waves. © Universal Audio

The Graphic EQ

Compared to the parametric EQ, the graphic equalizer comprises a number of set bands, typically around 30. The added flexibility of having this number of bands means that each has a fixed center frequency and a fixed Q, the gain (boost or cut) being the only variable setting in the form of a fader. Traditionally, it has served as a stereo master EQ compensating for the nonlinear reflections of the control room or the live venue.

The faders, when in place, displaying a graphic image (hence the name of this EQ type) of the boosts and cuts made, make the EQ quick and easy to adjust. In the form of intuitive software, the graphic EQ has found a broad use in computer media, but it is also used as an alternative to the parametric EQ in the studio—for example, emulations of the API 560 ten-band graphic EQ.

TIPS

✓ After equalizing each individual instrument, it is important to check the result by comparing the instrument in solo mode and as part of the mix. A nasal electric guitar is not necessarily thin and sharp when heard with the bass and drum tracks—it can change its character to raw and aggressive because instruments "borrow" sound from each other.

✓ The guitar shares the frequency range of the piano in the bass and the midrange, and so these instruments fight each other across the same frequencies. Assign each instrument its place in the mix, perhaps using complementary EQ. In addition, their low ends often require a low-shelf filter (or a low-cut filter) to prevent confusion with the drums and the bass.

✓ Not only the guitar and piano but other instruments with frequency content in the same frequency bands pile up on top of each other. If the bottom is muddy because of the bass guitar and the bass drum overlapping, then try panning the bass to 1 o'clock and the bass drum to 11 o'clock. Panning instruments that share frequency content to each side of the mix creates more space for each instrument. This method also works in the midrange and high-mids; for example, on the piano and the guitar.

✓ Think "call and response"; that is, avoid too many instruments fighting for space in the same frequency range of the mix. As with the guitar or the brass-section licks that fill the "gaps" between vocal phrases, it might be best to remove the guitar and leave the whole verse section to the keyboard.

✓ If you need to boost high-mids and highs heavily on an electronic keyboard to make it stand out in the mix, it's better to ask the keyboard player to play higher chord inversions. Alternatively, doubling with a bright string pad that is higher in pitch might fill the hole in the mix's frequency layers.

✓ A vocal that is a little too dark and woolly might benefit from a light reverb. This preserves the fullness if you find that EQing the top end makes it too thin.

✓ If the bass does not sound right after all possible EQing attempts, there's probably something else in the mix that muffles it. EQ is not only there to boost the top and bottom of the individual instruments—it should also be used to balance the frequencies in the entire mix.

✓ Multing works on most instruments that do not easily fall into place in the mix. If the track still sounds too thin when top is added or undefined when boosting the lows, then use multing by copying the instrument to another track. For example, dealing with the bass drum, the solution might look like this: boost the original track in the low frequencies (but do not emphasize the pedal strikes with a high-mid boost); boost the copied track heavily in the midrange and the highs (but not the lows); finally, optionally add compression and other effects to accentuate the strike of the bass drum.

165

20

Harmonics and EQ

What makes sounds into potentially musical tones is that they vibrate the air in which they sound with one predominant frequency, the fundamental, which is also called the root. In reality, though, such sounds comprise a number of frequencies. These are the partials (or overtones), which in musical tones are usually known as the harmonics. It is

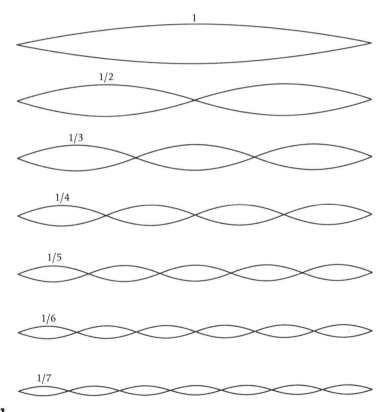

Figure 20.1

The nodes of a vibrating string.
Harmonics are caused by the nodes generated by a string or in an oscillating column of air (such as in a wind or brass instrument). A node is produced in a vibrating string at half its length (second harmonic, the first octave), one third of its length (third harmonic, the octave and a fifth), and so on. It is from this relationship that the name partial derives.If the fundamental, the first harmonic, is 400 Hz, the other harmonics, if present, will be 800 Hz, 1200 Hz, 1600 Hz, 2000 Hz, 2400 Hz, 2800 Hz, and so on.

only because the fundamental is by far the strongest that we perceive tones as having one frequency, represented by the fundamental.

Sine waves are pure tones, that is, they consist only of one frequency and thus sound rather colorless—even more boring than the A (440 Hz) of the tuning fork, which has two to three harmonics. All musical instruments have harmonics that become weaker the further they are from the fundamental. The amplitudes of the harmonics are different from instrument to instrument, and it is the number and relative amplitudes of the individual harmonics that determine the timbre of an instrument. This is what makes the middle C of the grand piano different from the corresponding note of the trumpet. Powerful lower harmonics create a smooth and rich sound, while powerful upper harmonics make the sound bright and piercing.

The numbers and relative amplitudes of harmonics are determined by the materials from which the instruments are made, the size of their sound boards, and the dimensions of their resonant spaces. Additionally, how the sound is activated is important, and the relative amplitudes of harmonics can change during the length of a musical note depending on particular instrumental or vocal techniques. For example, while the size and shape of the human voice box is one of the most significant factors making each voice being unique, a good singer can control the body's resonating cavities (particularly the mouth) so that the vocal timbre changes as the note is sung.

Instruments made of poor materials, worn out strings, and poor microphones are some of the factors that reduce the quality of the harmonics and thus the instrument's timbre. Samples (still) lack some of the harmonic richness that characterizes a musical instrument, which is why they often require more EQing to fit into the mix, and synthesis techniques are often incapable of producing the dynamic nature of instrumental tones (e.g., the changes in harmonic relations and therefore timbre).

Box 20.1

If a fundamental frequency, 1f, has additional partials at 2f, 3f, 4f, 5f, and so on (each being an integer multiple of f), these partials are known as harmonics. Sounds that are typically characterized as noise rather than musical tones (e.g., cymbals and snare drum) are described as inharmonic, because their partials are not integer multiples of a fundamental. Series of partials and harmonics include the fundamental; the term "overtone" is sometimes used, but this refers only to partials above the fundamental; in a musical tone, the fundamental is considered the first harmonic, while the second harmonic is the first overtone, and so on.

The Harmonic Series

Figure 20.2 displays the overtone series, starting with the octave, then the fifth, the second octave, the third above that, the fifth, and the seventh as the sixth overtone (seventh harmonic). The harmonics become gradually weaker, which is a good thing,

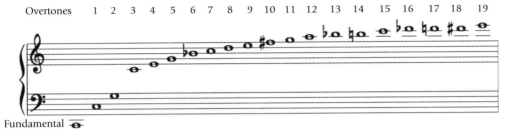

Fundamental

Figure 20.2

Harmonics are found to varying degrees in all instruments. In principle, the overtone series continues endlessly, but as overtones typically rapidly weaken in amplitude the further from the fundamental they are, only the lower overtones tend to affect the timbre of the instrument.

Chords are formed from the overtone series—for example, the chord of C (root, second overtone, and fourth overtone) and C7 (root, second overtone, fourth overtone, and sixth overtone). At the eighteenth overtone, the minor third is found, though it is so weak that the major third (fourth overtone) is the predominant character of the overtone series. The equal tempered scale, the dominant tuning system in use in the West today, modifies or tempers the frequency of the notes formed from the overtone series so that each semitone step is precisely 100 cents. This allows melodies and harmonies to be transposed from one key to another without altering the musical character.

because there are an infinite number of potential harmonics, including those that fit into the tonality of the musical piece and those that do not.

Overdriven guitar amps and overblown saxophones emphasize the harmonics, and this is the reason for their rich and complex timbre. It also explains why power chords (just the fundamental and the fifth played on the low strings) sound huge without the third on a heavily overdriven guitar amp. A guitarist also playing the third of the chord would sound slightly out of tune, since the distortion causes the upper harmonics to become too powerful, resulting in an inharmonic chord. Moreover, the third is already present as the fourth overtone, which is strongly highlighted by the overdriven amp.

EQing Harmonics

Although most instruments have their highest fundamentals between 1–2 kHz (see p. 154), the presence of harmonics means that there is a reason to use EQ higher than 2 kHz. The frequency of each harmonic is an integer multiple of that of the fundamental. Here are the harmonics based on middle C:

Harmonic	Fundamental C4	Octave C5	The fifth G5	Octave C6	The third E6
Frequency	261.6 Hz	523.2 Hz (2×261.6 Hz)	784.8 Hz (3×261.6 Hz)	1046.4 Hz (4×261.6 Hz)	1308 Hz (5×261.6 Hz)

Due to the progression of the overtone series, some overtone-rich instruments may become slightly dissonant when the high-mids and the high frequencies are boosted. The further away from the root (and the major chord, formed by the root and the second and fourth overtones), the more out of tune they will sound with excessive EQing. This applies in particular to an overblown saxophone, violin, overdriven guitar, Hammond organ, and some rich sounding voices.

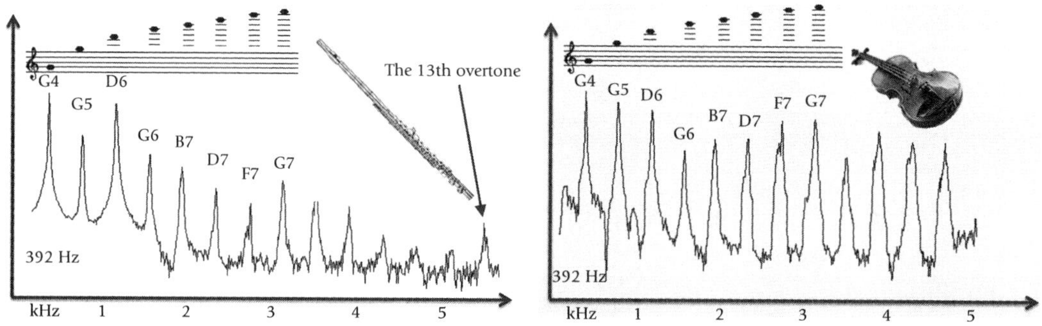

Figure 20.3

The harmonics generated from the same root (G4) on the flute and the violin. The y axis displays the strength in dB, while the x axis indicates the frequency in kHz. The charts show that the two instruments have the same harmonics but at greatly different amplitudes.

These spectrum plots show that the flute is softer sounding than the violin because it has weaker harmonics. Also, the thirteenth overtone of the flute, at 6 kHz (7f), displays a strong peak that results in a strident tone when boosted by EQ in the high range. © http://www.phys.unsw.edu.au/music/

The frequency spectrum below displays the differences in amplitude for the harmonics of the flute and violin. Their amplitudes relative to the fundamental frequency explain why the instruments respond differently to the same EQ. Therefore, a knowledge of the instruments and their harmonics aids using EQ effectively in order to reduce problematic frequencies and to emphasize the good ones.

21

Compressor/Limiter
and Expander/Gate

Dynamics processors are used to control and shape the dynamic range of a sound. The dynamic range is the difference between the weakest and the strongest level (measured in dB) of a recording. The dynamic progress of a sound is indicated by the ADSR envelope (often called the amplitude envelope; see p. 175).

There are three main objectives when altering the dynamic range of a recording:

1. When recording instruments on separate tracks by overdubbing, the balance between them is lost, and compression is one of the means to restore it.

2. When recording using close-miking techniques, even the slightest movement on the part of a singer will result in variation in volume. Moreover, both close-miking technique and DI input will enhance dynamic differences in the playing of an instrument, resulting in some notes standing out in the mix. In live performance in a room, these differences are leveled by the acoustics, but on close-miked recordings the compressor is used to control some of these dynamic fluctuations.

3. In the real world, dynamic range is often huge, and although quality microphones are able to closely reproduce this, some audio equipment and the speakers cannot, and this results in the signal being degraded by noise (when signal level is low) and distortion (when signal level is too strong). Dynamics processors are often helpful tools to compensate for such deficiencies.

Compressor/limiters and expander/gates are widely used to automatically control the dynamics of recorded tracks and to balance the individual instruments musically with regard to volume level.

In addition, the compressor and the limiter in particular are used to creatively shape the sound (that is, the ADSR envelope) of an instrument.

Compressor

The compressor is used to automatically smooth out an audio signal having (too) wide a fluctuation in level. When the amplitude of the input exceeds the threshold set by the user, it is reduced by a factor determined by the ratio. This reduces the maximum

Box 21.1 Compressing Musically

Originally, dynamics processors were designed to be used in radio broadcasts and for live performances. The first compressor, the Telefunken U3, was used in the PA system at the Olympic Games in 1936 in Berlin and served as a limiter (by automatically setting the maximum level) to protect other equipment from overloading. These simple types of compressors/limiters are also called leveling amplifiers.

Eventually, recording studies also needed to control levels. In 1960, the UREI 1176 (see figure 21.1) and the LA-2A were developed, and they became the prototypes of the "musical compressor" and were promptly put into service in rock and pop recordings. Ever since close-miking techniques became established in studios during the 1960s, the compressor has been indispensable in controlling the dynamics.

With an increased number of tracks, often recorded one at a time as overdubs, the balance between instruments can get lost. Here, the compressor becomes vital as a tool to reduce the dynamic fluctuations of the instruments and to help restore the integrity of each of the tracks.

Figure 21.1

The UREI 1176 compressor from 1968 is based on FET transistors and so responds quickly, unlike optical or tube-based compressors. The 1176 also adds a slightly bright tone to the signal. It is favored by engineers as a vocal compressor. © Universal Audio

amplitude of the signal, making space (overhead) to turn up the overall level, and as a result the weak passages become relatively stronger, because the overall dynamic range is decreased.

This is similar to manually turning down the signal on the volume level fader when it becomes too strong and turning it up when it is too weak—the compressor just responds faster and does this automatically.

Compressor Parameters

The compressor is controlled by the following parameters:

- **Threshold** is the amplitude of the input signal above which the compressor starts compressing; for example, if the threshold is set to −10 dB, any signal rising above −10 dB is compressed. When you compensate for the reduction of the signal peaks using the gain makeup, the overall level becomes stronger, since the low levels have been made relatively more powerful. Certain compressors have a fixed threshold and instead control the amount of compression through the input level (which, in practice, is the same as having control over a threshold level). Turning up the input signal thus corresponds to lowering the threshold.

- **Ratio** controls the ratio between the input and output signal levels. A ratio of 5:1 means that a signal that is 5 dB above the threshold level at the input stage will only be 1 dB above the threshold level at the output. Ratio thus determines the amount of compression.

- **Attack time** (0–500 ms) determines the time to full compression from when the compressor starts to respond to an input signal that exceeds the threshold. A slow attack lets fast transients (the instrument's attack phase) through unprocessed, and only the body of the signal (the

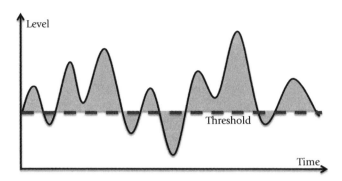

Figure 21.2

When the signal level exceeds the threshold, compression starts. The parts of the signal above the threshold are reduced by the factor indicated by the ratio.

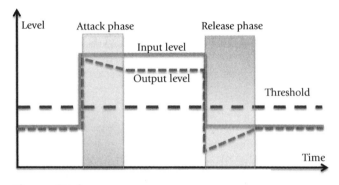

Figure 21.3

The solid line (green on the companion website) displays the input signal and the short-dashed line (red on the companion website) the output (i.e., the compressed signal). The vertical axis displays the volume level and the horizontal axis the timeline.

sustain through to release of the ADSR amplitude envelope) is compressed. A fast attack dampens transients, often causing an instrument to become woolly and confined sounding. Therefore, use slow attacks for acoustic guitar, snare drum, piano, and percussive instruments whose sounds are particularly characterized by their initial transients. You can use fast attacks on other instruments to dampen the percussive peaks and compress the entire signal, thus providing headroom to increase the overall level (by gain makeup).

- **Release time** (20 ms to 5 sec) is the time until the compression stops and the input returns to its original level as it drops below the threshold. Release times of 20–250 ms result in a more natural-sounding compression that preserves the original dynamics. A slow release at 300 ms or more can make the signal seem too compressed if a loud passage is suddenly followed by a weak one and the compressor does not have time to switch off. Quick release provides a more compressed output level, but as the compressor responds to minor changes in the input signal, it may result in pumping, with the compressor alternately turning on and off. Quick release is used quite a bit in some rock genres, as it controls the experience of loudness, that is, the sense of in-your-face dynamics and impact.

- **Auto** is included in some compressors automatically adjusting release and attack to the dynamics of the signal. The optimal setting of attack and release is the one that follows the amplitude envelope of an instrument (its ADSR; see p. 175). On well-designed compressors, this option may be the best and most musical approach until

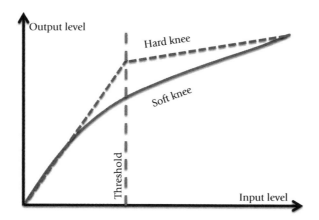

Figure 21.4

The knee determines how quickly full compression takes place. With a soft knee setting, a slight compression starts even before the signal reaches the threshold; at hard knee setting, compression starts instantly. Soft knee, therefore, sounds more natural and musical, as it tends to retain more of the transients. This principle is used in optical compressors such as Teletronix LA-2A and LA-610. Hard Knee is more immediate and can be used to provide power and impact to the signal.

you become skilled in assessing the effects of attack and release settings on various sounds and instruments. Furthermore, some compressors provide the choice between soft- and hard-knee compression.

- **Soft knee** compresses the signal gradually when it exceeds the threshold. This works for instruments with a slow decay, such as the grand piano and the acoustic guitar. Soft knee sounds more natural during the transition from non–compression to compression.

- **Hard knee** implements the compression quickly and works well on instruments with a short decay such as many percussion instruments.

- **Gain makeup** (sometimes called output) is used to compensate for the gain reduction caused by the compressor to the part of the signal that exceeds the threshold. To begin with, always set the gain makeup so that the input equals the output signal; this enables you to better assess what the compression does to the signal. When the level of compression is decided upon, raise the gain makeup level to utilize the added headroom provided by the compression.

- **Look ahead** is found on some compressors. This feature is designed to address the problem of variable attacks in the input signal—slow attack settings would result in smooth and gradual shifts in compression, while fast attack settings would destroy the transients. Instead of making a compromise in the settings for material containing both, the use of look ahead lessens inconsistencies when using either a slow or a fast attack setting. Obviously, it is impossible to look into the future—and certainly not in the audio industry. Instead, the audio signal is split into two and one is delayed. The undelayed signal is used to analyze and thereafter control the compression of the delayed signal, the latter being the only signal sent to the output. Thus, soft-sounding, slow attacks are preserved regardless of the presence of transients that would otherwise have activated the compressor. Similarly, look ahead can assist gates in activating on weak transients from a snare drum that might otherwise have been ignored (the gate assessing the transients as leakage from another drum in the kit). A look ahead setting of 1–2 ms is enough for the gate to respond. The cost of looking ahead is that the output signal from an analog compressor is delayed. In digital compressors, it is a minor problem that can be solved by the latency compensation of the DAW, which will delay all other tracks accordingly.

Using the Compressor

There are several methods to achieve a specific compression on an audio signal. Threshold and ratio are interdependent; a low threshold in combination with a low ratio can provide the same result as high threshold and ratio settings, because the threshold determines when compression starts (and therefore the degree of compression). An adjustment of the threshold, therefore, usually results in the need to review the ratio. Likewise, when slowing down attack times (that is, more of the signal passes through uncompressed), the threshold should sometimes be lowered or the ratio increased.

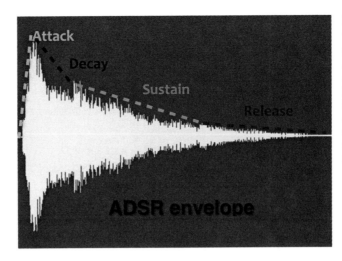

Figure 21.5
The ADSR envelope of a bass note. Attack, decay, sustain, and release typically characterize the amplitude envelope of a sound, although percussive sounds often have no sustain phase.

Fast attacks, in turn, provide more headroom, allowing gain makeup to be raised, with the result that the overall signal is more powerful.

Compression does not only provide an automatic smoothing of the levels. Since the ADSR envelope is changed, the sound of the musical instrument is also changed to some extent. Thus, compression can be used to creatively shape the sound.

The Limiter

The limiter is a simplified and specialized form of compressor. It functions as a severe compressor with a ratio of at least 10:1 and up to 100:1 depending on design. Moreover, it is characterized by fast attack and release settings (below 10 ms). Normally, threshold is set high enough so that limiting only takes place on strong peaks. On limiters with a ratio of ∞:1, the signal level can be controlled at an absolute level (all output is kept below the threshold). This is called peak limiting and is used in radio and TV broadcasting of live concerts, sport events, and so forth.

175

TIPS

✓ In principle, compression should not itself be heard—only the lack of it should be heard. This applies when compression is used to reduce the fluctuations in the level of the vocal due to the singer moving in relation to the mic. Likewise, compression can make a sensitive vocal heard even in a crowded and powerful mix.

✓ A procedure for setting "invisible" compression: start with a ratio of 3:1 and lower the threshold until you hear the compression clearly. Then, adjust the ratio ensuring you do not hear any unwanted effects of the compression (most apparent on transients).

Next, fine-tune the threshold (or the ratio) if the compression should be emphasized or reduced, and finally adjust the makeup gain.

✓ Generally, on the DAW, it might be easier to start with a preset (their names often suggesting what they are good at) and adjust the parameters until they sound right in the context.

✓ Customize the ratio to the actual recording. When modifying ratio (or threshold), gain makeup should be adjusted to reliably monitor the effect of the compression. Louder always sounds subjectively better, thereby concealing the fact that the compression might have destroyed the minor details of the signal.

✓ Threshold always depends on the level of the recorded signal, and so it should usually be adjusted. Attack and release work more transparently when set to slow for the vocal, medium for most instruments, and fast for percussion.

✓ Compression can also be used to creatively shape the amplitude envelope of an instrument (the ADSR envelope). Hard compression (a ratio of 5:1 and above) dampens the attack of an instrument and highlights its decay, and this is the method for making an acoustic guitar sound a bit like a bowed string instrument or for making a bass drum sound long and thunderous. If you want to preserve the natural ADSR envelope—particularly on acoustic instruments—compression should only be used lightly.

Box 21.2

In the first section of this book, "The Instruments" (pp. 5–116), there are more tips on using the compressor on individual instruments.

The Sound of the Compressor

The compressor was designed to solve the problem of too large a dynamic range, which can distort audio equipment. In principle, it should not color the sound of an instrument or vocal but rather remain as transparent as possible.

However, compression will always affect the amplitude envelope of an instrument to some extent. The grand piano is a good example. Due to its powerful attack and long sustain, the piano soon becomes unnatural sounding even when only moderately compressed. The attack is ruined and the decay sounds synthetic.

On other acoustic instruments too, compression often sounds unnatural, particularly in the classical music genre, which has perfected expressions of and variations in dynamics based on the authentic sound of the instrument groups. Listen, for example, to Mozart's Requiem or Beethoven's *Egmont* Overture; the emotional impact is created mainly by the expressive dynamics of the compositions, and this is precisely what the compression would ruin.

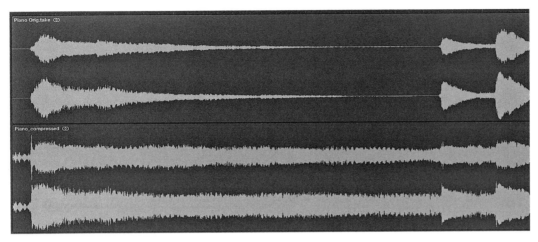

Figure 21.6

Two waveforms showing a stereo recording of a grand piano. The upper is the original recording; the lower is a strongly compressed version of this. The compression has completely changed the ADSR of the piano, resulting in a muted attack and a long release that provides a string-like sound.

Box 21.3

The piano on Toto's "Hold the Line" is heavily compressed. All attacks have the same level, being clearly attenuated by the compression, and they have plenty of fullness and sustain; only because of that can they assert themselves in the struggle against the powerful drums and the heavy guitar riff that occupy the same frequency range as the piano. This hard-compressed grand piano sounds great, as does the piano on "Lady Madonna" by the Beatles; usually, though, compression like this will be boring to listen to.

Led Zeppelin's "When the Levee Breaks" is an example of very strong compression added to a drum kit recorded with only two OH mics. The compression emphasizes the ambience of the room and the sustain of the kick and the snare, and it is clearly audible in the intro of the song.

A large dynamic range is a part of classical music, and it only becomes a problem when listening with background noise such as in the car. The popular music genres, in contrast, use the compressor as an effect to create presence and impact, for instance, to make the vocal close-sounding or the drums more in-your-face. Compression also makes the acoustic guitar cut through the rhythm section, and it emphasizes the decay characteristics of the bass, providing a denser and fuller bottom end.

However, compression may also have unwanted, non-musical effects. Groove, feeling, and swing are determined by the attacks and decays of the instruments, all of which are affected by compression. When compression is used on the rhythm group, the timing may be compromised, because one limitation of compression is that the release phase must be completed before the next attack exceeds the threshold—if the release is not completed, the attack becomes unnaturally dampened.

Too much compression will flatten out the difference in dynamics from attack to decay, and the music may end up pumping monotonously. The so-called Loudness War of the early 1990s saw the dynamic ranges of many rock tracks compressed to such an extreme point that fans and critics started to complain about poor sound quality and, in particular, loss of dynamic variation.

▶ Audio example 21.01 demonstrates the effects of over-compression on a vocal track.

Parallel Bus Compression

Parallel bus compression is a way of achieving a powerful compression of an instrument or the entire mix without completely ruining the dynamics. Parallel bus compression is achieved by mixing the unprocessed track with a heavily compressed copy of the track such that the transients are preserved while the softer sounds (sustain, decay, and room ambience) are brought forward to add fullness and impact.

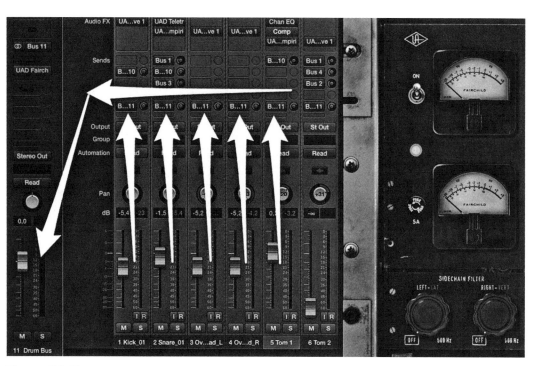

Figure 21.7

Parallel bus compression setup in Logic. The drums (channels 1–5) are sent via bus 11 to aux 1 with a Fairchild compressor inserted. All send levels should be set to unity gain (0 dB). The original drum tracks and the processed aux signal are shown sent to the stereo output in parallel. The aux channel volume level determines how much of the compressed signal is added to the mix.
The DAW's latency compensation should be active; otherwise the latency will result in a phase-like sound.

It is often used to fatten up the drum kit, to provide impact and fullness and to bring forward more of the recording room acoustics, since the natural attack (transients) of the drums is easily destroyed even when only slightly compressed.

Parallel bus compression is also used to place a vocal up front or to add contrast to the vocal between sections of a song; for example, the chorus is aggressively compressed while the verse is less compressed in order to avoid the effect becoming tiring.

This type of compression is also used in the mastering process to increase the level of the soft passages (particularly in classical and ambient music) while maintaining the original dynamics in the loud passages. Thus, the mix is fattened up in the parallel bus while the dynamics are preserved in the original tracks.

Parallel bus compression is also known as Motown compression, since the Motown studios started using it around 1970. The Motown rhythm section was more powerful than those on most other 1960s hits. In order to make the vocals clearly heard, Lawrence Horn, the engineer at Motown, started using heavy parallel bus compression on the vocals, while at the same time boosting the presence range around 5 kHz. Listen, for instance, to his recordings of Marvin Gaye, the Jackson 5, and Stevie Wonder.

Box 21.4

See pp. 219 and 242 for specific settings for parallel bus compression.

Gate and Expander

The gate and the expander have many of the same parameters as the compressor. Usually, the gate is used to automatically mute a signal to eliminate unwanted signal content below a certain level (i.e., noise). By setting the threshold such that the level of the unwanted part of the input signal is below the threshold level and the desired part is above, hiss and hum from a guitar amp or spill between drum mics, for example, can be automatically removed. However, any noise or spill occurring at the same time as the desired signal will still be present when the gate opens.

The gate can also be used to manipulate the amplitude envelope of an instrument (ADSR)—for example, by reducing a sound only to its attack if the gate is set to cut the decay. If the gate is set to respond slowly (slow attack), the transients will not open the gate, resulting, for example, in a guitar with an organ-like ADSR envelope. For the same reason, one must be careful not to cut off the ambience (the room reverberation) or the ringing from the snares of the snare drum.

A more sensitive tool for reducing unwanted sounds is the expander, which attenuates signals (noise) below the threshold and raises those (the instrument) above. The expander thus functions in the opposite manner of the compressor by increasing the distance between the strongest and weakest signal; the expander enlarges the dynamic range of the signal, while the compressor reduces it.

While the expander is capable of increasing the distance between noise and the desired signal in a not quite perfect recording, it does not brutally cut off the signal like the gate does when the signal falls below the threshold; thus, there is no sudden shift in level resulting from the opening and closing of the gate. Ratio determines the amount of the noise reduction.

The expander may also be able to (partially) repair a signal that has been compressed too much during recording, provided that at least a 5–6 dB difference between the weakest and strongest signals has been maintained.

Much as a high ratio makes a compressor into a limiter, a high ratio transforms an expander into a gate. More precisely, when the ratio is ∞:1, the gate closes abruptly for a signal falling below the threshold. Otherwise, the expander gradually reduces the signal—which is why it is often viewed as operating more musically, because it tends to retain transients.

Gate and Expander Parameters

The gate and expander parameters are:

- **Threshold**. When the input signal falls below the threshold value, the gate will be activated.
- **Ratio** (sometimes called "range") reflects the difference between output and input. That is, a 5:1 ratio results in a signal that is −1 dB at the input being attenuated to −5 dB at the output.
- **Attack time** is the time required for the gate to close (i.e., to activate to the required ratio) as the input signal drops below the threshold.
- **Release time** is the time required for the gate to open again when the input rises above the threshold.
- **Hold** controls how long the gate should remain open after the input signal has fallen below the threshold; that is, it delays the closing of the gate, thus preventing the instrument's decay and reverb tails from being cut off when they fall below the threshold level. On the gate, hold prevents the gate from stuttering (rapidly opening and closing) before closing smoothly.
- **Range** sets a maximum attenuation. 0 dB corresponds to bypassing the gate or expander, while 90 dB specifies almost a full mute of the signal once the gate is activated.
- **Key filter** (found on the more expensive gates and expanders) sets the gate to be activated only by signals in a specific frequency range—for example, a high whistle or a bass instrument. The key filter is also known as the side chain filter.

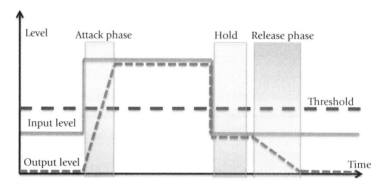

Figure 21.8

The solid line (green on the companion website) displays the original input signal, while the short-dashed line (red on the companion website) is the output signal after gating. Hold keeps the gate open even after the input signals falls below the threshold, while release controls the rate at which the gate closes.

Using the Gate and Expander

The art of using the gate or expander involves setting the threshold accurately so as to have the music above and the noise below. With the power of level automation in the DAW, it has become relatively easy to draw the threshold as the dividing line that separates noise (of varying levels) from the wanted signal.

Low ratios allow for soft expansion, while higher ratios work more like the gate, ultimately and at high ratios abruptly closing and cutting off the signal. Attack, release, and hold are the parameters that determine the transition (soft or hard) back and forth between processed signal and unprocessed signal.

Applications of the gate and expander:

- The gate removes spill between the mics on the drum kit. The expander reduces spill generally.
- They remove or reduce spill from headphones on recordings of vocals and the like.
- They remove or reduce noise from a guitar amp.
- The expander adds life (dynamics) to a track that has been compressed too heavily.
- The gate can be used to reduce a sound to just the attack when set to cut off the decay; the ambience of the room or the rattling from the snares will be captured only when other drums are hit.

▶ Audio example 21.02 demonstrates the use of a gate to remove spill.

Box 21.5

Often, accidents can lead to innovative uses of the audio technology.

When Phil Collins was laying down the drum track to Peter Gabriel's "Intruder" (1980) in Townhouse Studios, the thundering, gated drum sound that came to form the main character of the song was stumbled upon by chance.

The Townhouse Studios' new SSL desk was not only one of the first to sport compressors and noise gates on each channel, but the console also had a reverse talkback, so that the musician could talk to the control room. The talkback mic went through a very powerfull compressor, making it possible to hear the musicians talking from anywhere in the recording room.

One day, Collins started playing drums while the reverse talkback was on; the most amazing sound came out of the studio monitors, because the heavy compressor soaked up the ambience of the room as well. The desk was then modified, so that this compressor was fed it into a mixer channel, with a gate to cut off ambience tails, and this formed the powerful drum sound on "Intruder."

Later, producer Hugh Padgham also used this drum recording technique on Phil Collins's "In the Air Tonight" (1981).

Together with the reverse talkback mic and the heavy-duty SSL compressor, two Neumann U87s placed 4–5 m from the drums constituted the main part of the drum sound. The two Neumanns went through a powerful compression (UREI 1176s) that soaked up the ambience of the room, while gates cut off the ambience tails. Only a Neumann U47 close on the bass drum and a Shure SM57 on the snare drum added a touch of presence to the drum sound.

TIPS

✓ If the gate is used on the snare, the bass drum spill will often open the gate. A side chain filter or key filter can be set to filter out the low frequencies so that the bass drum does not trigger the gate. The side chain filter is a control signal used to determine which signals should open the gate (that is, it does not affect the sound of the snare drum track; see p. 31). Gate plug-ins normally have a side chain filter that makes setup simple.

✓ In live sound, correct gating is crucial, because it cannot be finely adjusted in the same manner as in the studio. Therefore, live engineers often use a contact mic on the snare drum whose sole purpose is to control the gate, thus letting even soft snare hits through while avoiding a closing of the gate triggered by spill from the other drums of the kit.

22

History of Reverb

Natural Ambience

The creative use of artificial reverberation was pioneered in 1947 by Bill Putnam Sr., who developed the concept of the "reverb chamber" or "echo chamber." Quite simply, he played back the recording into the studio bathroom, and, capturing this with a mic, he then mixed the reverberation with the original recording. Putnam's first "reverb" release, the Harmonicats' "Peg o' My Heart," became a hit and encouraged him to continue to experiment with the building of dedicated echo chambers in his Chicago studio and later in Los Angeles.

Box 22.1 Dry Recordings and Natural Reverberation

Up until about 1950, reverberation on recordings was only a by-product of the physical distance between the sound source and the microphone. The greater the distance, the more recording room acoustics were picked up.

Today, mic recordings from before 1950 sound very dry, but neither recording nor playback equipment of the era could reproduce reverb well; with the jukebox, which was widely used in the 1930s, recorded reverb sounded metallic and washed out. This is one reason why jazz recordings from the swing era of the 1930s were deliberately recorded very dry.

Not until the hi-fi era, starting in the early 1950s, was the recording and playback equipment good enough to reproduce reverb. Engineer Bill Fine was among the first to record classical music with natural reverb in 1951. He put one mono mic just behind and slightly above the conductor to pick up the acoustics of the hall. The recordings were released by the Mercury label in 1951–1967 under the title *Living Presence*, and they helped equate hi-fi with reverb and echo in the record buyer's mind.

In 1958, stereo became widely accepted as a playback format, and so reverb became even more interesting as a tool with which to create width and dimension in recordings.

These acoustic echo chambers were built as a room with non-parallel walls whose surfaces were painted in shellac to make them more reflective. A loudspeaker played back the music, and one or more mics picked up the reverberation.

Increasingly numerous experiments in the 1950s reveal the growing interest in reverberation although specific acoustics had been a characteristic effect in some recordings from the previous decades; the ghostly sound of Robert Johnson's recordings from 1936 was produced by him singing and playing guitar sitting on a chair, facing a reflective corner. An example from the 1950s was when the guitarist Duane Eddy used a huge water tank from a junkyard. In the front end of the water tank he placed a speaker and, in the far end, a mic capturing the guitar with the water tank echo included.

The option of controlling the amount of reverberation added to the mix would play a major role in the sound of pop and rock music. Echo chambers were used in 1950s rock 'n' roll and almost to excess in the doo-wop vocal genre, while in the 1960s reverb became a fundamental element of Phil Spector's sound and the Motown sound.

In parallel with echo chamber experiments, tape echo was also developed (see p. 187), and echo chambers and tape echo were the only ways to add reverberation and dimension to studio recordings until electronic reverb devices became widespread in the late 1960s.

Electronic Reverb

The first electronic reverb was the spring reverb, which used two long metal springs. The vibrations of the springs were transformed into an electrical signal creating a shimmering, metallic reverberation. The spring reverb was developed by Bell Labs for the Hammond organ in 1939, because organists complained about the dry sound of the Hammonds. It has survived due to its practical size and low cost, and today the spring reverb is still used in the Hammond B3 organ and guitar amps like the Fender Twin Reverb.

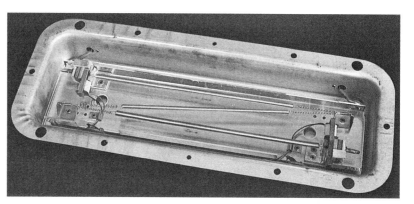

Figure 22.1

The spring reverb was used as a special effect on stage by the Doors and Emerson, Lake & Palmer in the late 1960s and early 1970s. Slapping the unit caused the springs to knock against each other, sounding like thunder and bombing.

EMT 140 Plate Reverb

In 1957, the German firm EMT made a technical breakthrough with the EMT 140 Reverberation Unit. It was the first plate reverb, and its uncompromising design was exactly what studios had been longing for: an electronic unit featuring a highly useful imitation of real-world reverberation.

The reverberation was created by the vibrations from a thin metal plate of 2 × 3 m suspended within a steel frame by springs at each corner. An electric transducer

Nachhallplatte
EMT 140

Figure 22.2
The EMT 140 and the EMT 250 both set a new standard in artificial reverberation. The 300 kg EMT 140, measuring slightly more than 3 × 3 m, was the most widely used electronic studio reverb until the 1970s. The EMTs are still highly sought after, easily fetching over $10,000 on the secondhand market. © EMT

controlled by the input signal (to which the reverb was to be added) made the metal plate vibrate, and a pickup forwarded the plate vibrations to the output. A damper device controlled by a servo motor allowed control of the reverb time up to 5 s. In 1961, the EMT 140 was given a stereo output when it was fitted with two built-in pickups.

EMT 250 Goes Digital

The first digital reverb to be produced was the EMT 250 Electronic Reverberator in 1976. It was smaller than the EMT 140, and, with its light-emitting diodes and big peg-shaped sliders, the EMT 250 looked like some futuristic gadget from science fiction movies of the time.

As an upgrade of the EMT 140, the 250 sported pre-delay and separate high and low frequency decay times controlled by the pegs. Furthermore, it was the first multi-effect processor with modulation effects such as chorus and phase in addition to echo and delay. In 1979, it was updated to the EMT 251, which featured an LCD display and a larger feature set.

The EMTs created a style standard in rock music and are still in demand; EMTs, therefore, are often modeled as plug-ins and are sampled for convolution reverbs.

From the early 1980s, digital audio completely changed the way music was recorded and mixed, and digital reverbs made it possible to emulate natural acoustics of any kind—or electronic reverbs like plate, spring, and tape echo—and unworldly spaces as well. Some of the most important reverbs and multi-effects were created by Lexicon. The Lexicon 224 (1978) and 480L (1986) were both class-leading in the top studios, the latter costing the same as an average family car. In 1999, the TC Electronic System 6000 set a new standard for studio reverbs, its complexity of parameters enabling the engineer to accurately imitate or create natural acoustics, electronic reverbs, delays, and any modulation effect.

23

Tape Echo and Digital Delay

Tape Echo

> ### Box 23.1 Slap Back Echo—The Sound of Rock 'n' Roll
>
> Slap back echo was the main ingredient of the Sun sound, which was developed by Sam Phillips in Memphis in the years 1954–1955. This was also the sound of rock 'n' roll, because slap back echo came to define the vocal sound of the genre. Phillips was responsible for introducing the rhythmic echoes pushing forward lead vocals on Elvis Presley's "That's All Right" (1954), Carl Perkins's "Blue Suede Shoes" (1956), and Jerry Lee Lewis's "Whole Lotta Shakin' Goin' On" (1957).
>
> Although, in 1950 guitarist Les Paul had already used tape recorders to create echo on his sound-on-sound recordings, Sam Phillips was the first to use this as the basis of a new sound. Moreover, he made the instruments quite powerful, making Elvis's vocal blend more with the instruments—quite unlike other contemporary pop songs that mixed the vocal level distinctly above the accompaniment. Instead, Phillips used the slap back echo to make the voice stand out and to provide fullness and a rhythmic drive.
>
> In 1955, RCA Records bought Elvis from Sam Phillips. However, they were unable to recreate "the Elvis echo" during the recording of "Heartbreak Hotel" because they used the large hall of the RCA Studios to add a long reverberation, completely unlike the short rhythmic effect of Sam Phillips's slap back echo.
>
> In 1954, Decca Records recorded Bill Haley's "Rock Around the Clock," and this is often viewed as the first rock 'n' roll hit. The sound of this song also seems quite bland, mainly due to the reverberation used, which made the loudly mixed vocal washy and ill-defined compared to the vibrant vocals of Sam Phillips's stars.

Tape echo was originally created using an additional tape machine that recorded and replayed a copy of a track. From the record head, the tape proceeded to the replay head (see figure 23.1), which then replayed the track with a short delay determined by the tape speed and by the distance between the two tape heads. Elvis's vocal on "Heartbreak Hotel" was delayed by 60 ms, corresponding to the delay between the tape heads of the Ampex stereo tape recorder running at 15 ips (inches per second).

Figure 23.1

The tape transport on the analog tape recorder. Feedback controls the number of repeats. The more play heads added, the more complex the repeat patterns.

Initially tape echo was used with commercial success in the form of slap back echo as part of the Sun sound (see box 23.1). Depending on the brand of the tape recorder and the tape speed, slap back echo adds a single distinct repeat delayed by 50–150 ms with almost the same volume level as the original signal. Eventually, variable tape speed was developed, and multiple playback heads were added, allowing multiple repeats. In addition, the replay signal could be sent back to the record head (called feedback) once or several times, creating echoes of the echo. Thus, slap back echo evolved into the more complex tape echo.

Echoplex was the first dedicated echo machine of the tape-based type (produced in 1959), while the Binson Echorec (1955) was the most advanced echo unit of its time. Its "tape" was a rotating magnetic drum, yielding better stability and durability than the tape-based units. The Binson was used by David Gilmour to create the floating guitar sound that defined the spacey textures of Pink Floyd from 1968 onwards.

Figure 23.2

The Roland RE-301 Space Echo from 1973 is still sought after and often emulated in plug-ins. The RE-301 has four playback heads, working much like digital multi-tap delays, in which several individual delay times, pans, and feedback can be adjusted. A tape of almost two meters was housed in a cassette on top of the unit, and this needed to be changed regularly as it wore out.
© Universal Audio

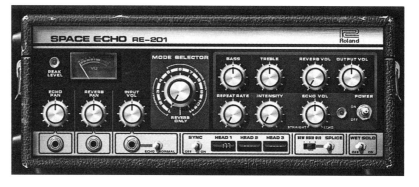

In the 1980s, the guitarist the Edge used delay as an integral part of the U2 sound—typically a 150–500 ms delay, with several repeats that were adapted to the song tempo and that gradually decreased in volume level. However, the Edge used the Korg SDD-3000 digital delay, which was a perfect solution for live performances because its adjustable delay times allowed the delay to rhythmically support the various song tempos. Moreover, the Korg SDD-3000 featured a second delay time, allowing rhythmically complex delays.

Digital Delay

By the end of the 1970s, digital gradually took over from analog tape delay, because it provided obvious benefits in sound quality, flexibility, and, in particular, reliability. Digital delay units comprised all types of echo and delay—chorus, flanging, and phasing included. Additionally, they were able to store presets and made stereo delay a relatively inexpensive option.

Digital delays are quite simple to construct—most units and plug-ins sound excellent—and this is also the reason why they appeared before digital reverbs.

TC Electronic's 2290 (1985) and Eventide's H3000 (1986) were the first dedicated digital studio units, making it possible to fine-tune more complex sets of parameters with the ability to save settings. The H3000 was a multi-effect unit, combining delay with pitch shifting, modulation, and filtering.

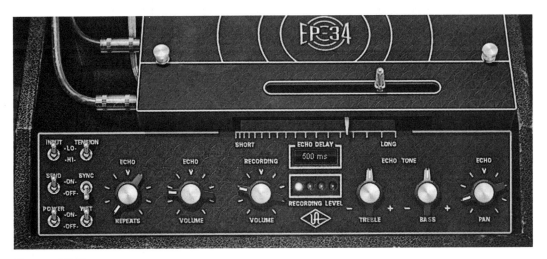

Figure 23.3
The sound of the classic analog tape echo units, such as the Echoplex and the Roland RE-201 Space Echo (an earlier model of the RE-301), is often emulated by plug-ins. The tape saturation, the tension of the analog tape (smoothed by the capstan controls), and the wow and flutter can all be adjusted to make up for some of the deficiencies of analog tape. Note the slider that on the Echoplex was used to manually move the replay head, thus determining delay time. © Universal Audio

Delay Types

With digital, it became possible not only to create delays of varying lengths but also, in principle, to recreate any tape delay with just a few parameters, since digital is not limited by the physical constraints of the analog tape recorder.

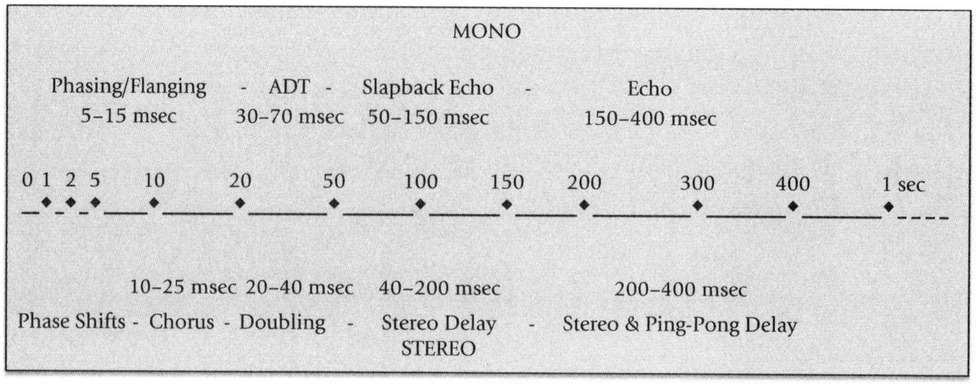

MONO									
Phasing/Flanging	- ADT -	Slapback Echo	-		Echo				
5–15 msec	30–70 msec	50–150 msec			150–400 msec				

0 1 2 5	10	20	50	100	150	200	300	400	1 sec

	10–25 msec	20–40 msec	40–200 msec		200–400 msec		
Phase Shifts -	Chorus -	Doubling -	Stereo Delay	-	Stereo & Ping-Pong Delay		
			STEREO				

Figure 23.4

Delay types displayed in milliseconds. At the top, the mono types; at the bottom, the stereo delays. The concepts of echo and delay are often confused. Echo refers to a delay that is heard as distinct repeats (that is, at 40–50 ms or longer), while the delay covers it all—that is, from indistinct repeats of a few ms to the distinct repeats of echoes.

In general, studio delays cover most delay types, and their software versions are often split into several plug-ins representing the various types:

- **Flanging** has a delay of 5–15 ms, to which frequency modulation is added.
- **Chorus** has a delay of 10–25 ms, to which frequency modulation is added.
- **ADT** (automatic double-tracking; see p. 9) has a delay of 30–70 ms.
- **Slap back echo** consists of one single repeat delayed by 50–150 ms. The longer delay types have been developed from the original tape-based slap back echo. At first, multiple repeats became possible, then digital enabled features like cross feed, modulation, and tempo sync. Stereo delay, ping-pong delay, and sample delay are among the most common types:
  - **Stereo delay** comprises separate controls for the L (left) and R (right) settings. If these two delays are set differently, for example, to 540 and 380 ms, the effect of width is also added to the signal. Feedback controls the number of repeats.
  - **Ping-pong delay** bounces the delayed signal between L and R. The ping-pong delay has two separate sets of controls that can be patched by cross feed to feed the L delay with the R delay and vice versa.
  - **Sample delay** delays the L and R sides separately with sample accuracy. Normally, it is used to add width to mono recordings by shifting the sound balance between L and R.

⊙ Audio examples 23.01b–23.01c demonstrate first flanging, then chorus, compared to the original dry signal (23.01a).

⊙ Audio example 23.02 demonstrates slap back echo.

⊙ Audio example 23.03 is a demonstration of stereo delay.

The Parameters of the Digital Delay

- **Delay time** is the time delay between the input and the output signal. Delay times of more than 40–50 ms are heard as separate echoes, while at shorter delay times the echoes are indistinguishable, eventually becoming phasing. When enhanced by modulation and high feedback settings, this is used, for example, by dance genres as a metallic "spiral effect."

- **Tap tempo** is used to adjust the delay time to the song tempo by tapping a button.
- **Tempo sync** automatically adapts the delay time to the song tempo if correctly set in the tempo box (bpm) of the DAW. The delay can be set as note durations on most plug-ins, the number of fourth notes (quarter notes or crotchets) equaling the number of beats per minute (bpm). A stereo delay set to a fourth note on the L side and an eighth note on the R side corresponds, respectively, to 500 and 250 ms delay at 120 bpm and creates a rhythmically shifted delay that fits perfectly to the song tempo. However, rich delay effects are not achieved by setting the delays to exact multiples of each other. With the tempo sync off, the delay can be freely adjusted so that the repeats occur a little after (or before) the song pulses. The combination of 500 and 320 ms at 120 bpm tempo will be fuller sounding, but take care that it does not disturb the timing of the song. Delays at dotted quarter, dotted half, and dotted eighth notes may be even fuller sounding, as this provides fascinating rhythmic subdivisions of delays between the beats.
- **Feedback** is a signal sent from the output back to the input of the delay device, creating echoes of the echo that gradually decrease in volume level. Feedback determines the number of repeats, set in percentage (0% equals no feedback, thus only the one repeat); the higher this setting, the longer the feedback loop. Feedback is used to create complex repeat patterns that are often used as an effect on guitar, vocals, or sax solos; in combination with reverb, this can provide great results.
- **Cross feed** sends the L output to the R input and R output to the L input. Immediately after the dry signal, the initial delayed signals are heard, and they are then followed by further delays, the number of which is determined by the cross feed setting.
- **Mix** or **wet/dry** sets the ratio between the dry and the delayed signal. With the effect on an aux channel, output mix should be set to wet (that is, 100%) while, in the mixer channel, wet/dry determines the ratio between the original signal and the added delay effect.
- **Filter** is usually a high-cut filter attenuating the top end or a low-cut filter attenuating the low end. The high-cut filter can be used to make the repeats less distinct, and the low-cut filter removes muddiness from the bass range. High-cut is also called high-damp in some plug-ins that emulate the vintage quality of analog tape echo, which not only attenuated the top end but also compressed and added harmonic distortion at high input levels (tape saturation), making the repeats less distinct. Thus, more effect can be added, which is the main reason that analog tape echo sounds fuller. The delay may also be modulated with an LFO, described further in the modulation section (p. 213).
- **Speed** or **rate** is the speed of the LFO that determines the frequency of the modulation.
- **Depth** is the degree of modulation.
- **Flutter rate** and **flutter intensity** mimic the fluctuations in speed that are inherent in analog tape transports.

191

Calculating Delay Time

Delay times above about 30 ms produce an audible rhythm, and therefore it is important that the repeats relate to the song tempo. This does not necessarily require that the repeats be within milliseconds of the song's pulse, as small deviations can help create width. However, the repeats should not act against the song's pulse.

A song tempo of 120 bpm will have one hundred and twenty fourth notes per minute (one minute is 60,000 ms). The formula for calculating time between beats is thus:

60,000 divided by the number of beats per minute

At 120 bpm, this results in:

- The fourth note lasting 500 ms (60,000 ms divided by 120 bpm = 500 ms).
- The sixteenth note lasting 125 ms.
- The dotted eighth note lasting 375 ms.

This way, the bpm setting can be used as the initial setting of the delay time.

Using Delays

The use of delay is highly genre-specific. As short delays are clear and aggressive sounding, they are often used in the hard rock genres, whereas reverb is preferred in mainstream pop productions, as it provides a softer feel and a blending of instruments. Short delays in particular—calibrated to the song tempo—provide both attack and dimension without the fluffy wrapping that can result from heavy use of reverb.

On rock vocals and guitars, short delays are often preferred to reverb, the delay adding drive and attack, whereas reverb tends to make an instrument distant sounding. This also applies to acoustic instruments, though they tend to require reverb as part of their sound and to soften the spaces between delays.

Longer delay times with high feedback settings, however, may create a mess in the harmonic structure of a song, since the repeats overlap with the next chord change. Long delays, though, do provide a rich floating feel, and this is as useful for sax solos and heavily distorted guitar solos as it is for ballad vocals.

Delays are almost never used in jazz (delay would confuse the delicate rhythmic feel of the genre) and never in classical music (which always relies on natural acoustics).

Automating the Delay

Often, the volume levels and the on/off function on a delay are automated. A distinct delay on the vocal may seem too much in the long run and automation can be used to vary its level in the mix, for example, between verse and chorus. Additionally, delays are often used to highlight a single word or a phrase ending, and automation is the simplest tool for achieving this.

Combining Delay and Reverb

Adding a touch of reverb to the delay almost always sounds great; a reverb filling between repeats becomes a more coherent reverberation. Most DAWs are able to route the output of an aux directly to another aux channel. Use this approach:

1. Route, for example, the vocal via the bus send to aux 1.
2. Insert a stereo delay with a fourth- and an eighth-note delay (adapted to the song tempo) at aux 1.
3. From aux 1, set up a bus send to aux 2. Initially set send to unity gain for a powerful signal.
4. Turn the aux 1 volume level completely down and set it to pre-fader; this results in the aux 1 signal still being routed via the send at unity gain level to aux 2, but it is no longer sent to the stereo mix bus.
5. Insert a reverb plug-in on aux 2.

Thus, the delay effect goes to the reverb, and the mixture of the two is forwarded to the mix bus. If the repeats seem too distinct, the frequencies above 8–10 kHz can be attenuated using a high-shelf filter on an EQ inserted after the reverb plug-in on aux 2.

Alternatively, if the combination should only be used on a single instrument or vocal, both plug-ins are inserted directly on the channel, the reverb after the delay. Set the wet/dry mix to your liking (although you will probably favor the delay).

Combining Delay and Pitch to Make Mono Wider

The combination of a pitch effect and a short delay adds width to a signal, much like chorus, but without the sweeps and diffuse effect. Use a short delay of 30–50 ms (feedback set to zero) with different L and R delay times. The processed (both dry and wet) signal is sent to a pitch device with a detune of up to +10 cents at the L and −10 cents at the R.

This combination provides width to harmony vocals, keyboards, guitars, and many other instruments—in smaller quantities, it sounds great on acoustic instruments. Moreover, this effect can be used to camouflage intonation issues on both vocals and instruments.

Box 23.2

See pp. 5–116 on how to use the delay effect on individual instruments.

TIPS

✓ Unlike reverb, a short delay of a single repeat or a few repeats does not make a track seem distant. On the contrary, it adds dimension, as it makes the sound stage wider, deeper, and higher.

✓ It is essential that the delay does not fight the song's pulse. The repeats should adapt to the rhythm of the song or fill out rhythmically between beats.

✓ The faster the song tempo, the shorter the delay time and the fewer repeats can be accommodated. At slow tempos, such as in pop ballads, long delay times work fine, and there is also space for more repeats. However, pay attention to overlapping delays that may make chord changes dissonant sounding.

✓ Recordings are usually made without effects. However, if an effect is an integral part of the guitar solo or the keyboard sound, it should be recorded, though preferably on a separate track in order to preserve the option of shifting the effect in the mix.

✓ Backwards echo was used creatively by guitarist Jimmy Page, who also mixed most of Led Zeppelin's songs. He flipped over the multitrack tape (that is, the left reel became the right, and vice versa) and recorded a tape echo triggered by the vocal or the guitar on an empty track. When he flipped the tape back, this created an effect of the echoes increasing in volume level, abruptly ending, and being followed by the tone or the word that triggered the tape echo. For this reason, backwards echo is also called preverb. This effect is found on the Led Zeppelin songs "You Shook Me" and "Whole Lotta Love."

✓ Likewise, backwards reverb was made by flipping the tape, recording reverberation, and then flipping the tape back again. With the DAW, this is accomplished by recording the reverb of an instrument on a separate track and then using the reverse function to reverse the ADSR envelope of the reverb.

✓ The 3/16 delay setting provides a distinct character to a song; in particular, it gives depth to a rhythm guitar playing fourth or eighth notes. The same applies to chord arpeggios but does not really work with bent notes.

24

Ambience and Reverb

Most instruments have evolved in interaction with various types of acoustics over hundreds of years. Gregorian chant and the organ have been tailored to the huge reverberation of the cathedral; the symphony orchestra interacts with the concert hall's acoustics; the lute and wind instruments come to life in small chambers; and the piano is adapted to the salon.

This interdependence with acoustics characterizes most acoustic instruments, and we have come to expect it as a part of the instrument's sound, not least when the instrument appears on recordings.

For this reason, while tracking an electric guitar can be done quite well with the guitar amp isolated in a small booth or behind screens and carpets, the acoustic guitar

Figure 24.1

An anechoic chamber is designed to completely absorb sound and is entirely isolated from external noises. The anechoic space is useful for measuring acoustic signals without reflections and exterior influences, thus simulating an open field without spatial characteristics.

Being in an anechoic space is disturbing to many, because echoes and reverberations aid in locating ourselves in space and making sense of the surrounding environment; in evolutionary terms, the ability to assess the spatial characteristics of, say, a predator's roar would aid in an assessment of the beast's proximity and location. © Shure

and the piano may sound dull and confined when not exposed to the ambience of a space.

This becomes even more evident with the drum kit, which requires a bigger room to breathe in. Since the drum kit and grand piano play a major role in popular music, most commercial studios are designed with the acoustic requirements of these instruments in mind. Overhead mics and room mics placed at a distance are crucial for reproducing the character of the drum kit and capturing a powerful drum sound, and the grand piano really comes into its own when captured in good acoustics.

Accordingly, the larger studios invest in building acoustically well-balanced rooms to accommodate acoustic instruments and entire bands—and a few world class studios like the Abbey Roads and Ocean Ways of this world have even larger recording spaces with variable acoustics to accommodate the symphony orchestra and other classical ensembles.

Nevertheless, the most widely used recording technique of rock and pop music is close-miking, almost eliminating the acoustics. The benefit of this approach, among others, is that in the mix spatial effects can be created independently of the recording room acoustics. Without reverberation, most instruments sound one-dimensional and confined and do not blend with each other. Artificial reverb, therefore, is used to re-create an acoustic space around them and to glue the instruments together in the mix. Fortunately, most electronic instruments and even vocals often sit better in the mix when processed with electronic reverberation like plate reverb.

The rock and electronic genres in particular have utilized the fact that instruments can be recorded on separate tracks without spatial information, making it possible in the mix to create new spaces and sound images that do not reference any real-world acoustics. With the development of electric and electronic instruments, it was no longer a requirement to place the music in natural acoustics, and this led to the experiments and creative use of the recording studio that have characterized the rock, pop, and fusion genres since the 1950s.

Box 24.1 The Acoustics Depict the Surroundings

In a natural acoustic space, we hear the direct sound source followed by the reflections off the boundary surfaces of the room. These reflections are caused by the direct sound hitting walls, ceilings, and objects in the room, and they are colored by the materials on these surfaces. Carpets and curtains attenuate the mids and the highs, resulting in a soft-sounding space. Hard surface materials, on the other hand, will reflect the mids and the highs, resulting in a brighter and harder sound.

The street also has reverberation, and even a forest has its own distinctive acoustics generated by the reflections from near and distant tree trunks and by treetops attenuating early reflections. In this way, all sound is colored, and a spatial location is disclosed by the acoustics; each of the multitude of reflections generates new reflections, adding complex colorations to the original sound, and from these patterns of reflections our brains decode information regarding the size and properties of the space.

Digital Reverbs in the Studio

Digital modeling of real-world acoustics is used to add acoustics to recordings. Only the major studies, like Teldex studios (Berlin [see figure 24.4]) and Abbey Road (London), have large recording spaces with natural reverberation. AIR Studios (London) even features a former church that is used to record symphony orchestras, musicals, acoustic instruments, and so forth.

Basically, two types of digital reverbs are used: the algorithm-based reverb, based on acoustic theories, and the convolution reverb, based on the recording of actual acoustics, which is used as a basis for the reverb parameters. Both reverb types are based on how the reverberation is created in natural surroundings. In this chapter the algorithm-based reverbs are addressed, and in the next convolution reverbs will be addressed.

The Parameters of the Digital Reverb

The digital reverb models various types of acoustics with algorithms; for example, the hall reverb, which has a number of editable parameters. The algorithms are based on theories of room acoustics, with parameters representing the physics that create the reverberation in the space. The more advanced digital reverbs are capable of simulating most of the dimensions, forms, materials, and other aspects of the space. In addition, they can create effects, such as reverse and gated reverbs, that are found neither in nature nor in man-made spaces.

The basic parameters that are editable in most units and plug-ins are the pre-delay, early reflections (ER), decay (or reverb time), and mix.

Pre-delay

Pre-delay represents the time between the direct signal and the start of the reverberation. In natural surroundings, the pre-delay is generated if, for example, spoken words travel from one side of a room, which is dampened, toward the opposite side, which is reflective. In concert halls, the direct sound is what arrives first at the listener's ears, followed shortly afterward by the reverberation; this time the gap is known as the pre-delay, and it provides a sense of the size of the room.

Pre-delay makes the reverb come forward in the mix, because the pre-delay separates the original signal from the reverberation by a number of milliseconds. Between 10 and 15 ms is a good starting point for vocals and most instruments, because this corresponds to reflective surfaces that are approximately 3.3–5 m from the sound source.

Increasing the pre-delay means the dynamics of the source signal are preserved. A snare drum with a large amount of reverb will sound a little distant without pre-delay, but, set to 20–30 ms, its dynamics are preserved, while a distinct reverb tail is added that is suitable, for example, for a slow ballad.

If a vocal track *must* have a lot of reverb, adding pre-delay will improve the intelligibility of the lyrics.

The longer sound travels through the air, the more its high frequency content is attenuated. This effect of real-world acoustics results in the pre-delay being enhanced, the direct signal being stronger while the reverberation is dampened. With reverb, by

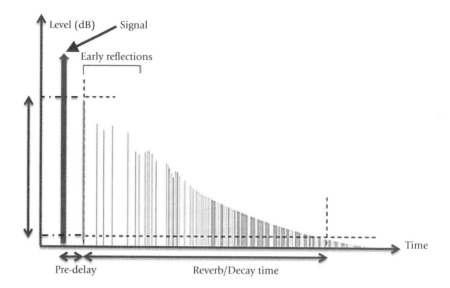

Figure 24.2

The main parameters of reverberation. The signal (*far left*) sent into the reverb is followed by the pre-delay, the early reflections, and finally the decay. The long, smooth reverb tail displayed here is characteristic of the hall algorithm.

dampening the high end using either a low-pass or a high-shelf filter, the pre-delay is given more attention, and, at the same time, more depth is added to the mix. In the last stages of the mix, the pre-delay should often be fine-tuned to highlight the reverberation that might have been drowned out during mixing.

Early Reflections

Early reflections (ER) are the initial reflections from the surfaces closest to the sound source. They precede the actual reverberation, providing an (unconscious) image of the location of the sound source relative to the nearest surfaces. The volume of the ERs provides a sense of the qualities of the materials of these surfaces as well—that is, the materials' abilities to absorb and reflect sound waves. Strong ERs correspond to hard, reflective materials on the closest surfaces, and the arrival time at the listener is dependent on the distance of the sound source from these surfaces.

ERs are measured in milliseconds. In large quantities, they sound tinny and hard because they create an echo-like space within the reverberation.

ERs are part of a realistic recreation of a space and are therefore important in acoustic music genres but are rarely used in electronic music such as trance or dance.

Decay Time/Reverb Time

This temporal parameter reflects the size of the room and the ability of the surfaces to reflect or attenuate sound. The decay time is the time taken for the reverberation to decrease 60 dB (that is, for all practical purposes, to a non-audible level).

In sophisticated reverb units, the decay time is split into several frequency ranges, because the walls, ceilings, and furniture will reflect low and high frequencies differently depending on their materials, and this results in decay times with different timbres and lengths. In less complex units, this can only be adjusted somewhat with EQ.

The direct signal, together with the early reflections, provides an impression of the acoustic space and the location of the sound source, while pre-delay and decay time provide an impression of the size and the materials of the space. Our brains decode the character of the space quite precisely by assessing the interactions of the ERs and decay time; a long ER period before the main reverberation typically provides the impression of a greater space, and if a long decay time is also added, this creates the impression not only of a large room but of one with walls that are highly reflective because the reverberation is built up of dense, numerous, and modulated repeats such as you would hear in a cave or in underground parking.

If the decay time is reduced, the walls will seem more absorbent because the reverberation fades out faster. In contrast, a combination of a long decay time and a short ER period creates the impression of bathroom acoustics because the sound is reflected quickly but fades out slowly due to the highly reflective tiled walls. Bathrooms were used as echo chambers (p. 183) in the rock 'n' roll era of the 1950s—the legendary producer Joe Meek was renowned for his use of the bathroom as an echo chamber, often recording singers there.

Mix

Mix determines the mixture of wet (the effect) and dry (direct sound source signal).

If a plug-in is inserted on a single channel, mix determines the quantity of reverb added as a percentage. If the plug-in is inserted on an aux track, it is important that it is set to 100% wet, or else it will double the direct signal and will increase the volume level of the sound source and possibly also create phase issues.

Less Common Parameters of the Digital Reverb

The above are the basic parameters of the algorithm reverb. In the following is an additional list of some other common parameters, though there can be some variation in the names given to them.

Diffusion

Diffusion controls the density of the reverberation and its spread in the stereo image by adding a degree of randomness to the distribution of the reflections in time and space.

Diffusion can help provide mono recordings with more width, and it also smooths out strong transients, making them sound less metallic. Use a high diffusion on percussion and less on vocals and horns.

Density

Density controls the density of the early reflections. Increasing density is similar to modeling the closest reflective surfaces as having irregular shapes and spacing between them.

Room Size

Room size determines the size of the space that creates the reverberation. In the perceived size of the space, room size interacts with ERs and decay time.

199

Modulation

Modulation is used to create fluctuations in the reverberation, primarily in the reverb tail.

Dampening

Dampening boosts or dampens the lows, midrange, or highs. This is a form of dynamic filtering—that is, a gradually increasing absorption as the reflections of the reflections decrease in volume level. The alternative to this is EQing, though EQ only attenuates the selected frequency range, whereas dampening mimics the gradual attenuation of the upper frequencies of room reflections, thereby relatively enhancing the lower frequencies.

Dampening of the high end simulates absorbing materials in a room, like carpets and curtains; rooms furnished like this sound warmer, providing a softer and less metallic reverberation.

Without low-frequency dampening, a simulated room seems bigger with massive surfaces, as in, for example, a parking garage that has a distinctive rumble in its reverberation. Dampening the range below 200 Hz reduces rumbling and provides an impression of a smaller space with hard and reflective surfaces that particularly reflect the midrange and high range.

Figure 24.3

The more parameters included in a reverb algorithm, the better and more nuanced it will sound if properly used. Hardware studio reverbs like the TC Electronic System 6000 and Lexicon 960 are among the most complex. The Lexicon 960 is renowned for its non-naturalistic reverbs like Random Hall, which has an uneven and almost echo-like decay that is great for solo instruments. The System 6000 is renowned for its highly realistic concert hall emulations.
© TC Electronic
© Lexicon/Harman

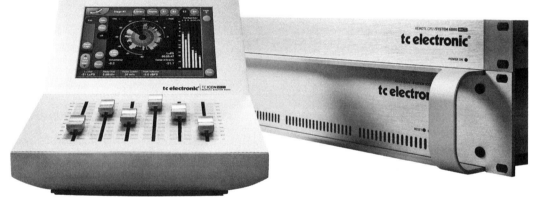

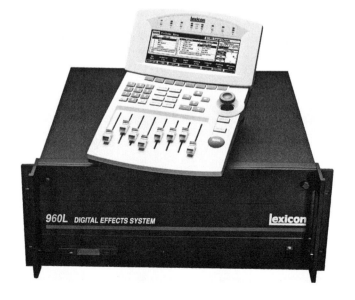

EQ is almost always found in reverb units in the form of at least low-pass and high-pass filters. Attenuation of the low end is often used to avoid muddiness, and cutting the highs reduces thin and metallic-sounding reverberation. Dampening of the frequency range between 4 and 9 kHz should be used if the reverb enhances the sibilants on a vocal track.

If EQ is not part of the reverb, this can be accomplished by inserting an EQ on the channel.

Always place it after the reverb to prevent any (bass or treble) frequency boost overloading the reverb.

Insert or Send

Basically, the reverb should always be inserted on an aux channel that is fed from the individual tracks via the bus send. In this way, many tracks can share the same reverb, and you can EQ and compress on the individual tracks without worrying about the order of the inserts. This also saves processing power. Although the signal being transmitted via the bus is mono, the return (from the reverb) is usually stereo; therefore, the aux should always be a stereo channel. However, it sometimes makes sense to insert the reverb on the track itself, if you want to highlight the spatial location of an instrument that is panned. A mono reverb on a panned channel will highlight the directionality of the sound. Always place the reverb after the compressors but before the EQ.

Reverb Types

The algorithm-based reverbs mimic the behavior of reflections in real-world acoustics, as the algorithm is based on a generalized characteristic acoustic like a church or a living room.

Presets are stored sets of parameters of an algorithm that are suitable for a particular instrument or that simulate a particular space. Generally, this is reflected in their names, and sometimes they are even based on the analysis of a specific space.

Most digital effect units and plug-ins contain algorithms for the following real-world acoustics:

- Room.
- Chamber.
- (Concert) hall.
- Ambience.

Some of the following artificial acoustics are provided too:

- Plate reverbs.
- Nonlinear reverbs (gated and reversed reverbs).
- Special effects.

Room

The room algorithm mimics short and dense acoustics from our everyday life: smaller spaces like living rooms and offices that have a mixture of absorptive and reflective materials. Early reflections already occur 5–10 ms after the direct sound, since the distance to the nearest wall is short. Thus, this algorithm builds up fast, and its dense ERs characterize the reverberation. If the algorithm is set to long reverb times, it will sound very different from the hall algorithm, which has a quite different pattern of ERs.

The room algorithm is well suited for drums, horns, electric guitar, and percussion—in general it is used to glue together different instruments without being a distinct-sounding reverberation.

Chamber

The chamber algorithm is named after the medium-sized halls used for chamber music, often found in mansions and townhouses from the 1700s and 1800s. As a medium-sized room with irregular surfaces, the chamber provided the ideal sound for string quartets and chamber ensembles. Because the ERs are dense, emerging from various distances and angles, and the decay is randomized with a tail that fades fast and in a nonlinear fashion, the chamber algorithm adds a lot of color.

These medium-length reverbs (0.7–1.5 s) are suitable for vocals and most acoustic instruments and are also used on electric instruments.

Hall

Hall algorithms are the long reverbs mimicking the acoustics of the concert hall or auditorium; that is, from 1.2 s reverb time for the concert hall to 3–6 s for the sports hall. Concert hall and church presets are built on this algorithm. ERs are scarce, as it is at least 10 m to the nearest wall, and therefore the reverberation builds up gradually, the low frequencies having longer reverberation times than the high frequencies. The algorithm is characterized by a smooth decay, its long tail dying out slowly as the reflections of the reflections become weaker.

Figure 24.4
The Teldex Studio (Berlin) is among the most imitated acoustics in digital reverb units due to its ceiling height and balanced acoustics. Teldex still uses an echo chamber equipped with Neumann 184 mics and K&H speakers. © Orchestral Tools

The hall algorithm is suitable for acoustic instruments and is also used for keyboards, vocals, and a huge snare drum sound. However, if used on the drums, it requires a slow tempo (the plate algorithm works better at faster tempos).

Outside of the algorithm's "native" parameters, plenty of other settings may be useful. If it suits the mix, even the room algorithm can be used with a long decay time and the hall algorithm with a short decay time.

Ambience

The ambience algorithm mimics a variety of indoor and outdoor acoustics. It adds spatiality mainly through the early reflections and rarely has much real reverberation. It is primarily used for real-world atmospheres in movies—ranging from the interior of a Mercedes E220 SX through to stairways and sidewalks to various office interiors.

Plate

The plate algorithm imitates the electronic reverberation device invented in 1957 by EMT. Plate has very dense ERs and a bright and short decay time that provides clarity and definition to drums, percussion, electric guitar, and vocals.

The diffusion setting is used to make the reverberation more or less dense. The higher the diffusion, the denser the reverberation, whereas low diffusion settings can result in echo effects in the reverb tail which rarely match the song pulse. Read more in chapter 22 "History of Reverb."

The nonlinear (often named NONLIN) gate and reverse algorithms have a different pattern from the natural reverberations.

Gated Reverb

The gated reverb algorithm is a dense reverb with a sudden decay, as the reverb tail is cut off abruptly using a gate in which the threshold is set quite high. Widely used by Bruce Springsteen, Michael Jackson, Prince, Phil Collins (see box 21.5), and others on the snare drum, synth brass, and vocals, the gated reverb algorithm became a defining characteristic of the 1980s sound in pop and rock.

Reversed Reverb

The reversed reverb algorithm is a backwards reverb resulting in an increase in volume level of the reverberation and ending abruptly. Inspired by 1960s backwards tape effects, it is used as an effect on drums, guitar fills, and the like. The pre-delay of both gated and reversed reverb algorithms is set to zero in order to merge the sound source with its reverberation.

Special Effects (FX)

The special effects algorithms, often called FX, combine the above algorithms with modulation, feedback, panning, and so forth to create artificial spaces and they often have imaginative names like Huge Tunnel, Sci-fi, Plate Tectonics, or Visit from the Gods.

▶ Audio examples 24.01b and 24.01c demonstrate the use of plate reverb and hall reverb compared to the original dry recording (24.01a).

How to Use Reverb

The use of reverb might be the crucial spice that saves the mix and transforms a flat, unblended recording into a vibrant and interesting whole. On the contrary, if overdone, it can be what makes a mix sound washed out and undefined. The use of reverb is largely determined by the music genre as well as personal taste. However, there are some rules of thumb that apply if you want your mix to sound professional.

A good start is to determine which type of acoustics best suits the recording. Would the song benefit from an intimate club atmosphere (room algorithm), an arena setting (hall algorithm), or the sound of a distant galaxy (a combination of hall algorithm, delay, and modulation)? By considering the imaginary space of the song, it becomes easier to choose the most suitable reverb algorithm as a starting point. Next, the selected algorithm is fine-tuned by using the parameters described above to match the position of the sound source, the room size, the materials, and so to the recording. If the music genre does not require a clearly defined sound (as many acoustic genres or blues do), then there are no set rules for the use of reverb—only the technical parameters impose restrictions on the possible acoustics. However, the reverb time should always be adjusted to the song tempo so as not to mess up the next beat or chord change.

Below are some general recommendations for the use of reverb on some instruments. These can be used as a starting point.

Instrument	Algorithm type	Decay/Reverb time	Pre-delay
Vocal	Plate, short hall, ambience	0.6–3 s	10–20 ms
Drums	Plate, short hall	1.0–2.5 s	10–60 ms
Electric guitar	Room, plate, short hall	0.6–3 s	10–20 ms
Piano	Concert hall, plate	2–4 s	5–50 ms
Acoustic guitar	Plate, hall	1–3 s	10–20 ms
Strings	Room, hall	1–2.5 s	20–80 ms

Specific recommendations for the use of reverb can be found in "Mix Settings and Effects" under each individual instrument (Part I of this book). In addition, p. 237 deals with how to handle breadth and depth in the mix.

Box 24.2 "Kiss"—A Song without Bass and Reverb

You do not always need to fill up the arrangement with dense instrumentation and a fully featured acoustic space; many successful songs have used a minimalistic and "dry" aesthetic.

Prince's "Kiss" (1986) started as a folk-like song recorded on cassette tape by Prince with only vocal and acoustic guitar. He composed this song for Maserati, a group he had signed to his Paisley Park Label.

During the night, before Prince got involved in producing, the group and engineer David Z had recorded the song based on a groove on the Linn 9000 drum machine. The next morning, when David Z and Maserati appeared in the studio, Prince had taken back the song and finished his own recording. As usual, he had recorded his own vocal from within the control room using headphones and a Sennheiser 441 dynamic mic. He had also replaced the guitar with his own.

Then they started to minimize the recording. The bass was replaced by the Linn 9000 kick drum processed through the reverse reverb of an AMS 16 unit set to 150 ms; this occupies the bottom end, so that you hardly notice that the bass line is missing.

Similarly, "When Doves Cry" also has no bass, and this is in line with a practice that includes the Rolling Stones' "Honky Tonk Women" (1969) and AC/DC's "You Shook Me All Night Long" (1980), both of which have no bass in the verses.

Furthermore, the hi-hat was discarded in "Kiss", leaving only nine tracks in the recording, and the mix was equally simple and quite dry. Apart from the reverse reverb and a little tape delay on the guitar, there was no reverb used, not even on the vocal.

"Kiss" helped to start the dry sound of the 1990s.

TIPS

✓ Not every instrument in the mix needs to have reverb added. Reverb has a spill effect, particularly between instruments sharing the same frequency range.

✓ The more reverb added to an instrument, the further away it will seem. This can be utilized to push some elements (e.g., choral parts, a guitar, or a synth) to the background of the mix, thereby releasing space for other instruments in the foreground. This also generates depth in the mix.

✓ An "in-your-face" vocal or other instrument that should also blend in the mix is created by using a short reverb time. Start with the room algorithm and experiment with pre-delay settings. For this purpose, it is often better to use a short delay having one single repeat. The solution might also be to only use ambience. If the vocal seems too dry and confined, an ambience algorithm might provide both width and depth while at the same time preserving definition.

✓ Find the appropriate reverb time by adjusting its length to the song's tempo. Normally, reverb should die out before the next beat. Reverb hanging on too long clouds the mix, while reverb stopping too early does not quite glue the elements of the mix together. A tambourine playing eighth notes (quavers), therefore, should have a short reverb (and very little of it), but, if it is playing on the 2 and 4 beats, a powerful and long reverb can be used.

✓ Reverb should be considered a rhythmic element—or, more correctly, an element that interferes with the rhythm, affecting the musical phrasings and the groove—so be careful.

✓ Basically, there is nothing wrong with using different reverb types in a single mix—used with taste, this may make the music more interesting. Only if the instruments are perceived as being in different "worlds" can it become a problem.

✓ Pitch shift added to the reverb might provide the snare with body and/or clarity.

✓ The reverb tends to react strongly to strong treble content. In order to avoid sibilant explosions, insert a de-esser (see p. 14) before the reverb plug-in on the aux channel (in this way, only the send signal is de-essed).

✓ By adding a tiny bit of a long hall algorithm to one single instrument (e.g., the acoustic guitar), it is often possible to create extra depth without interfering with the song pulse and without adding muddiness.

✓ In the mix, reverb should enhance the timbre of an instrument. A dark reverb on a dark-sounding instrument makes it undefined and muddy, and a bright reverb added to a trebly instrument will make it thin and without body.

✓ Even minor overloads of the reverb input can produce distortion, and this also causes the width and depth to collapse.

25

Convolution Reverb

Convolution reverb (CR) is the digital version of the good old echo chamber that, in the early days of the sound studio, was the only way to add reverberation after the recording had taken place. In the major studies this was a large (usually basement) room with shellac-treated walls. Here, the recording was played back through a loudspeaker, and by moving the microphone relative to the loudspeaker, reverberations of different lengths could be added. CR, though, allows not just one but countless real acoustics that are available to paint onto the tracks from a CR plug-in.

Generally, convolution reverb is more authentic than the algorithm-driven reverbs, which, in turn, are more flexible, since they have more parameters to adjust. CR is based on the sampling of acoustic spaces, and this can be seen as a snapshot of the reverberation of a specific space into which a recording can then be placed. If it is a concert hall, the tracks become colored by its special acoustics; in fact, the CR can be any sound, and the tracks will assume its character—just like when adding any other effects to a recording.

The samples of such acoustic spaces are called impulse responses (IRs). Since an IR is a sample of a distinctive sound, anything can be used as an impulse response, not just recordings of renowned concert halls and cool studio acoustics; it might also be the sound of a particular guitar amplifier, an exotic mic or preamp, traffic noises, or birds singing. A synthetic acoustic guitar (a software instrument) can thus be made more acoustic-like by adding to it the IR of a real acoustic guitar.

The benefit of CR is that it borrows real world acoustics, allowing you to add reverberation from the best or the most exotic spaces on the planet to your recording as long as the IR is available for use. There are limitations, though, as the IRs, to some extent, are limited to the original IR sample, which means that there are fewer parameters available for editing. For example, the reverb time can be no longer than the length of the reverberation time of the space sampled, though it can be made shorter. However, with the increasing capacity and speed of computers, more of the properties of the acoustics can be sampled, adding more editable parameters and thereby making convolution reverbs yet more flexible.

Likewise, although the time taken for the computer's CPU to calculate various parameter changes is decreasing, the higher latency of the CR plugin remains an issue (compared to an algorithm reverb plugin or a hardware device). Latency, however, is today typically below 5 ms, and so it can be considered pre-delay that itself can be

Figure 25.1

Convolution reverb eats up a fair bit of CPU power. Altiverb was the first commercially available CR (2002), but its acceptance by the studios was a long time coming, because it was not until 2005 that computers were fast enough to render an IR. Logic's Space Designer arrived in 2003, along with the Waves IR-1, and, subsequently, CRs began to emerge as integrated plug-ins in DAWs (e.g., MOTU's Ethno Instrument and Studio One's Open Air). © Altiverb © Logic Pro

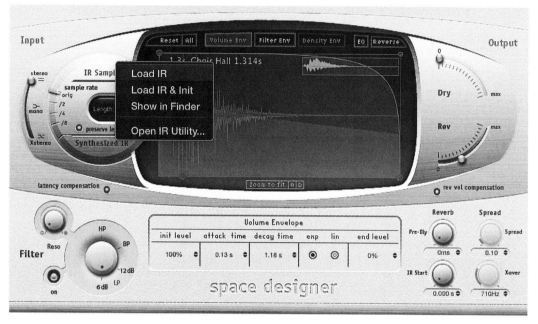

reduced in the settings of the convolution reverb, or the processed track can be bounced, CR included, to a DAW audio track and moved forward in time accordingly.

Impulse Response (IR)

An impulse response of the reverberation from a church or bathroom is produced by activating the acoustics with an impulse that ideally should cover the entire audible frequency spectrum. For this, a shot from a starter pistol, a burst of full-range sine-sweep frequencies, or a balloon popping is used. After recording the resulting reverberant sound, the trigger sound is removed. The residual signal is then a sample of the acoustics, called an impulse response because it is the room's response to the impulse. Since reverberation covers a wide dynamic range, 24-bit recording is needed, and most IR libraries are sampled at 96 kHz or 192 kHz.

Even though CR plug-ins have their own file format, most also import standard formats like WAV and AIFF files, which are the formats that IRs of concert acoustics and exotic spaces are recorded with.

Figure 25.2
Altiverb provides the acoustics of Wembley Stadium, the interior of a Ford Transit, Notre Dame Cathedral, the Sydney Opera House, cave acoustics from Malta, and so on. Its recording of the renowned acoustics of the Concertgebouw in Amsterdam (*left*) takes up 20.6 mb, and the IRs from the concert hall at Sydney Opera House (*right*) 21.3 mb. These IRs were captured by six DPA 4006 omni mics and sine sweeps played through a Genelec 1037 speaker. © Altiverb

IR Libraries

A convolution reverb is no better than its IR library. IRs recorded with quality equipment by engineers who understand acoustics can sound heavenly—almost like being in the space they were recorded in. They sound purer and lack the metallic harmonics and grittiness that are often a part of the reverb tail of algorithm reverbs. The reason why IRs taken from real acoustic spaces sound quite different from algorithm-based reverbs is due to the early reflections (which are crucial to real-world acoustics) being more complex than what an algorithm reverb can create. A vocal track with the IR of a cave or a volcanic crater added really sounds like this was the place where the singer was baring her soul.

However, this will not make algorithm reverbs obsolete. They are designed to make instruments and vocals blend and at the same time stand out well in a mix. Besides, the music we listen to has made us accustomed to algorithm reverbs, so, like the electronic EMT plate, they still sound real to us. Therefore, the IRs of Lexicon, TC Electronics, and other algorithm reverbs themselves represent a large part of the IR libraries.

The Vienna Multi Impulse Response (MIR) provides a great example of the potential of convolution. For each space in the Vienna MIR, numerous IRs—up to five thousand—are recorded in part by triggering impulses at different positions on stage (to serve as the virtual stage) and recording the impulses from different places in space (the virtual listening position).

Since the objective of the Vienna MIR is authentic acoustics, instruments are often used as the impulses, sounding at different pitches and volumes, and for this reason the Vienna MIR sounds great on acoustic instruments.

Owing to the numerous IR recordings, the Vienna MIR has some additional parameters, including variable listening and sound source position. These parameters are controlled by vectors that allow certain movements of the instruments (corresponding to

Figure 25.3

A Vienna IR displaying the positions of instruments and mics for a symphony orchestra. The ovals represent parameters that are variable by the use of vectors.

the IR recordings). In this way, stereo width and depth, the position of the sound source, and the listening position can be varied. Compared to the algorithm reverb, this makes the pre-delay and the room size a lot more flexible.

Special FX

When leaving real-world acoustics and using any sound as an IR, convolution opens up a whole new universe of spaces and sounds. Just as an IR will transfer an acoustic space to an instrument, any sound may be transferred to an instrument or a mix. The sound of traffic noise, for example, can be added to a drum track—or vice versa; as the IR is actually an audio file, any recording of an instrument, the flushing of a toilet, or some other everyday noise can be used. A drum loop sounds quite otherworldly as an effect added to a vocal or an acoustic guitar.

Resonances from the soundboard of an acoustic guitar or a piano can be transferred to entirely different instruments, and although this does not convert an electric guitar into an acoustic guitar, some of the acoustic guitar's tonal character will be added. Similarly, the IR of a toilet being flushed may be the missing ingredient that makes a lo-fi drum groove fit into the mix.

In this way, CR opens up a whole new tonal universe. The IR approach is already widely used in sound design in games and movie soundtracks, and on location where film images are recorded, sound engineers record additional IRs and later mix these realistic spaces with more unrealistic spaces. Birds twittering and nature sounds, for example, can be added to an IR traffic effect to provide the anticipation that later in the film a park will be bisected by a highway.

How to Create an IR

Recording authentic acoustic spaces requires quality preamps and mics, and, when using sine sweeps to excite the space, good amps and loudspeakers too. Omni mics are best when capturing ambience, but all mic characteristics will work if they are used in accordance with the principles of stereo recording (see p. 141). If the IR recordings must capture concert hall acoustics, the mics are placed in the sweet spot among the audience's seats, the impulse being fired from the stage position. Following the same principle, "the virtual stage" and "the virtual listening position," the obvious impulse and record positions for other types of IR recordings, are also decided upon.

The ideal impulse is very short and contains all the frequencies across the audible range, the response thus being distributed evenly across the entire frequency spectrum. In practice, short impulses result in poor signal-to-noise ratio (the level of the background noise becoming too high). Following the impulse, most professional sweeps range from 6–15 s, and Altiverb provides both sweeps and instructions for their use on the company website.

IR recordings can also be recorded using applications like Logic's IR Utility and Voxengo's Deconvolver, which also generate the sweep signals. These applications can additionally be used to create IRs of external effect devices without the need for speakers or mics. Compiling a library of classic hardware reverbs and effect units—including units most could never afford to own—thus becomes possible with IR techniques and convolution processing.

TIPS

✓ Use the best available equipment, in particular good mics, mic stands, and audio interfaces. Handheld recording devices like the Zoom also provide reasonable results.

✓ If sweeps are used, use calibrated loudspeakers and a good amp.

✓ Record at as high a resolution as the equipment allows, preferably at 96 kHz / 24 bit or better.

✓ At the location, find the sweets spot(s) by clapping your hands, and place the microphone(s) in this position. Stereo recording is normally required.

✓ The recording location should be quiet and peaceful. Be aware of fans, traffic, and so on. Do not move or make any noise while recording and for at least 10 s afterward.

✓ Remove objects in the space that may obstruct the dissemination of sound waves (your own body included).

✓ Trim the impulse responses in your DAW (or Audacity, Sound Forge, etc.), removing the original impulse and then saving to the required file format. A deconvolver application, like Logic Response Utility and Voxengo's Deconvolver, removes the sine sweep from the response and leaves just the room's reverberation.

26

Modulation Effects

The most commonly used modulation effects are flanging, chorus, and phasing. Beyond these, there are some variations in modulation parameters and countless combination effects, such as ensemble and modulation delay.

Chorus and flanging are created by a modulated delay that is mixed with the original signal. In modern chorus and flanging devices, the modulation is generated by varying the processed signal in time with a low frequency oscillator (LFO), creating a series of frequency phase-outs slowly sweeping through the frequency range from the low-mids to the high-mids. Most of the coloring thus consists of a series of peaks and dips in the frequency response (the comb filter effect; see p. 272), while at the same time there is a continually altering volume level and frequency content that is particularly evident in stereo.

The phaser only applies the phase shifts that are generated by an LFO. Since no time delay is used, phasing has fewer frequency phase-outs.

The effect of the Leslie speaker is also a modulation effect generated mechanically by the rotating speaker, which creates the Doppler effect (see p. 102), the depth of the effect being determined by the rotation speed.

Finally, tremolo and vibrato are also modulation effects, tremolo being modulated in amplitude (volume level) by the LFO speed and vibrato being modulated in pitch. These are the simplest modulation effects, and they are particularly used as guitar effects and occasionally on the synthesizer.

Flanging

Flanging is generated by mixing the original signal with one or more delayed and pitch-modulated copies of the signal. The time delay is in the range of 3–15 ms, the modulation being distributed evenly across the entire frequency range.

Box 26.1 Tape Flanging

"Itchycoo Park," the hit single by the Small Faces from 1967, was one of the first recordings to use flanging. The song was recorded at EMI Studios (now Abbey Road Studios) by engineer Ken Townsend, and the effect was applied to the entire mix in the bridge section after each chorus to create a psychedelic painting of the effect of mind–altering drugs. Along with spacey reverbs and echoes, flanging was an essential effect in psychedelic rock; for example, it was used on the Beatles' "Lucy in the Sky with Diamonds" (1967) and by Jimi Hendrix on several tracks of the album *Axis: Bold as Love* (1967). Flanging re-appeared in 1992 as an iconic effect on Nirvana's "Come As You Are."

Flanging required that the same signal was recorded onto two tape recorders (see figure 26.1). When replaying these two signals to a third tape recorder, the engineer slowed down one of the recorders by placing a finger lightly on one tape flange (the edge of the reel, hence the name flanging) or, alternately both flanges, causing the two machines to get out of sync. By trial and error (and listening), the early engineers hit upon a delay of 5–15 ms, creating the flanging effect when mixed together on a third tape recorder.

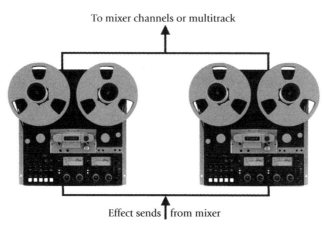

To mixer channels or multitrack

Effect sends from mixer

Figure 26.1

The equipment needed for flanging was expensive even for the professional studio. In 1970, the Revox A77 two-track cost about $1,000, equivalent to about $6,400 in 2017. Not until the late 1970s was an electronic circuit imitating flanging and chorus developed.

The number of parameters differs from device to device, as do their names, but here are the most frequently used:

- **Delay** determines the delay time of the modulated signal and thus the extent of the peaks and dips across the frequency range (the depth of the comb filtering effect).
- **Speed** refers to the speed of the LFO. Usually it is set to slow, since the faster settings produce too much of a trembling effect.
- **Feedback** loops the signal back into the processor for additional processing.
- **Depth** (or **intensity**) controls the level of flanging—that is, the mixture of the original and the processed signal. Also called **dry/wet.**
- **Width**, on some devices, controls the stereo width.

Chorus

Like flanging, chorus is created by mixing the original signal with one or more delayed and pitch-modulated copies of itself. Apart from the delay here being 10–25 ms, chorus operates like flanging, and the parameters are the same, though normally with no feedback (which is why chorus is a subtler effect than flanging). In the stereo chorus, delay and modulation settings in the L (left) and R (right) channels differ, thereby creating extra width in the processed signal.

Chorus is mainly used on electric guitars and keyboards, almost sounding like voice doubling, since it spreads the mono signal to stereo. Acoustic pianos, twelve-string guitars, and mandolins naturally produce a slight chorus effect, as they have two (or more) of the same string; even small deviations in pitch of the doubled strings may create this effect.

Figure 26.2
When introduced in 1979, the Roland Dimension D became popular in the studios for its chorus and flanging effects. Today, it is modeled in a number of plug-ins. © Universal Audio

In the same way, a chorus effect is created when an instrument, like an acoustic guitar, is doubled during recording because of the small deviations (most falling within the 10–25 ms range of chorus). In general, when instruments with almost the same tone and pitch are mixed, as in a choir or string ensemble, and there are several musicians playing the same part (first and second violin, soprano, tenor, etc.), a slight chorus effect will be produced. This can be used to add body and a large width to a recording.

Phase Shift

Phase shift creates its effect by shifting the phase but without delaying the signal. The shifts are distributed over the entire frequency range, though not evenly; this is probably one of the reasons why chorus and flanging are more commonly used.

In the 1970s, before digital delay became available, if the engineer did not have access to three tape machines, the analog phaser was the only way of getting a modulated effect, but in a limited fashion. The prestigious Maestro PS1A Phase Shifter (1971) allowed little control over the effect even with its three speed switches. This changed with the Roland Jazz Chorus amps in 1978, and soon chorus found its way onto countless 1980s recordings as an effect on guitars and most keyboards.

Shortly afterward, the Roland Boss pedals became widespread both on stage and in the studio (such as the BOSS CE-1 Chorus, which is available today in the form of plug-ins).

The Haas Effect and Doubling

Although there is a gradual transition between the phase and delay effects, the Haas effect objectively defines when the shift from phasing to audible delay takes place. The Haas effect—describing a psychoacoustic phenomenon—states that a sound delayed less than approximately 30 ms is not perceived by our hearing as a separate event when heard along with the original sound. But when the sound is delayed more than about 50 ms, the two sounds together are always heard as separate events.

Practically, this means that a short delay of less than 30 ms may be used to fatten up a track. Such a delay will add more width to a mono track when the original signal (dry) is panned to L and the delay (wet) to R.

A true doubling requires that the instrument or vocal is re-recorded on a separate track (as an overdub) as identically as possible. However, the small variations in timing and pitch between the two performances make the overall sound bigger. The problem with doubling, though, is that it also makes the vocal sound less raw and less powerful. Doubling is often used with inexperienced singers to produce a smoother and fuller sound.

Though the result is not identical to doubling, a delay of between 30–70 ms added to the vocal will imitate the doubling effect. The delay level should be as strong as the original signal, and feedback must be set to minimum. At 75–200 ms, the delay turns into slap back echo (see p. 187).

TIPS

✓ The flanger, chorus, and phaser broaden the sound textures of chord instruments. However, they also diffuse the instruments, making them less distinct in the mix.

✓ Flanging is a very pronounced effect, but even a subtle flanging may bring life to an instrument. Experiment by adding small doses to the bass, cymbals, or strings.

✓ Chorus is commonly used on guitar and keyboards; however, a little might also benefit the lead vocal and background vocals. If the harmony vocals are not quite clean (in terms of pitch), a little chorus will help to camouflage this.

✓ The Haas effect is very effective and a little overlooked in its application to the toolbox of mix effects. Solo instruments love the doubling—both the real and the Automatic Double-Tracking (ADT, see p. 9). Do not be afraid to try this on vocals, guitars, horns, background vocals, and so on. This form of doubling is also the principle used in the large band or symphony orchestra to make the sound of the instruments bigger (numerous first violins, second violins, etc.).

✓ Pan a mono keyboard or a rhythm guitar L and at the same time send the track to an aux channel with an inserted chorus or flanger plug-in. Pan the aux to R, set the delay to 7 ms and the output to wet (100% effect), and set speed/rate to 0.8 Hz and depth to about 20%. This provides a slow and not very deep modulation of the delayed signal, making the aux signal alternately closer and more distant sounding relative to the dry sound on the L channel—a continually changing stereo image is thus produced.

27

Distortion and Tape Saturation

In the context of sound recording, distortion has two widely different meanings.

In general, the objective with the proper audio equipment is linear reproduction. We want the signals that we send through the audio equipment to be reproduced without loss of quality. Only when we are editing should there be a change in the signal. Everything else is undesirable, and distortion is considered a reduction in the sound quality.

▶ Audio example 27.01 shows the effects of undesirable distortion produced by digital clipping.

However, when we want to shape the sound artistically, distortion becomes part of the toolset as an effect to be used creatively. The most sought-after distortion is harmonic distortion, produced when the output signal contains frequencies not present in the input signal but which are integer multiples of the input frequency. An input signal of 300 Hz thus gains added frequencies at 600, 900, 1200 Hz, and so on at the output. As this corresponds to the harmonic series (see p. 168) of the 300 Hz fundamental, it explains why harmonic distortion often sounds great.

Amplifying equipment using tubes in particular creates harmonic distortion, and this distortion is utilized in tube-based guitar amplifiers, pre-amps, compressors, and so forth.

Enhancing Sounds with Distortion

Harmonic distortion enhances the harmonics of an instrument. In particular, the second (the octave) and third harmonics (the fifth) are the most powerful, although, as in the harmonic series, their volume level is weaker than the source signal.

Most often, harmonic distortion is used to enhance the sound of the electric guitar, Hammond organ, and saxophone, and—if added discreetly—it will also make a vocal or the bass step forward in the mix. This is due to the highlighting of the harmonics, which is perceived even before the effect is heard as actual distortion.

Used as a noticeable effect, distortion fools our brain into thinking that a signal is more powerful, even when it has the same measurable level as the undistorted signal. Thus, a distorted guitar track played with the same reading on the level meters as a clean guitar will seem more powerful. This is the reason why distortion provides energy and makes a sound brutal and raw.

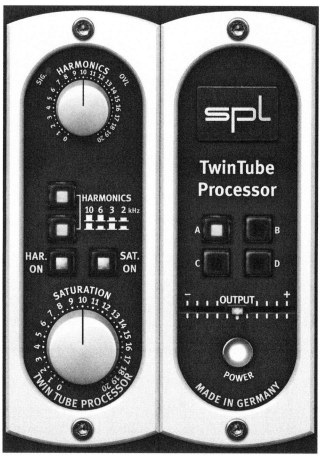

Figure 27.1

SPL TwinTube and iZotope Nectar plug-ins add a pleasant harmonic distortion with excellent control of the harmonics. © spl

Tape Saturation

A major part of rock history can be traced through the sound of the electric guitar and drums. Their sound is also associated with the analog distortion provided by tube (pre-) amps, tube-style compressors, and other outboard devices that are fed with high-gain signals.

Tape compression, or tape saturation, is another form of distortion of the input signal. This occurs with hot input signals recorded to analog tape. Analog tape stores sound on magnetic particles that are twisted and turned by the magnetic field of the record head. However, there are limits to how strong a signal tape can handle, and at a certain level saturation is reached and the magnetic particles lose accuracy in their storing of the audio signal. This particularly affects the transients, which are cut off, much the same way as in a compressor set to short attack. As most of the brightness of an instrument is located in the attack, the saturation smooths out the sound, and so the decay is heard as being comparatively stronger.

This is what we describe as a rich, warm analog sound. Tape saturation is part of the secret of the great drum sounds of John Bonham (Led Zeppelin) and Roger Taylor (Queen), particularly evident on the toms.

In the 1960s and 1970s, when analog tape was the only choice, this was not as desirable. The engineers knew that tape would reduce transients depending on how hot the signal sent to the tape was. They also knew that a tape played again and again would gradually wear off some of its coating, resulting in a loss of treble.

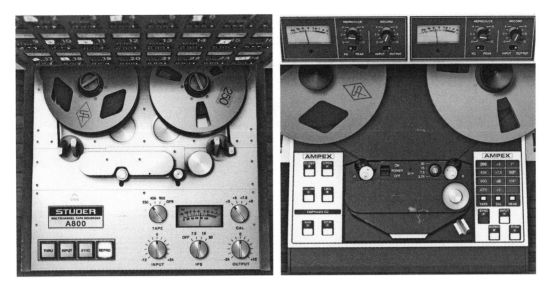

Figure 27.2
In 1978, the Studer A800 set a new standard for twenty-four-track multitrack recorders. The A800 achieved a breakthrough in sound quality with accurate and fast winding. Furthermore, its reliability and durability means that the A800 is still alive and kicking in many studios. While the analog machine weighs more than 400 kg, including the 2.5 hp motor, the Universal Audio's plug-in is weightless, only taking up a few mbs. The UA A800 is shown here together with the modeling of the Ampex ATR-102 two-track tape machine. © Universal Audio

However, digital recording equipment was not yet developed, and consequently the studios had to live with analog. Today we have the choice, but analog equipment is expensive, and despite its shortcomings, we now miss the warm sound it provides. Fortunately, tape saturation plug-ins, costing a lot less than 1% of, for example, a Studer A800, are modeled by the bucketload, and, furthermore these plug-ins also allow us to freely control the quality of the analog sound.

▶ Audio example 27.02 demonstrates the use of tape saturation.

Parallel bus compression is another method of adding small doses of harmonic distortion. The individual tracks from the drum kit are sent to an aux channel containing a compressor such as an LA-2A, 1176, or similar. Set to fast attack, the compression attenuates the transients from the drumsticks, and this results not only in fullness, as the decay is heard as being relatively stronger, but also in an enhancement of the ambience of the recording room.

Since the strongest parts of the signal, the transients, have been attenuated, this provides headroom, and the entire signal can be raised by gain makeup. Because of this attenuation, the gain makeup will bring forward the decaying of the signal, so release can be set to medium; however, if the objective is an over-processed drum sound, a longer release is required.

Once the parallel compressed aux channel has been routed to the mix bus, the mix ratio between the compressed drums and the more natural and dynamic-sounding tracks can be set. Usually, a ratio of 2–4:1 and a gain reduction of 3–6 dB is enough to add a touch of analog sound to the mix. Higher ratios and lower thresholds provide a more hardworking and eventually rough drum sound, with a risk of pumping occurring because of the decay and the ambience.

Parallel bus compression is also used on vocal tracks and guitars. (Read about parallel bus compression on p. 178.)

Countless plug-ins that mimic harmonic distortion and tape saturation are available, such as tape plug-ins from Universal Audio and Waves that model Ampex and Studer analog tape machines. Additionally, there are the SPL Transient Designer, Sonnox, and the Trans-X, which process transients in numerous ways.

Distortion Used as an Effect

Heavy distortion is a very strong and dominant effect that also occupies a lot of space in the stereo field. A high-gain guitar put through a Marshall rig fits neatly into many genres because of its rich harmonic distortion. Together with an overdriven Hammond through a Leslie speaker, this still works fine in some genres, because the two easily blend in the mix, but by now the sound stage is filling up, and these two instruments risk dominating the mix.

If the bass is also distorted heavily, it all starts to go wrong, because the distortion results in a loss of clarity and an inability to distinguish between instruments. If a previously solid bottom end becomes indistinct, most mixes will collapse. As a rule, there should always be some non-distorted instruments to provide the foundation for powerful distortion in one or more instruments.

However, distortion can also form the basis for a form of noise aesthetics, with even the vocal being heavily distorted. To achieve this, pedals and plug-ins that overdrive the input signal are used. Often the lo-fi aspect of these aesthetics is enhanced by phase distortion and other plug-ins like Bit Crusher (which reduces the audio resolution from 24-bit to 8-bit or less [see p. 265]).

If the sound needs to be extremely discordant, equipment that creates intermodulation distortion (IM) is best suited to the task. IM is produced when the audio output's added frequencies are related to two different input frequencies. As an example, input of 300 Hz and 2000 Hz will produce 1700 Hz and 2300 Hz at the output, and this risks sounding like dissonant noise rather than music.

Box 27.1 Third-Order Intermodulation Distortion

Most amplification circuits produce significant odd-numbered harmonics (a form of the nonlinear distortion that is present—but undesired—in most amplification). This inherent feature can be used to produce intermodulation effects at the output by inputting two sine waves of equal amplitude but slightly different frequencies. The most significant distortion occurs around the third harmonic (specifically, the IM effect produces tones that are the sum of and difference between the fundamentals and their harmonics). IM measurements describe the ratio (in dB) between the power of the fundamental frequencies and the resulting third-order distortion.

Harmonic distortion—also called second-order distortion—occurs at multiples of the fundamental tones, particularly in tube-based amps. As described above, harmonic distortion is a much-valued effect widely used in recordings.

A deliberate noise aesthetic has been cultivated, for example, by the German concept group Einstürzende Neubauten. Punk, grunge, glitch, and some dance and metal genres also use this aesthetic in smaller doses to reinforce an aggressive tone and as an expression of repressed energy.

TIPS

✓ A slight harmonic distortion can be used to emphasize the acoustic guitar or dobro played with fingerpicking.

✓ Harmonic distortion also enhances the reverberation of the snares on the snare drum.

✓ A clean and dynamic (digitally recorded) vocal might benefit from a tiny bit of harmonic distortion providing edge and making it even more highlighted in the mix.

✓ A few overdrive plug-ins have a specific low-pass filter similar to the bias control on a tape machine. On analog tapes, the bias setting was used to improve the linearity of analog tape. In digital, this is used to add a touch of analog; that is, a nonlinear response is added to the recording.

✓ Camel Crusher, produced by Camel Audio, is a free plug-in. It can be used as a distortion effect on guitar, drums, and the like. Combined with its straightforward compressor, it is useful to fatten up the tracks, smoothly or aggressively.

28

Varispeed and Pitch Processors

The term "varispeed" originates from the days of tape machines and analog studios. Increasing the tape speed made both the tempo and pitch higher, and lowering the speed lowered the tempo and pitch.

In the analog era, varispeed was often used to enable a vocalist to reach higher notes. By recording slightly slower (and at a lower pitch), the singers were able to reach pitches above their actual range. A recording slowed down 2–3 semitones sounded fine when the tape machine was set back to normal replay speed and only resulted in a slight change of timbre in the voice. However, voices recorded at lower speeds than that soon sounded like the Chipmunks (see below) in normal playback mode, since not only did the pitch become brighter, but the articulations became faster.

Conversely, a deep voice recorded at higher speed would sound like a 300 kg gorilla having a subwoofer mounted in his chest when played back at normal speed. Setting the tape machine to half speed (pitching down one octave) also worked fine if the guitar was required to sound like a mandolin—this also allowed the playing of fast arpeggios—and only the articulations would sound slightly unnatural.

Varispeed was first used as a production technique to make an artist sound younger than his actual years. As early as 1958, David Seville topped the charts with "Witch Doctor," a song that was recorded at half-speed that at normal playback became the iconic sound of the Chipmunks. In the mid-1960s, The Beatles used this technique to artistic effect such as when altering the timbre of the vocal in "Lucy in the Sky with Diamonds" (1967) and on the backing vocals of "Magical Mystery Tour" (1967).

Most DAWs have standard varispeed that is able to perform the major changes in speed that result in unnatural-sounding vocals and instruments, as with analog tape. In the DAW, though, varispeed has a new feature that is not possible with analog tape: the "speed only" mode changes the playback speed without changing pitch. This is a great help in recording a fast guitar solo or a synth arpeggio in sixteenth notes at 158 bpm. However, changes of more

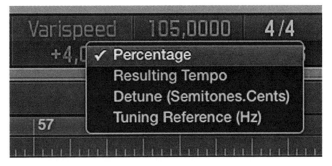

Figure 28.1
On the DAW, varispeed can be activated both during recording and playback. MIDI can be affected by varispeed.

than 3–5% provide poor playback quality, particularly on chord instruments. The speed-only feature can also be used to slow down or speed up the entire mix without changing the pitch; this should be used only lightly, if you still want a natural-sounding recording.

Pitch Shift

Pitch shift is available as a plug-in in any DAW. Pitch shift changes the pitch of a sound without changing its speed. The interval is usually within one or two octaves up or down, with fine tuning in cents. Normally, pitch shift cannot be used to change the key of a recording, but in small quantities it can be used as an alternative to chorus in order to create width without the sweep effect of the chorus. In Part I of this book dealing with individual instruments, suggestions for the use of pitch shift are given.

Pitch Correction

Everyone does it, but no one likes to talk about it. According to producer Tom Lord-Alge, autotune is used on most recordings in pop and rock, since even the slightest intonation problem can be heard on a recording, whereas in live performances this is only noted by a few. Despite this, the question of autotune still gives rise to mixed feelings. In 2009, Christina Aguilera appeared wearing a T-shirt with the text "Auto Tune is for pussies," and Jay-Z released his "D.O.A (Death of Auto-Tune)" in 2009.

Particularly with the voice, we might expect transparency, and the professional pride of many singers holds them back from using such pitch correction. Therefore, it is rarely

---

Box 28.1 How Auto-Tune Was Born

Boy bands and singing models have always been a widespread phenomenon in pop music. The many amateurs in the industry have often been an obstacle to making the nice, polished sound that is one of the most important qualities of the genre. Rock music shares this problem to some extent, though a few years in the rehearsal room and a practiced stage routine rectify most of this before aspiring rock stars are ready to make a serious recording.

Auto-Tune was developed in 1997 by Antares to correct intonation and pitch inaccuracies. Since Auto-Tune was the first to manufacture such a form of pitch processor, the technique itself was named autotune. From the beginning, no one was particularly proud of using a tool that corrected the pitching of a vocal track no matter how much the original singing was off-key.

Auto-Tune is rumored to have appeared on Robbie Williams's "Millennium" (1998) without Williams knowing. The then-large rack was smuggled into the studio after Williams had performed the best he could. That same year, Auto-Tune became a popular effect with Cher's "Believe." At first, the producer, Mark Taylor, tried to preserve the "Cher effect" (as the technique was called) as a business secret, claiming that the effect was made by a Digitech Talker FX pedal. A few months later, it was revealed that the effect was created by Auto-Tune at its most aggressive setting, correcting pitch immediately. The result was the abrupt, robotic sound we are now familiar with. As this robotic effect, pitch correction is used in a large number of recent teen pop songs. Auto-Tune has also perhaps had the indirect effect of making mainstream pop increasingly characterized by monotonous tunes lacking scale runs, pitch leaps, and vibrato, as these musical patterns and devices are inherently difficult for Auto-Tune to handle.

used in "live" genres like folk, blues, jazz, and that section of rock seeking to do more than just make a nice three-chord tune with a cute melodic phrase repeated throughout the whole chorus. In these genres, autotune would destroy a range of stylistic elements—from blues intonations through to scale runs and the subtle and almost inaudible sliding between notes that is portamento.

Pitch Correction (and Special Effects)

The pitch correction feature shifts pitch to the nearest note in the scale set (usually the semitone scale). At mild settings, the attack of a tone slips through unaffected, and it is the main part of the tone that is corrected, as well as the out-of-tune tail end of a phrase. By using slow attacks, pitch correction can fix minor intonation issues without side effects. Often, the best approach is to locate problem areas and then use pitch correction only there by automating on/off.

Pitch correction can also be used as an effect to make the voice sound synthesized if the pitch is altered abruptly or significantly. At extreme settings, pitch correction very firmly assigns a fixed frequency to each note, quite unlike the natural human voice, which uses lots of intonations and sliding tones (portamento or glissando). Harsh pitch correction, therefore, provides a robot-like character to the voice, and this can be used as an effect—for example, making the voice sound like it is played by a synthesizer, leaping between distinct notes (the "Cher effect").

In this respect, as a creative effect, pitch correction provides new opportunities to allow the automated features of digital to interact with the human voice. For this reason, it is particularly used by hip-hop and R & B as part of the genre's machine aesthetics.

Auto-Tune is available as a plug-in for the DAW and as a stand-alone rack for live performance processing.

Today, however, Auto-Tune is no longer the only product in the pitch correction market. The Antares version was shortly followed by Melodyne, Logic's Flex Pitch, Cubase's VariAudio, Waves Tune, and Digital Performer. Stand-alone hardware units are also available in the form of the TC-Helicon VoiceOne, which is also capable of adding harmony vocals to a lead vocalist.

Auto-Tune and Melodyne currently produce the most advanced pitch processors, with both being equally great at discreetly correcting pitch issues on vocals that have gone astray here or there. They have a wealth of editing functionality, since both

Figure 28.2

Pitch correction in Logic is quite simple compared to the editing parameters of Auto-Tune and Melodyne. With respect to the scale selected, the response controls how fast pitch correction is addressed. If it is set to 80–150 ms, the attacks slip through unaltered before pitch correction, thus creating fewer side effects. The correction amount continually displays the amount of correction taking place.

processors convert an audio track into individual note elements (called blobs), which are represented in the editor with pitch, time, velocity, and ADSR.

Auto-Tune is most widely used for automatic pitch correction, whereas Melodyne, at present, is the more complex tool, suited to the creative shaping of vocals and instruments, drums included. In Melodyne, the properties of a tone (formants, harmonics, etc.) are displayed as editable graphic elements, with the processing of pitch, timbre, and timing limited only by your imagination.

Both provide correction of formants when shifting the pitch of a sound; this removes the Mickey Mouse effect when the pitch is increased and makes it possible to shift the

Figure 28.3

Melodyne makes it possible to affect the most detailed elements of a tone such as the internal dynamics (the ADSR envelope) and time stretching, thereby completely changing its timbre.

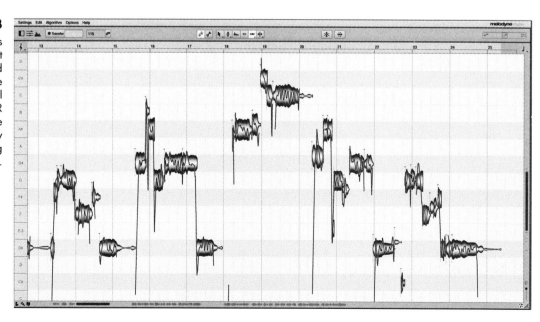

pitch quite a lot while leaving it sounding natural. A male singer can be given the character of a female voice, and vice versa.

Manipulating Sound with Pitch Processors

Besides tuning vocals, pitch correction software also opens up a lot of creative possibilities reaching far beyond the "Cher effect."

In the following, a few creative uses of pitch processors are listed. When the functionality only applies to a specific software platform, this is referred to.

Add a Harmony Vocal or Edit the Melody Line

A melody line can be changed and even rewritten by dragging (re-pitching) the note blobs (the editable blobs representing each pitch of the vocal track).

A harmony vocal can be created by manually shifting the notes of the melody line up by a major third (four semitones) or down by a minor sixth (eight semitones). Afterwards, the notes falling outside the key need to be shifted a semitone (use your ears or your knowledge of the scale as a guide).

All this is done in a copy of the track, which can be edited independently of the original. To make the harmony vocal more distinct sounding, the pitch, timing, and amplitude of some of the harmony phrases can be edited. A subtle adjustment of the formants (supported by Melodyne, Auto-Tune, and Flex Pitch) may work wonders for the tonal character of the harmony part.

Editing Percussive Sounds

In Melodyne, the Percussive Mode is an algorithm specifically intended for percussive sounds. In the edit window, the generated blobs represent the pitch of the beats over time.

This is an obvious tool to use to tune the individual drums of the kit in the mix if they do not quite match each other. Of course, this can also be used to modify the tonal character of an individual drum, say, to make the bass drum extremely low in pitch or to pitch the snare up or down to fit the mix in terms of timbre. This can also be used to double one or more drums, afterwards dropping the pitch; mixed 3–6 dB below the original beats, this will add fullness.

Pitching up or down can be used on the entire track or just a few bars to provide an effect during a breakdown or bridge. In terms of the sound character, Melodyne performs this trick much better than the standard pitch plug-ins of DAWs. Moreover, in Melodyne, the processing can be limited to a single drum or even a few beats of the track.

Used in tandem with other features, like extending the length of the snare beats (time-stretching), increasing the volume of some of the snare blobs, or changing the timbre with Melodyne's formant tool, Melodyne can shape the drum kit or any percussive sound either drastically or with more subtlety, to make the tonal character of the beats match the mix.

Vocal Leveling

In Melodyne, the Amplitude tool (easiest to use in the percussive mode) can be used manually to adjust levels on the individual blobs. This can be used to make the vocalist sound more consistent, thus reducing the need for compression (with its resulting artifacts).

Additionally, the Split tool can be used to separate sibilants, breath noises, and plosives from the vocal and to then reduce their levels.

Create Double-Tracking by Editing

A natural-sounding double track (see p. 9 on analog ADT) can be made from a recorded vocal track using a copy in which subtle differences, which are naturally a feature of double-tracking, are mimicked.

For this purpose, subtle changes are applied to the timing, pitch, and/or volume of the individual blobs (notes). Melodyne allows all three functionalities to be manipulated, as well as the formant (start by setting the Correct Pitch Center slider and the Quantize Time Intensity to 50–60% and adjust for the most convincing ADT effect).

Melodyne is great for fine-tuning the individual blobs; however its Add Random Deviation feature can generate the desired doubling effect for the selected blobs much more quickly. If needed, the formant tool can be used to additionally change the tonal character of the doubled track. Also, a slight volume variation in some of the blobs can be used to highlight certain words or phrases—all together, this results in added body on the original track.

To add space (and avoid chorus effects), the original track and the doubled track can be panned slightly to the sides of the stereo field. If two (or more) doubled tracks are created, keep the lead vocal in the center and pan the two doubles slightly to the sides.

Generate MIDI from an Audio Track

Most pitch-correction tools can generate MIDI data from an audio track, so if you hum or play a tune, MIDI can be extracted from the recorded audio performance in order to have a virtual instrument play it.

This allows you to transform your singing into a piano solo, a flute part, or any another instrument you yourself do not play. Likewise, the bass part can be doubled by a bass synth to beef up the bottom end.

PART IV

Mixing and Mastering

29

The Mix

In producing music in the studio, the recording phase splits a song into its parts, as each instrument is recorded on a separate track while focusing on the details of each part. After that, the mix is the stage at which the parts are assembled—hopefully creating a whole from the separately recorded tracks. Therefore, the mix should:

1. Clean up the recorded tracks, assigning each instrument/track a clear role in the mix.
   Mix tools: muting/deleting parts of the recording, re-recording, or re-amping
2. Balance the individual instruments/tracks with each other. This requires an assessment of which instruments should shape the song.
   Mix tools: setting levels, compression, fading, and panning
3. Place the instruments in tonal layers, both separating them and making them blend with each other by adapting their frequency content to the entire mix. The tonal layers (bottom, mid, and top) largely correspond to the roles of the instruments in the various bands.
   Mix tools: EQ and reverb
4. Place the instruments in space and assign width and depth to each relative to the overall mix. A naturalistic or artificial space should be created as suits the genre.
   Mix tools: reverb, delay, panning, and modulation

The mix process is therefore made up of many partial processes, some of which are described in the instrument chapters (Part I of the book). For example, in the "Mix Settings and Effects" sections of those chapters, the use of EQ, compression, and effects is described for specific instruments.

Here, we deal with the overall mix process.

The Basic Mix

Make a Sketch

Start the mix by making a fast and intuitive balance between the recorded tracks. A fresh and objective perspective is important, so even if you know the tracks well, try a playful approach. Leave out EQ, reverb, and any effects at this stage.

Listen to this sketch a few times; what mood is being expressed by the raw mix? what is the basic idea of the song? which of the instruments are best able to support the concept of the song? This first impression is used to determine which instruments should have the main role and the direction in which the mix (the use of EQ, compression, reverb, etc.) should take the recording.

Finally, the positions of the individual instruments within the stereo field are outlined using panning. Ideally, a picture of the final mix should already be taking shape. If not, then either the recording has shortcomings or the recorded instruments do not form a whole—failings that might require some tracks to be re-recorded, new instruments added, and so on.

This rough outline is the basis for shaping the individual instruments so that they fit into the mix.

Cleaning and Building Up the Mix

As it is quite normal to record too many tracks, the mix process is also a cleaning out of unneeded elements; maybe a guitar should be muted in the verse or the keyboard left out of the chorus, for instance, as there is already plenty of activity. It may even be necessary to leave out the entire solo section. Often, too many overdubs drain the energy from the rhythm section and the vocal. By leaving out some instruments, the mix may suddenly jump out of the speakers with a lot more dynamism and clarity. Moreover, variation in instrumentation and timbre creates contrast and helps the music develop and tell its story.

The vocal is the key element of most recordings, and experienced engineers often build the mix around it. Others will start with the rhythm section, which requires an understanding of how much space the vocal will take up and perhaps requires going back to the rhythm section later to make space for the vocal.

If the recorded tracks get their character from a groove, a riff, or the interaction between the guitar and vocal, these elements should also be balanced in the early stages of mixing. And no matter where you start, the balance between melody and accompanying instruments is the most crucial aspect of the mix.

Box 29.1 The Artist Should Leave the Studio

Most good mixes are made without the musicians being present. Musicians start getting bored, restlessly hammering on the furniture, fiddling with instruments, and telling jokes. They are typically not familiar with the process of mixing and thus make suggestions that might be right but at the wrong time. Most often they are plain wrong. A popular audio engineer meme, circulating on the internet, has a youthful wannabe popstar expressing his sentiments to the engineer thus: "I'm gonna hire you to mix my album because you're the pro . . . But I'm not gonna trust your judgment. Then I'll disagree with you and make you change the mix and blame you when it's bad." If you haven't experienced this already, be warned!

It is best, though, to have the producer involved. Producers are experienced in translating musical ideas to a recording and have an intimate knowledge of the genre. For the non-established artist, however, it is often the engineer in control. Replacing the guitarist's and drummer's focus on their own instruments with a cool evaluation of what works in the mix, the experienced engineer is more likely to succeed in making the individual tracks coalesce into a whole. However, it is always a good idea to involve the musicians in the last stage of fine-tuning, as they know the music intimately and are aware of details that the engineer may have missed.

This approach thus depends on the particular arrangement of the song. However, common to all approaches is that in any of the stages of the mix, each instrument and the effects added should constantly be assessed in relation to the whole. Music listeners do not focus on fancy flanging on the bass; most go for an experience of the musical whole and may not even notice the sophisticated fill-ins from the '59 Telecaster floating on the triplets from the vintage Echoplex EP-4.

Levels and Summing

Proceed with the fine-tuning of levels in the various sections of the song, and always keep a safe distance from the red fields of the meters. As a starting point, each individual channel should have more than 6 dB headroom (i.e., below unity gain), so there is room for the boost added to the signal from EQ and compression.

When tracks are added (called summing), the overall level becomes louder, so the level of the stereo bus must also be kept within safe bounds. As some DAWs have poor summing quality, always maintain 4–6 dB headroom on the stereo mix bus; overloading digital systems produces intolerable distortion, and even before it turns into audible distortion, the dynamics are reduced and the stereo image starts to collapse.

Figure 29.1
Although the professionals use Pro Tools, Logic, Cubase, and so on, they often route the individual tracks via direct out to an SSL api or Neve mixer that has better summing properties and a larger headroom than the DAW. Another option for the summing mixer is to have a quality analog unit with great dynamic range. Shown here is the Crane Song Egret with eight channels of summing and D/A conversion. © Crane Song

The levels in the mix should continuously be adjusted, because the added EQ, compression, reverb, and so on all affect the level and definition of an instrument in the mix.

TIPS

✓ Switching to mono can be helpful in checking levels, as panning interferes with the volume levels. Mono is also revealing as to whether or not there are timbral overlaps between instruments. Two guitars panned L (left) and R (right) may seem distinct in stereo, but mono reveals whether they should be further separated.

✓ Maintain listening ability and focus by mixing at a low volume level and only turning up the level if details should be checked. At low levels, the quality of the mix is put to the test; it is all too easy to make it sound cool at high levels.

✓ The level of the vocal varies from genre to genre. In genres like blues and bluegrass, the vocal is generally kept low compared to pop ballads, but even vocal stars of the caliber of Michael Jackson have used low vocal levels in the verses to create contrast between the verse and chorus. Ensure the right level by comparing to reference commercial releases. The same applies to the use of EQ, reverb, and delay.

✓ If you start to doubt that the mix level of a track is right, hearing the mix in a different way might be helpful. Listen to the mix from different monitors or from an adjacent room—perhaps while you are washing up or cleaning the windows. The final test of the level balances between instruments is made through various systems (boom box, computer speakers, headphones, car stereo, etc.) and in different situations.

✓ Make alternative mixes, one having louder/weaker vocals or louder/weaker drums, guitar, or whatever is appropriate. Come back to the mixes after a few days and you will find it easier to determine which mix works best.

Utilizing the Stereo Field

Panning makes the mix sound wider in the stereo perspective, as do time-based effects such as doubling, chorus, and flanger. When reverb and delay are added, both of which create depth, the mix will sound three-dimensional.

When the individual tracks are panned toward L and R, the instruments are separated and additional space is created in the center of the stereo image. The panning may imitate the setup of the instruments on stage, though better results are often achieved by using panning creatively; what works with the instruments in this recording, and what sounds best?

The lead vocal, the kick and snare drum, solos, and the bass are usually panned to C (center). Guitars, piano, violin, and saxophone are some of the many instruments fighting for space in the midrange and high-mids, and they should be separated by panning. This also gives more width to the entire mix. A recording having only two chord instruments, like a guitar and a piano, is given width by panning them to L and R. Most instruments residing above the low-mids benefit from panning because this, along with EQing, separates them tonally.

Instruments recorded in stereo or with two or more mics should always be panned to some extent—often full L and R. Thus, the drum kit overheads are normally panned full L and R, while the toms are distributed across the stereo field. It is an obvious choice to pan the hi-hat, snare, and toms to match the setup of the kit from L to R.

Likewise, a horn section can be panned after its setup.

Panning significantly affects the experience of fullness, definition, and transparency of a mix, and so it is usually done together with EQing and the balancing of levels.

EQ

EQing Musically

EQing should be seen as a way to define the clarity and presence of an instrument in the mix, and the key to a great mix is very much a clear distribution of instruments in the bottom, middle, and top of the frequency range. In the EQ chart shown in figure 29.2, this is subdivided into sub-bass (20–60 Hz), bass (60–250 Hz), low mid (250 Hz to 2 kHz), mid (2–4 kHz), high mid (4–6 kHz), and high (6–20 kHz)—terms generally used in this book for these specific frequency ranges.

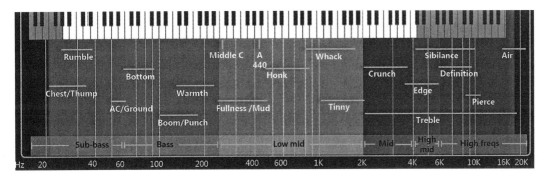

Figure 29.2
Use EQ to place the instruments from sub-bass up to the midrange, then to the high frequencies. The chart is further elaborated on pp. 153–156 to include the range of a number of instruments.

After EQing, an instrument should still sound natural. It is easy to determine whether the voice or an acoustic instrument sounds natural, but the options for electric instruments are much wider, and for a synth or a software instrument there are almost no rules.

Always be aware of instruments overlapping in certain frequency ranges. Most often it is necessary to cut out frequencies from one or more instruments, thereby creating space for all of the others. Two overlapping instruments will lose clarity—several will create a general lack of transparency. Sometimes, re-recording is the only solution to make an instrument stand out when trying to give it a clearer role in the arrangement.

Already during recording it is important to ensure that the instruments are distributed in clearly defined layers according to their role in the arrangement. Chord inversion might be the solution: one or more of the instruments are transposed up (or down) so that they are separated from each other in frequency.

Chord inversion reduces the need for EQing because the mix becomes more transparent. Excessive use of EQ often indicates that the recorded instruments were not

235

placed optimally in the tonal layers to begin with; that is, an instrument might have been recorded with a sound that does not conform to its tonal role in the arrangement. Excessive use of EQ can ruin the dynamics of an instrument, and if this is due to excessive EQing during recording, this becomes doubly disastrous for the dynamics.

The best approach to minimize the EQing in the recording process is to choose the right mic and to place it so that it picks up the sound that suits the instrument best.

Transparency in the mix is often a matter of balancing the complementary frequencies (complementary EQing; p. 163); as an example, a slight attenuation at 250 Hz might have the same effect as a boost at 5 kHz.

Always pay attention to the interaction between levels and EQ. EQing actually boosts or attenuates the level of a signal, though only in a limited frequency range. What makes the inexperienced engineer use a lot of additive EQ (i.e., boosting) is that an instrument at a higher volume level initially always seems better sounding in the mix than the subtractive EQ, which cuts frequency content. However, the subtractive approach is the least destructive to the dynamics, and generally, this will produce the same result as a boost if the right frequency range is chosen for the cut.

Box 29.2

See "Mix Settings and Effects" in the chapters for each instrument in the first part of this book and chapter 19, "EQ and Instruments" (p. 153).

✓ When EQing each individual instrument, it is important to check the result by switching between the instrument and the entire mix. Use the solo button.

✓ If heavy treble boosting is required on the electric piano, it is often better to have the keyboard play a higher chord inversion or to overdub using a string pad that provides a bright timbre.

✓ If the low range remains muddy because of the bass and the bass drum overlapping each other, try panning the bass to eleven o'clock and bass drum to one o'clock in order to reduce the effect of the added frequencies. This approach also works in the midrange and high range, though is less pronounced in its effect.

✓ A vocal that is inadequately defined in the mix often benefits from a bright reverb. This maintains the fullness where boosting the treble easily makes the vocal thin-sounding.

✓ An instrument still sounding thin with added midrange and high or undefined when adding bass and low-mid will benefit from multing. Make a copy of the instrument on a separate track and add bass and low-mids to the original track, while adding midrange or high-mids to the copy. Moreover, the two channels can be panned and enhanced with varying amounts of compression or different shades of reverb.

Depths and Widths

Reverb, Delay, and Other Spatial Effects

Depth—when the music is perceived as coming from behind the speakers, not just between them—is added to the mix using reverb and other spatial effects. This is due to our everyday experience that the greater the distance to a sound source, the more the sound is affected by reflections (early reflections and reverberation) from the surfaces that sound waves meet before they reach our ears.

Depth is also found on recordings that use many mics in the basic tracks, because the mics capture sound from the more distant instruments. In rock recordings, this applies largely to the drum kit, since most other instruments are recorded using close-miking. In the recording of jazz and acoustic music, it is much easier to create depth, since these genres are often recorded live in the studio using multiple mics in acoustically vibrant rooms. In this situation, the spill between mics is not necessarily a problem; often it provides depth and dimension to the recording.

In the mix, spatial effects are used to compensate for the acoustics having been removed by close-miking. After the individual instruments have been placed in the stereo field, they are placed in a full, three-dimensional acoustic space by using reverb, delay, and other spatial effects such as chorus and flanging. Reverb and delay add width and depth to the music, while chorus and flanging create width beyond what panning accomplishes.

In the acoustic genres, reverb must provide a naturalistic space for the music, whereas in pop and rock the use of spatial effects is not limited to imitating the acoustics of concert halls. Accordingly, in the latter genres, there are no set rules for the use of reverb and spatial effects; the use of the same reverb is not required for all the instruments—several types of space can be created—and the use of artificial spaces is more widespread in these genres.

However, it can at times be useful to use one specific reverb for several instruments in order to glue the instruments together and to establish a shared acoustic space. It is practical to put the shared reverb on the aux channel, using the send (via the buses) on each instrument channel to control the amount of effect added. On the DAW, this saves processing power while also making it possible to experiment with the overall amount of reverb by only using the aux volume fader.

Short ambience reverbs are great for bringing to life a snare drum, guitar, horn (section), or vocal, all of which should sound relatively dry and stand forward in the mix. Conversely, long reverbs make an instrument appear further away and consequently more remote in the mix.

Reverb is not necessarily required on all instruments, as reverb has a spill effect. If added to one single instrument, it is often perceived as also being on other instruments sharing the same frequency range.

Reverb affects instrument rhythms, phrasing, and grooves, meaning that a longer reverb can be added to the instruments of a slow ballad than to those of a fast piece. Also, more reverb can be added to slow pieces; this might wash out the fast groove or the riff of a horn section in faster music but will provide a floating character to a saxophone or a guitar playing long notes in slower music.

Grooves and instruments emphasizing rhythm should generally have a reverb that is shorter than the timing between the beats. Reverb that overlaps the beats will generate a cluttered sound stage and make those instruments with a strong rhythmic profile diffuse; if the perfect reverb is a little too long, use a gate to cut the tail before the next beat.

In general, instruments with a great deal of low end, like drums and bass, should not have reverb. If they must be given just a little (to provide depth), a low-cut filter inserted at the aux channel after the reverb can be used to cut the frequencies in the 200–300 Hz range in order to avoid any muddying of the bottom end of the mix.

Often, short delays with only one repeat work better than reverb. Delays provides both width and depth and do not rob an instrument of its dynamics or make it remote sounding. Stereo delays with more repetitions provide a large amount of fullness but at the same time affect the rhythm of the instrument.

Unless it is used as an effect, neither reverb nor delay should be heard in itself, its purpose merely being to make the instruments blend and to add depth, width, and fullness. If attention is drawn to the reverb itself, too much has probably been used. In the final mix, it may be difficult to assess the amount of reverb actually used, since there is more than is actually heard, most of it being masked by the instruments. Only when it is not there is it felt to be lacking; the space provided to the instruments by the reverb collapses, making the mix narrow and confined. Check the balance between dry and wet by muting the reverb auxes and the reverb on the individual instruments at selected points during playback.

Reverb has its greatest effect when there are only a few instruments in a mix. Therefore, it may be necessary to raise the reverb in the busy parts and reduce it in the more sparsely populated parts of the mix where there are fewer instruments competing for space. This can be done very simply by automating the output level of the reverb aux.

Reverb—like anything else being adjusted in the mix—can be an addictive effect to use, so take a break, do something else, or clean your ears by listening to a good mix that has passed the test of time. When you listen again to your own mix, it should be obvious whether too much or too little reverb has been added.

Box 29.3

Read more about reverb and delay in the chapters for the individual instruments in the first part of this book. See also chapter 23, "Tape Echo and Digital Delay" and chapter 24, "Ambience and Reverb."

TIPS

✓ An instrument that is panned to one side is given width in the mix with stereo reverb or delay, the effect being equally distributed on both sides.

✓ Send an instrument that is panned full L to an aux with a stereo reverb inserted. Leave the R side of the aux in place and pan its L to C. This preserves width and, at the same time, the effect of the reverberation coming from the right side, opposite the instrument; this causes the brain to interpret it as if the instrument is in a dry place (the L side) projecting its sound to an acoustically vibrant place (the R side). Moreover, this provides space for additional effects on other instruments in the L side, thus avoiding instruments drowning in each other's effects.

✓ A short and dull bass drum might be revived by using a short, room-type reverb. Use a high-cut filter, cutting off the highs above 2–3 kHz to avoid metallic reverberation.

✓ Delay is usually best when it is consistent with the song tempo (activate tempo sync in the plug-ins of the DAW or the tap feature). On vocals, a delay with a single repeat normally works best, particularly when the tempo exceeds 110 bpm. Otherwise, try setting up a stereo delay lasting a sixteenth note on the L side and a half note or longer on the R side. If necessary, boost the highs above 5 kHz to highlight the tail of the delay.

Box 29.4

The mix places great demands on concentration and the ability to maintain a musical reference point. During hours of concentrated mixing, most engineers will become spectrally disoriented and lose the ability to assess whether the drums are too powerful or if too much treble, bass, or reverb has been added. Breaks are a must, and it is a good idea to occasionally listen to a reference mix to reset the hearing.

The Sound Stage

The stereo image is not a particularly large painting and is very flat. In the foreground of a typical rock or pop setup, there is space for the vocal, with a couple of weaker instruments slightly behind in the middle ground, while the sides are occupied by one or two guitars and a keyboard. Frequency-wise, at the bottom end the bass drum is joined by the bass, whereas in the midrange the keyboard and guitar are placed, and here space might be available for an extra (acoustic) guitar and a saxophone. At the top, the hi-hat, harmony vocals, strings, and similar are added.

When the height and depth are included, a little more space is provided, and the three-dimensional sound stage can now be populated.

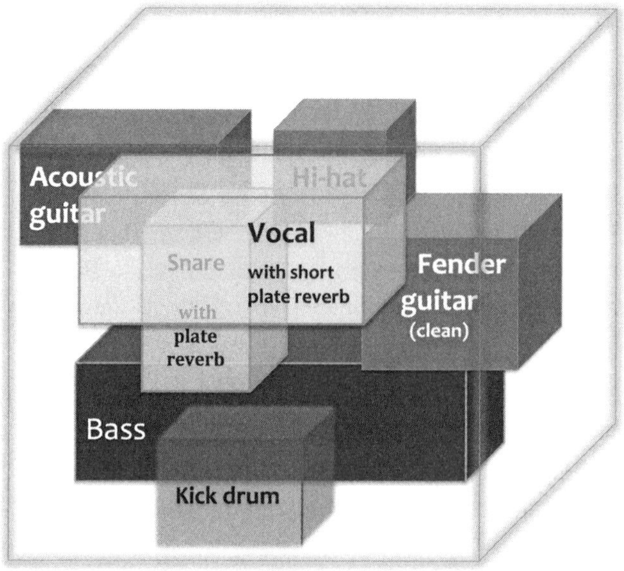

Figure 29.3

The sound stage containing the instruments in three-dimensional space.

The lows, midrange, and highs are controlled by EQ. Width is controlled using pan, reverb, delay, chorus, and so forth, and depth is controlled by reverb and the spill between mics. This example is filled in with the typical pop and rock instruments, but it applies whether the music is opera, jazz, or folk; there is only so much space available within the sound stage.

When using reverb, the instruments previously squeezed into the stereo image are given more room to breathe, with the result that the instruments blend better.

Even though we have been talking of the stereo image becoming increasingly larger, this does not change the basic principles of the mix; in the foreground the lead vocal or the soloist, a couple of weaker instruments in the middle ground (instruments supporting the character of the song, such as the riff or an ostinato), and then some instruments placed purely in the background (bass, chord, and rhythm instruments).

Try out which of the instruments give life to the recording. Would the overall mix benefit from the bass drum being put forward or laid back relative to the bass? Should the guitar only be heard as an integrated part of the rhythm?

Experiment with levels by placing instruments in the foreground, middle ground, and background according to their role—minimal changes might make quite a difference. The mixer is a tool for balancing, while EQ defines and clarifies the layering of instruments from bottom to top.

Making the Individual Tracks on the Mix Sparkle—EQ Revisited

When the tracks have been set up with respect to levels, compression, and spatial effects, it is time to take a look at the EQ again in order to refine the sound of the instruments and to make them sparkle in the mix. By holding back on (a part of) the EQing in the first stage above, the all-too-easy temptation to make the sound too big on each instrument (so that they sound like solo instruments, are fighting for space in the overall mix, and are making the mix cluttered) can be avoided.

One of the tasks in EQing is to compensate for the dampening of the high-frequency transients introduced by the use of compressors. Also, assess the mix with regard to the sound layers represented by the color bars in the EQ table in figure 29.2; what belongs to the sub bass, bass, low-mid, midrange, high-mid, and the highs? A final check of EQ and levels will fine-tune remaining minor issues, and always check the instrument you are EQing against the entire mix. The whole is greater than the sum of its parts, and a guitar that sounds thin and nasal in solo mode may sound great in the mix.

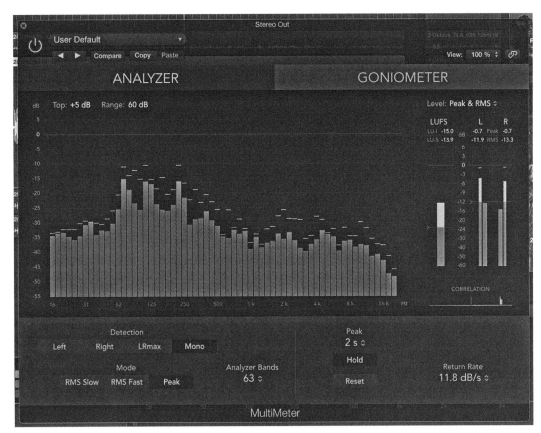

Figure 29.4

A multimeter inserted on the stereo bus provides a graphical representation of the frequency content of the mix. With practice, it can be helpful in understanding the sound of the mix. The mix shown here has pointless sub-bass content below 20–30 Hz, which should be removed with a low-cut filter. Moreover, the mix is bass-heavy (rumbling) from 80 to 500 Hz and also lacks midrange and high-frequency content (transparency).

Stereo Groups

Once the mix begins to come together, it can be useful to combine several instruments or vocals in groups. A group is designed to make it easy to control several tracks via a group fader. This technique can be used thus:

- The drum tracks are assembled into a group so that the level of the entire set can be tested in the mix by simply adjusting the level of the group fader.
- The harmony vocals are assembled and controlled relative to the vocal and the accompaniment.
- The amount of reverb and/or delay on the vocals is adjusted relative to the overall mix.
- The guitars or the entire rhythm section are grouped, and their volume levels are tested relative to the vocals or a solo.

The tracks can also be grouped according to their role in the sound layers. Thus, the groups can be used to discretely fine-tune the low end, the midrange, and the high end. Similarly, groups can be created according to the genre, such as a string or a brass section, the many string instruments in folk music, groups of percussion, and so on.

Always wait to set up groups until the final stage of the mix, after fine-tuning the individual instruments but before the final refinements. With groups, it also becomes simple to make various mixes of a song, since the instrument groups can quickly be assigned varying degrees of attention in the mix; putting the guitars, the drums, or the vocals to the front or to the back of the mix or adding more or less reverb might change the fundamental character of a song.

Compression

In the mix, compression is used on many instruments, but the amount of compression depends greatly on the instrument and the genre. Therefore, compression is mainly dealt with under each instrument in Part I of this book; in this chapter, only parallel bus, mix bus, and side chain compression are addressed.

Parallel Bus Compression

In the mix, it often becomes necessary to address a group of tracks in a way that takes advantage of the parallel bus feature, which allows you to create anything from subtle nuances to profound changes in the sound of instruments and vocals.

Most often, parallel bus compression is used to make drums fuller and up-front sounding. This is achieved by routing the drum tracks via the send bus (which is set to unity gain = 0) to an aux channel. In the case of hard compression (ratio settings of 5:1 or higher, or low threshold settings), the overhead tracks should be left out to prevent the cymbals from sizzling and pumping. On the aux channel, a compressor is added and brought into the mix in parallel with the original tracks. Use a compressor with a specific character (such as an 1176-type, Fairchild, Joe Meek, or clones thereof) to smooth out the dynamics. If none of these are available, experiment with those you have and select optical, FET, or variable-mu tube types (if available). Setting the compressor to an audible reduction of the dynamics (i.e., smoothing of the attacks) and balancing the level of the aux channel with the unprocessed original drum tracks will result in a longer sustain of the drums, adding fullness to the mix in addition to a distinctive harmonic distortion if a tube compressor (or a plug-in model) is used.

Finally, adjust (using the individual sends) how much of each drum track should be sent to the compressor at the aux. (See the details of the setup on pp. 178 and 219.)

Parallel bus techniques can be used for many purposes (and not just for compression), the idea being to preserve the character and dynamics of the original tracks while adding heavy processing on top of this. Thus, an instrument can be made otherworldly through its effect while being held firmly in place by the original (dry) track:

- The bass drum can be made long and thundering with large amounts of compression.
- The vocal can be given an aggressive character and, when mixed with the original track, be given fullness and put forward in the mix.
- Using a distortion plug-in on the aux can add a slight harmonic distortion for a more vintage and rich sound. A soft harmonic distortion causes many instruments to be more pronounced in the mix without occupying more space.
- A thin acoustic guitar can be given more sustain with medium to hard compression while maintaining the natural attack.

Mix Bus Compression

Properly applied, mix bus compression is an excellent tool to make the mix more coherent by making the instruments blend while at the same time adding fullness and a slightly stronger output. The compression of the entire mix can provide anything from presence to a pumping, in-your-face impact.

However, mix bus compression should not be confused with mastering. Mix bus compression is only intended to please the client in the studio and to give an idea of how the final mix will sound when mastered. In other words, remove it when producing the final mix ready for mastering.

Hard compression will always create undesirable side effects, because it changes the attack in particular and the ADSR envelope (p. 175) in general. Also, the levels between instruments in the mix will be affected.

However, a moderate processing using the right type of compressor might provide very pleasing results. The compressor should be inserted at the stereo bus early in the mix process—in principle, from the very start, as the compressor affects the balance between the instruments and the decay from reverb and instruments. If it is first added after the levels are mixed, this can change the balance that has been carefully set up. Still, many prefer to wait until the basic levels and EQing are in place, but before reverb is added, to use mix bus compression.

Four types of classic analog compressors are widely used for mix bus compression: optical, variable-mu tube, VCA, and FET. All of them are modeled in the plug-in format (some approved by the manufacturers of the hardware model), and the differences between them relate to the ways in which they process level changes of the music.

Optical Compressors

These are used mainly because they are both transparent and musical sounding, providing a gradually increasing attack as the signal exceeds the threshold, and, with a rather

Figure 29.5
The Fairchild 670 variable-mu tube compressor. It features twenty tubes and takes up six rack units. Attack and release are interlocked in six choices (called time constants), two of which are application-dependent—that is, they adapt to the dynamics of the music, thus being useful at the mix bus. Its soft compression and harmonic distortion are reminiscent of soft limiting. Transients slipping through before compression sets in are softened by tube circuitry that glues the mix together in a rather musical way. © Universal Audio

tube-like sustain, the input-to-output signal processing is nonlinear. Widely used optical compressors are the Avalon AD2044, Joe Meek SC2, Tube-Tech Cl2a, and Millennia Media TCL2.

Variable-Mu Tube Compressors

This type of compressor is based on tubes. The best have a distinctive sound: a slight yet appealing harmonic distortion and a warmth and fullness that is difficult to achieve using the other types. Famous variable-mu tube compressors are the Fairchild 660/670 and the Manley Variable Mu, and they can be used for both a transparent and a harsh compression effect.

VCA Compressors

Voltage-controlled amplifier compressor designs are quite different from the variable-mu tubes, since they use transistors, which provide an accurate representation of the signal—that is, the input-to-output processing is linear. At the same time, they are quite flexible and great at gluing together the different parts of the mix. The classics are the Neve 33609, SSL G-series, API 2500, and Focusrite Red 3.

FET Compressors

The field effect transistor (FET) compressor combines several of the above features. Although it is transistor-based (solid state), the FET almost has the character of tube compressors when the gain is overdriven, though they are slightly brighter sounding. The attack times of the FETs are faster than those of the other three types, which is why the FET is often used as a limiter. However, a few types can be used with great results on the mix bus, among them the Cranesong STC8, Universal Audio 1176, and Classic Compressor, produced by LA Audio (much sought after for its vintage sound, which is reminiscent of the UREI 1176 and Fairchild).

Mix Bus Compression Settings

Usually, the mix bus compressor is set to a gentle compression, as it is processing a complex signal that should maintain its dynamics. Only the peaks should be tamed a little. Start by setting ratio as low as 1.5:1 or 2:1 and then adjust the threshold for a gain reduction of 2–3 dB.

Attack should affect transients from the snare, the vocal, or any other acoustic instrument. Release is a little harder to set by ear; however, here the reading of the meter comes in handy when it is set to display the gain reduction. The VU meters particularly smooth out changes in output level, thereby providing a visual representation of the amount of compression. Adjust the release so that the VU returns to unity gain just before the next attack.

If the meter does not return to unity gain in time, the compression is not released before the next attack, resulting in an audible ducking or attenuation of the attacks. This is particularly important to pay attention to for music characterized by acoustic instruments, percussion included, and, with varied and complex music, auto release is

Figure 29.6
The Universal Audio SSL mixbus compressor is modeled after the stereo compressor of the SSL G-series consoles. Here, ratio is set to 2:1, release to auto, and attack to 1 ms. © Universal Audio

likely to work better; automatically adapting to the dynamics of the music, the auto setting provides a smooth and musical release.

A compressor responds primarily to the peaks of the bass instruments, since the low frequencies have the most energy. This means that the bass drum will trigger compression on the overall mix, resulting in an audible ducking of high-frequency content as well that is particularly destructive to transients. To prevent the low frequencies from triggering the compressor, a side chain with a high-pass filter is inserted (if not already part of the compressor) to filter out the low frequency content of the signal. The side chain only controls the compressor, having no effect on the signal itself (see p. 246).

When applying mix bus compression, pay particular attention to the vocal, which has probably already been significantly compressed. As the vocal is on top of the mix, the added compression in the mix bus may ruin some vocal peaks.

TIPS

✓ If you do not own a suitable mix bus compressor or are uncertain how to use it, it would be better to leave it to the mastering engineer, who knows what compression and limiting do to a mix and who has the proper tools.

✓ The mix bus compression should be adapted to the song tempo and to the character of the music. When compressing the individual tracks of a mix, the attack and release settings of the compressor have lesser impact on the song timing; however, at the mix bus, the groove and the song pulse can be adversely affected.

✓ Set gain makeup to match the level of the processed signal to that of the unprocessed signal. Thus, when bypassing the compressor, it is easier to hear what the compression does to the mix. When the settings are fine-tuned, turn up the gain makeup (not the level of the stereo master, which would increase the compression) to utilize the headroom left.

✓ A slow release on an up-tempo song will choke the mix, while a release that is too fast may cause pumping effects that work against the pulse of the song. A quick attack and a medium release setting will attenuate the transients and boost the relative level of ambience and longer sounds.

Side Chaining

The side chain allows a mix function to be controlled by another signal than the one being processed. Since this might not seem obvious, here's an example: disc jockeys use side chain to automatically attenuate the music when talking over it. Practically, this is done by sending a copy of the mic signal to the side chain of a compressor inserted at the music channel. Talking into the mic automatically results in the compressor dimming the music, and just after the last word, the music returns to normal level. This is also known as "ducking."

In other words, the side chain is merely controlling the compressor—it is not a part of the mix. Most often a track that is already in the recording is used, and in addition to controlling a compressor, it can also be used to control a gate to modify the gain of a track when activated by the control signal.

Side chain is widely used in the electronic dance genres to control effects; for example, controlling the ON/OFF of a reverb or delay added to the vocal or a filter that gradually processes the sound of a synth. Also, de-essing uses a side chain; an EQ boosting the sibilance of the vocal is set up as a filter in the side chain, and the boosted sibilant track is sent to a compressor inserted on the vocal track, thereby automatically attenuating sibilance in the original vocal track (see p. 11).

Quite a few compressors have a built-in side chain filter; usually, this is a low-cut filter (with optional settings of off, 100 Hz, and 250 Hz), since it is mainly the low frequencies that trigger the compressor.

⊙ Audio example 29.01 demonstrates the use of side chain compression with a kick drum used to key the compression of a bass guitar.

The following are four examples on how to set up side chaining.

Side Chain Used at the Bass

Side chain is often used to control the balance between the bass drum and the bass for a tighter and more consistent low end and to gain a few extra dBs of headroom. This is done by letting the bass drum trigger a compressor that attenuates the bass on each beat of the bass drum. This is also an example of the technique known as ducking.

This example is based on Logic Pro, but the concept is the same in any DAW that has plug-ins with optional side chaining (sometimes also called "key in")—and is based on bass and bass drum as audio instruments, but is even simpler when it comes to audio tracks. Not until the bass drum and bass are completely mixed is the side chain set up to automatically control the balance between them.

a. In Logic, it is not possible to make an audio instrument track function as a side chain—only for audio tracks is this possible—and therefore the bass drum instrument is routed to bus 1.

b. Insert a compressor at the end of the plug-in chain on the bass instrument track. Since its purpose is to act solely as a side chain compressor, use its default settings (no auto gain, no limiting, etc.).

c. Connect the side chain of the compressor (in the upper right corner) to the output of bus 1, to which the bass drum has been routed.

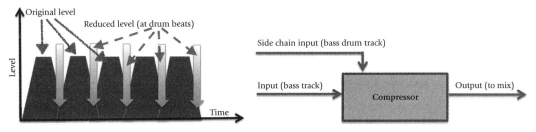

Figure 29.7
The bass drum is routed to the side chain input; its attack controls the attenuation of the bass track, and so the bass is briefly dampened by the drum beats.

d. Set attack to 0 ms, because the bass should be attenuated instantly when the bass drum triggers the compressor.

e. Set the compressor to hard knee and peak mode, since it is the peaks that will trigger attenuation. In addition, set the compressor gain to unity (0 dB) so that the bass level remains the same.

f. Set ratio between 4:1 and 10:1 (depending on the required attenuation). A 3–6 dB reduction is usually enough, while a ratio of 10:1 will almost mute the bass.

g. Set release according to how fast the bass should return to normal level—usually 20–50 ms. Longer release times may cause the bass to pump. Automatic release can be used on rhythms and tone lengths that are more varied than is standard in bass and bass drum grooves.

h. Adjust the threshold so that all attacks trigger the compressor by using your ears while checking the gain reduction meter. Only the peaks of the signals should make the compressor respond, so there is no benefit in setting the threshold lower than that.

247

Finally, the settings are fine-tuned to make the ducking work seamlessly in the mix. Not only does this tighten up the bottom end and reduce boominess from the summed bass frequencies—since the bass and bass drum often fight for space in the same frequency range—the setup also improves the feel of the timing and creates a few dBs of headroom to make the mix a little louder without the side effects resulting from strong compression of the entire mix.

Delay Automation on Vocals

Side chaining can be used to automate the delay added to the vocal. Insert a compressor with a side chain as the final plug-in on the aux containing the delay unit. Select the vocal track as the side chain input; the vocal track will now make the compressor attenuate the delay signal such that the level of the delay is attenuated when the vocal is active, returning to normal levels when there are no vocals. Thus, only at the last word in a phrase will the delay be evident.

Compressor settings:

a. Turn off auto gain.
b. The peak or RMS setting depends on the tempo (delay time) and the length of tones. Start by using peak.
c. Attack is set to 0–0.5 ms.
d. Set the release time so that the delay pops up immediately after the last word in a phrase.
e. Set the ratio to about 4:1 for the compressor to have a marked effect.
f. Experiment with the soft/hard knee and threshold settings, both of which depend on the material. Start with the hard knee.

A little experimentation is required to find the appropriate level of compression without the delay pumping. However, this method is a great alternative to manually drawing the delay level automation for the whole vocal track.

Frequency-Dependent Compression—The Pennywhistle

Frequency-dependent compression is normally associated with de-essing vocals, but it can also be used to tame a boomy acoustic guitar, electric bass, or cello. In particular, it is effective for reducing resonances in a recording that are due to acoustic problems in the recording space or with the instrument itself.

The pennywhistle can be used to illustrate the concept of frequency-dependent compression. This instrument can sound penetrating and metallic in the 1–4 kHz range, which is enhanced when it is recorded using close-miking, since the acoustics do not contribute to smoothing out its sound.

However, this sound can often be tamed using a compressor controlled by a side chain EQ:

a. Insert a compressor with side chain as the last plug-in on the pennywhistle track.
b. Select a parametric EQ as the side chain input controlling the compressor.
c. Set the side chain EQ to boost the frequency range of 1.6–3.5 kHz. Note: this only equalizes the signal controlling the compressor, not the signal itself.

d. Set the compressor ratio to 10:1 (approaching limiting). Threshold should be set low so that the entire signal is compressed. Set attack to 0.5 ms and release to 200 ms.

The effect of this is that the pennywhistle is attenuated when it has excessive frequency content in the 1.6–3.5 kHz range.

Make the Strings Sound Like a Banjo

Using effect devices in combination with side chaining can create interesting effects like making a twenty-five-person string ensemble sound like a banjo by running the strings through a gate that is triggered (i.e., opened) by a hi-hat. If the hi-hat plays eighth notes, the strings will also do that—almost sounding like the staccato that is characteristic of chord playing on the banjo.

Box 29.5 Mixing and Time

If, from the start of the recording, there is a clear aim for the sound of the final mix—and each instrument has a clear function in this—a recording may almost seem to mix itself. The musical performance is the raw material, so pay attention to an uncertain performance or a vague idea in the song, which requires a lot of editing and processing just to come together in the mix.

Depending on the raw material recorded and the genre, a mix may last from a few hours to several days. Renowned mixer Tom Lord-Alge spends about one day mixing a song (on top of the time used by his assistant to set up the tracks, the analog equipment, and the plug-ins according to the template that fits Lord-Alge's working methods). Here is an eight-hour model that can be used as a guide:

- Three hours setting up the rough balance between instruments (level) and their basic sound (EQ, compression, and reverb).
- A few hours more to fine-tune details of balance and processing, including the final decision on which instruments should dominate the mix and which should form the accompaniment.
- Subsequently checking the mix in the car and other play-back systems, if necessary making time to go back and make corrections.
- Involving musicians in the fine-tuning in the final stages.
- Finally, making different mixes with various balances between vocal and instrumental groups.

249

Leave a Little Headroom to the Mastering Engineer

Inexperienced engineers add stereo bus compression with the sole aim of making their mix LOUD—both to impress the musicians and out of fear that their customers will not understand why their mix is not as powerful as the commercial releases.

A great compressor/limiter (e.g., Waves L1 Ultramaximizer, Logic's Adaptive Limiter, or UA's Fairchild plug-in) might be able raise the stereo output to the volume level of a true master copy. They can also make the instruments blend better in the mix and make them richer in the low end and up-front in the midrange and the highs. This is fine for a customer mix, but to make this the final mix and send it to the mastering studio would be a mistake, limiting the opportunities for an experienced mastering engineer to make a great master copy.

Thus, when producing the stereo mix ready for mastering, it is important to bypass stereo bus compressors/limiters and to leave at least 3–6 dBs of headroom to the master engineer.

Box 29.6 Toto's "Africa"—A Complex Analog Recording with No Mastering Compression

Toto's "Africa," recorded in 1982 at the Sound Factory, Los Angeles, used three analog twenty-four-track machines kept in sync by timecode. In addition to the tripled vocal tracks (by David Paich) and the rest of the band, there were six tracks of the Yamaha GS1 (a pre-DX7 synth) using the kalimba preset, recorders, and quite a few percussion tracks.

This was before DAWs and the easy options of countless numbers of tracks and mix automation.

Like Queen's "Bohemian Rhapsody," "Africa" was a little ahead of its time, requiring that the song be mixed in sections, as the mixer channel count couldn't accommodate the large number of recorded tracks; the verses and the choruses were mixed separately and then spliced together on the analog tape master.

Since the console had no automation, the band assisted by "riding the faders," crowding around the desk and doing the mixes over and over until they got it right.

In common with working practice at the time, "Africa" was not processed with master compression (this was before the Loudness War began), which is why the great dynamics of the band performance are not flattened out, producing a song with a very strong musical expression, especially when the understated verse gives way to an explosive chorus.

30

Mastering

Mastering is the final touch on the mix before it is released, aiming for a cohesive sound and a higher, average volume level. Mastering also balances low end, midrange, and highs so that the finished product can be played back without excessive fluctuations in both level and balance between frequency ranges. Good mastering should translate across a variety of playback systems and media.

While adding tightness and punch, mastering also makes the instruments blend better, ensures consistency between tracks, and ultimately brings diverse elements together as a whole. However, mastering cannot correct fundamental imbalances that are already present in the mix.

Until about 1990, when even small record companies began to discover the benefits of allowing a mix to undergo this final touch and to be exposed to a set of critical ears that had not been involved in the recording and mixing process, nobody outside the mastering studios really knew what mastering was all about. Gradually, though, mastering spread to home studios, and by about 2000 mastering became almost synonymous with loudness.

However, in the professional industry, the mastering engineer is still the expert that is brought in for a fresh and objective perspective—someone knowing nothing about the compromises, limitations, and poor excuses that popped up during the recording and mixing.

The Mastering Studio

Mastering makes a good mix better and may improve a poor mix quite dramatically as well. In the mastering process, the mix is optimized using EQ, compression, limiting, and other tools to process the stereo width and depth.

The requirements of the mastering room are a completely linear space with a controlled reflection pattern and no standing waves. This requires balancing the acoustics using diffusers, absorbers, bass traps, and so forth (see p. 279). The monitors should not make bad music sound good; they should be neutral, clinical, and transparent, revealing clicks, noise, and the faintest distortion, and they should expose imbalances and flaws in general. They should also provide a perception of a three-dimensional sound stage; that is, they should accurately monitor both the stereo imaging and the depth.

Figure 30.1

Mastering engineer Bob Katz in front his racks of Crane Song, TC Electronic System 6000, Pendulum, Weiss EQ, and so on. Bob Katz wrote *Mastering Audio: The Art and the Science* in 2002, and on several YouTube videos he explains some of his tips and tricks. © Bob Katz

Passive monitors are used—monitors that have passive crossover components that split the audio signal and send each frequency band to a separate amp. Commonly used speakers are B&W, PMC, Quested, ATC, Neumann, and some of the larger Genelecs and Dynaudio monitors. Reference speakers like Dunlavy, Duntech Sovereigns, and Wilson Watt are also found in mastering facilities.

Overall, the acoustics and monitors of the mastering facility must ensure that the end result transfers: that it maintains the same balance and sounds right on any media or playback system.

Like the acoustics and monitors, mastering processors are quite different from those of the recording studio, generally being specialized, high-end processors able to deal with complex stereo mixes and to make both smaller and larger changes without signal degradation. Analog mastering processors usually have detented dials, allowing the change of parameters in fixed increments that can easily be recalled.

The D/A and A/D converters typically are from Prism, Benchmark, Lavry, and Antelope. The EQs and compressors are, among others, from Weiss, Crane Song, TC Electronic (the System 6000), Massenburger, Millennia, Brainworx, Tube-Tech, Manley, and Pultec, often connected in a chain like this:

D/A converter >> analog compressor >> analog EQ >> A/D converter >> digital multiband compressor >> digital EQ >> digital brickwall compressor >> limiter (often soft clip)

The specific processors in this chain are those preferred by the mastering engineer. Some devices may be set up for parallel processing (such as compression), and, almost always, a limiter is the last device, ensuring that the now mastered output is not distorted when sent off for mass production. The signal strength is crucial throughout the chain, since each processing stage affects the volume level. Therefore, levels are constantly monitored for clipping and distortion. The initial D/A converter is not used if the mix from the studio is on 1/2″ analog tape.

Using plugins (for example, Waves Masters Bundle or MD3 Stereo Mastering from TC Electronic), it is now feasible to imitate some of the processing that takes place in mastering. However, this does have fundamental shortcomings, since maintaining a powerful and dynamic signal without signal degradation is quite a challenge if dedicated and quality analog and digital processors are not present.

In addition to a clean signal chain, the required reference monitors and optimal acoustics are probably not present in the home studio; if mastering takes place in the same room as the mix, the acoustics will enhance any shortcomings of the mix. Also, the experience and knowledge of the mastering engineer should not be underestimated; for commercial releases, professional mastering will probably always pay off.

Figure 30.2

A typical mastering setup. Freed from the mixing desk, the hardware can be placed within easy reach of the listening sweet spot. © Bob Katz

Mastering for CD

Technically, mastering is the preparation of the final mix for the glass master (CD), including the addition of PQ codes, ISRC codes, and CD text. When mastering for MP3, the highest possible resolution is used (at least 256 kbps in the AAC encoding format is currently recommended), and Apple has also come up with the high-resolution SRC-encoding format of 44.1 kHz and 32-bit floating point to preserve the dynamics of 32-bit while eliminating the need for dithering.

When mastering for CD manufacture, three types of masters are distinguished:

- **The production master** is the final mix from the mix studio (a 24-bit/44.1 kHz audio file or 1/2″ analog tape) accompanied by a timesheet with track numbers and their durations and any notes for the mastering engineer.
- **The pre-master** is the mastering engineer's final master, which adds the ISRC and PQ encodings necessary for manufacturing a glass master. The pre-master is sent to the CD factory as a 16-bit/44.1 kHz audio file, DDP image file, or CDR together with the PQ sheet.
- **The glass master** is produced by the CD factory as a digital, bit-by-bit transfer from the pre-master. This is used as the copy master for the production of CDs for sale.

Box 30.1 CD-text

CD-Text is an extension added to the Red Book specifications of the audio CD in 1996 which specifies artist, song name, album, performers, arranger, and so forth. Along with the PQ code and ISRC data, the CD-Text is embedded as metadata on the CD's lead-in. CD-Text is only read by some CD players, mostly those in cars and CD-ROM drives.

iTunes, Windows Media Player, and similar software do not read CD-Text; they read only the automatically retrieved data of the titles subscribed to in the Gracenote Database.

MP3 files also contain CD-Text, while audio files such as WAV and AIFF do not contain such metadata.

Mastering for Online Streaming

The way we listen to music has changed dramatically in recent years; not only have we to a great extent replaced CD and downloads with streaming (in 2015 revenues from music streaming surpassed sales for physical formats of music in the United Kingdom and United States), but also listening to music on domestic audio equipment has been replaced by an extensive use of mobile telephones and computers as the playback medium.

Since the streaming services consider the individual tracks as part of an overall broadcast, this is gradually changing the way we master with regard to levels. Also, the data reduction used for streaming (mostly AAC, Vorbis, and sometimes MP3) can affect the quality of the delivered master.

Data Reduction

Generally, in streaming, the levels of data reduction determine the price:

- Low bit rate (high data reduction): mobile telephones / free.
- Medium bit rate: mobile desktop / subscription.
- High bit rate: desktop/subscription.

Data reduction, used even at high bit rates, will discard the highest and lowest frequencies and reduce stereo information almost to mono by matrixing into MS stereo while reducing the side information. Also, weak sounds (like reverb tails) that are partially masked by louder elements will be discarded.

Generally, the data reduction will distort loud peaks, and in practice, when mixing and mastering, it is almost impossible to address the deterioration introduced by the lowest bit rates. This would require heavily limited masters killing the transients and musical detail that are audible when reproduced at higher bit rates. Moreover, low bit rates are most often used for poor-quality earphones and for mobile telephone and computer speakers.

In practice, the deterioration introduced by the medium and high bit rates can only be addressed by keeping the level below −0.3–0.5 dBFS to avoid intersample peaks in the conversion to lower bit rates (MP3 and AAC).

Loudness Normalization

From 2013, streaming services gradually adopted different practices for loudness normalization inspired by television broadcast efforts to tame fluctuations in loudness between commercials and program content.

While FM radio processed a song by raising the perceived loudness so all music tracks sounded loud, online streaming instead measures the level of each track and adds loudness normalization to create a more pleasant and more consistent listening experience at a lower volume level.

In the pursuit of being "louder than the competition," FM radio often squeezed any internal dynamics out of a song regardless of how the track was mixed or mastered, making excessively loud masters sound even more distorted and crushed. In contrast to that, streaming services maintain the internal dynamics of a song.

The peak to loudness ratio (PLR) meter is used to determine the loudness normalization scaled in LUFS (loudness units referencing full scale). It is the average level that indicates how loud the music sounds, while peak levels tell us almost nothing about the perceived loudness. PLR calculates the difference between true peak level and the average loudness of a track resulting in an overall PLR level.

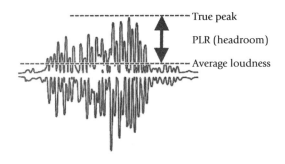

Figure 30.3

In 2013, Sound Check (SC) was integrated into Apple's iTunes Radio to make songs play back at consistent levels based on the peak to loudness ratio (PLR). SC also performs normalization in the iTunes app when SC is selected in Preferences. The sound check levels are stored in the ID3 tags; when SC is turned off, iTunes ignores the data in the tags. Users of Spotify, Tidal, and Apple Music can choose to switch off loudness normalization, but this is not an option in YouTube.

Confusingly (at time of writing), the streaming services adjust to different levels on the PLR:

- Apple: −16 LUFS (equivalent to an average loudness of −16 dB below 0 dBFS).
- YouTube: −13 LUFS.
- Spotify: −14 LUFS.
- Broadcast and television: −23 LUFS.

Spotify, as an example, streams tracks at around −14 LUFS. For a track with a loudness level of −6 LUFS, Spotify will decrease the level to −14 LUFS, while a track at −20 LUFS will be increased to −14 LUFS, thus securing a consistent playback level if, for example, a quietly mastered Miles Davis track is followed by a loudly mastered Metallica track.

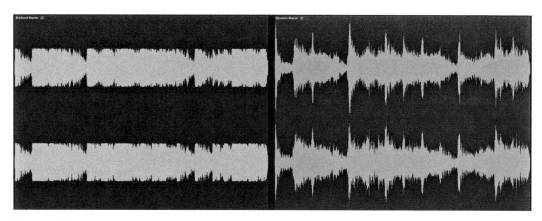

Figure 30.4

Contrasting music genres after normalization. As the PLR scale measures the average level, the quietly mastered jazz track on the right ends up sounding both louder and more dynamic than the heavy rock track on the left, since the jazz track takes advantage of the headroom.

The headroom (between loudness and true peak) leaves space to maintain dynamics in the mastering process, and this encourages engineers and artists to maintain dynamics, unless there is an artistic reason to compress or limit a music track. Therefore, to maintain sound quality and to make the track play back as loud as possible, make sure its PLR falls within the online platform's PLR max true peak level and the normalization level. Further reducing the dynamics of the music will not result in the final playback level being louder.

A track with both loud and quiet sections that varies significantly above and below the average reading might measure the same level on the PLR scale as a track having a consistent level at the average reading (i.e., no internal dynamics).

In the streaming environment, it is not the louder tracks but tracks that are more dynamic that stand out. From an artistic perspective, this means that, by including sections that drop in level, you can also have sections that are significantly louder than the average. In the long run, this might contribute to a return of internal dynamics in popular music, which have been largely absent since the Loudness War began in the late 1990s.

Mixing and Mastering

The newly introduced loudness meters—produced, for example, by Nugen Audio, TC Electronic, Sonnox, and iZotope—have become important tools for audio engineers who deliver to streaming services and broadcast media.

Raising a signal by 1 LUFS is the same as simply raising it by 1 dB, as 1LUFS equals 1 dB. Similarly, the loudness meter will read −14 LUFS when fed with a −14 dBFS sine tone.

Though dBFS and LUFS are similar, they are calculated differently, since LUFS tries to approximate the perception of loudness in human hearing by using some extra measurements:

- **Integrated loudness** measures the average loudness throughout the duration of a track.
- **Momentary loudness** (similar to the RMS/VU meter) measures the loudness of the past 400 ms.
- **Short-term loudness** measures the loudness of the past 3 s. During (longer) periods at a constant level, the integrated loudness and the short-term loudness will be similar.
- **True peak** measures peaks (intersample peaks included). The traditional peak meter does not read intersample peaks that exceed 0 dBFS (music mastered at a very hot level). True Peak meters use oversampling in order to measure those peaks above 0 dBFS.

Practically, this means that a track mastered to an overall integrated loudness of −11 to −12 LUFS and a short-term loudness of maximum −8 LUFS will fall within the optimal loudness normalization of the streaming services.

The Creative Process

Although a lot can be achieved, mastering can neither perform miracles nor fix everything wrong with the mix. While mastering can certainly make a mix stand out and sparkle, if the mix is fundamentally unbalanced (e.g., levels between instruments), it is always better to redo the mix.

At the initial stage, listening is vital, and this is equally so for the dialogue with the producer and the musicians to find out what their expectations of the mastering are. What sound are they looking for, which parts of the mixes are they happy with, and which parts have shortcomings? If you are unsure about which of two mixes will sound better after mastering, the mastering engineer will invite you to provide both. Often, it is agreed that some elements should be changed by going back to the mix to provide a better end result. If you are unsure about certain elements of the mix, it might be appropriate to provide the stems (see below). Using stems is an effective approach to addressing balance, EQ, and compression issues.

The better the mix, the better the result achieved in the mastering.

Generally, several of the following are accomplished in the mastering process:

257

- Customization of levels—normally along with compression and limiting to add punch and loudness.
- Placement of songs in a musical order for an album (taking the key, tempo, etc. into account) and adjustment of levels between tracks to make the individual songs match and the album sound whole.
- Adjustment of overall tonal balances by EQing to create a natural (i.e., genre-adapted) sound that adds openness, fullness, transparency, and so forth or to highlight or attenuate an instrument or group of instruments in the mix (some of this can also be achieved by varying compression in specific frequency bands).
- Removal of any resonances caused by the acoustics of the recording and/or mix studio across specific frequencies.
- Addition of an analog character to the mix.
- Fine-tuning of fade-ins and fade-outs and the addition of crossfades.
- Cutting and splicing of parts from different mixes.
- Adjustment of the pauses between songs to the tempos and feels of the songs (i.e., creating a musical flow).
- Adjustment of the stereo balance, often widening the stereo image of a one-dimensional mix.
- Addition of ambience (depth and width) using reverb.
- Removal of noise, hiss, and clicks (particularly in the lead-ins and the fades) and, in rare cases, noise reduction (crackles and other clicks).

Mastering Tools

Mastering EQ

This is used to smooth out imbalances in the mix's tonal layers and as a creative tool to improve the overall sound of the mix. Imbalances are often due to the fact that instruments are fighting for space in the same frequency ranges. Though it is impossible to separate a bass and a kick drum sitting in the same frequency range—this should have been dealt with in the mix—they can be balanced so that the mix maintains its weight and fullness without muddiness and loss of transparency. Likewise, imbalances resulting from the acoustics of the mixing room can be corrected.

In mastering, parametric EQ is the type that is mainly used, making it possible both to work with defined frequency areas (using a narrow Q) and to balance across a broad treble or bass range (a wide Q). Often, phase-linear EQ types are used to minimize the phase distortion resulting from EQing. Wide Qs are preferred in order to avoid ringing at the cut-off frequencies; a narrow Q is used only to surgically cut unwanted frequencies or to boost an instrument that is underexposed in the mix. For example, a surgical cut might be used to remove a room resonance triggered by the low bass string (at 41.2 Hz, the frequency of the low E) or a 60 Hz rumble from the mains.

Finally, it is often necessary to use the high-pass filter to reduce issues in the sub-bass range (below 60 Hz). This usually arises when several instruments have not been

Box 30.2 The Critical Frequency Ranges of Mastering

- The sub-bass range below 60 Hz is more felt as a physical impact than it is heard, and it provides tightness and impact (the kick drum and the bass), though the frequencies below 30 Hz may only rumble and choke the signal chain (see p. 156, low-cut or HPF).
- The range 60–200 Hz provides punch and warmth to most instruments but, if overemphasized on the instruments of the rhythm section, will make the mix woolly and boomy, while too little makes it thin and cold. This range contains the lower fundamentals of most instruments, and EQing may radically change the balance between instruments.
- The range 200–500 Hz gives fullness and weight to vocals, guitars, and piano. Too much enhancement here makes for a muddy and cluttered mix; too little makes it thin and weak. This range contains the mid/high fundamentals of many instruments, and EQing may radically change the balance between instruments.
- The range 500–1000 Hz gives body and definition to many instruments, but too much gain here makes them honky and nasal sounding, while too little makes them undefined. This range includes the higher fundamentals of most instruments, and EQing may radically change the definition of instruments.
- In the 2–4 kHz range, clarity, attack, and bite are to be found. Emphasizing this range too much will make instruments sound aggressive and tinny, while under-emphasizing it will make them sound soft or even stuffy. This range is important for the intelligibility of words and thus is vital to the vocal track.
- The range 4–10 kHz provides openness and clarity. Too much enhancement makes the mix sibilant and cutting; too little results in a lack of presence and crispness and might make the music seem distant.
- The range 12–16 kHz provides air and transparency. Too much gain in this range makes the music sound hissing and piercing; too little will make it sound confined and nontransparent. See p. 154 for more on tonal layers and the frequency ranges of the instruments.

subjected to a low-cut filter when mixing, mixing that, moreover, might have been done on nearfield monitors with inaccurate low-end reproduction.

In EQing, the settings should normally be the same for L (left) and R (right) to avoid phase issues; that is, use a stereo EQ or EQs with a stereo link (meaning that one set of knobs controls both channels).

Often, the use of EQ can be restricted to a boost of the sub-bass, typically combined with a cut in the 100–250 Hz range (to reduce boominess) and the addition of air in the 12–16 kHz range.

Compression and Limiting

Compression and limiting are used for two widely different purposes:

- To make the music more homogeneous and dynamically consistent.
- To make the music loud and powerful.

Uneven dynamics—for example, the snare, vocal, or guitar suddenly seeming prominent on some beats—cause the mix to be perceived as incoherent. By contrast, a well-chosen compression glues instruments and vocals together in the mastering. The processing also brings out the details of a track—nuances that are indistinct and not heard in the mix—and hopefully the essence of the music as well. This may also bring out noises and sibilance that are not obvious in the mix, and so de-essing might be necessary.

Figure 30.5
At the top, the original stereo mix waveform is displayed, while the middle is moderately compressed, and a hard-compressed waveform is at the bottom.

Compression smooths out the dynamic fluctuations of the mix and also frees up headroom so that the overall level can be raised to the digital maximum of 0 dB. Clipping of transients is seen on the hard-compressed waveform.

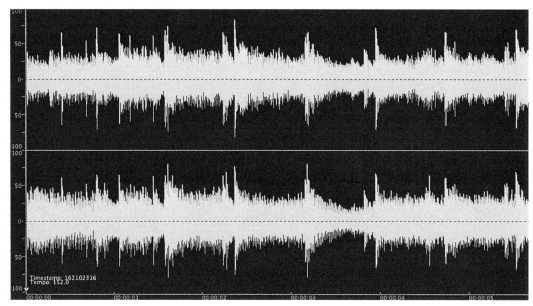

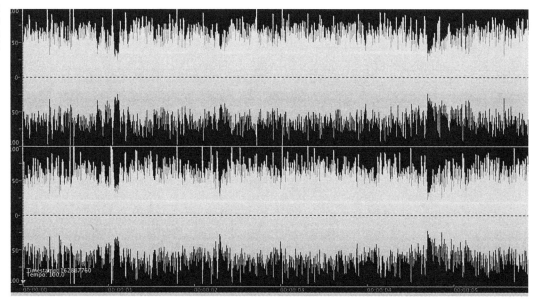

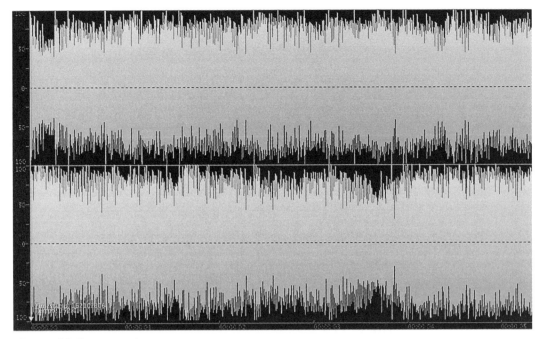

Figure 30.5 (Continued)

However, too much compression will produce a sound that is no longer dynamic. Mastering involves finding the sweet spot of loudness where the level is powerful and punchy but fits the music genre without the dynamics being leveled out and transients flattened. This is the reason why compression is not used when mastering classical music, so that the dynamics of the loud passages of the mix are preserved, although occasionally parallel compression might be used to make soft passages in the music clearer when listened to in a noisy environment (such as when driving). In jazz and acoustic genres, compression is also used to a lesser extent, though here it varies greatly with the type of rhythm section, style, and so on.

Most pop and rock releases are heavily compressed during mastering.

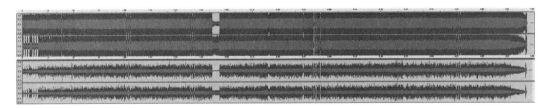

Figure 30.6

Metallica's album *Death Magnetic*, released in 2008, made both fans and professionals respond negatively because the music was so over-compressed and so pumping that there was no musical expression or dynamic variation left. This can be seen on the upper stereo waveform of the song "My Apocalypse."
A mix that is so powerful has undergone a very hard brickwall limiting that allows all music elements to reach 0 dBFS, banging hard up against the threshold and thus being clipped. The waveform becomes squeezed, and the total output becomes LOUD! According to Ted Jensen, mastering engineer on the album, the mix received for mastering was already heavily limited. In contrast, the Guitar Hero version of "My Apocalypse" was quite different and, soundwise, technically far better than the CD release. The Guitar Hero version is seen in the lower stereo waveform and is 10 dB lower in average output.

261

Multiband Compression

Low frequencies contain more energy (i.e., a stronger electrical signal) than the high frequencies. Consequently, the lows trigger the compressor more than the midrange and the highs of the music. This is why many compressors have a side chain (see p. 246) that filters frequencies below 100–200 Hz when activated in order to prevent low frequency content from unintentionally triggering the compression.

When complex frequency content in particular is compressed, this unintentional compression can become an issue, since you would not want a powerful bass note to trigger the compression of a weak stroke on the acoustic guitar just because they occur simultaneously.

For this reason, the multiband compressor is designed to enable frequency-dependent compression of complex signals like a stereo mix. In mastering, this can be used to create a punchy mix without completely squeezing the dynamics of the music. Multiband compressors split the audio signal into a number of frequency bands—usually three bands on high-end compressors—so that the low end (below about 300 Hz) can be compressed hard, the midrange (0.3–4 kHz) moderately, and the high end (4 kHz and above) more discreetly, since the compressor bands are set individually for threshold, ratio, attack, release, and gain makeup. The split signals are then merged and sent to a limiter that controls the peaks that might result from the combined signal.

Hard compression of the bass and the kick thus provides a tight and full low end, while vocals, cymbals, and piano, for example, can be discreetly smoothed in their dynamics without being destructively affected. Thus, multiband compression can also be used as a tool to balance the tonal layers of the mix without using EQ, since gain makeup can be used to enhance the individual frequency bands by, for instance, opening up the midrange or attenuating the low end.

The benefit of multiband compression is that you can avoid pumping and squeezing of the instrument attacks by compressing only selected frequencies. The drawback is the more or less audible signal degradation of the crossover frequencies in less well-designed compressors; this is quite obvious, for example, with Logic's Multipressor. The Waves Phase Linear Multiband does a good job, but in order to completely avoid signal degradation, quality equipment like the TC Electronic System 6000 is required.

As plugins, multiband compressors are widely used at the mix bus. However, using them is a bad idea for the production master (from the mix studio) that is delivered into the hands of the mastering engineer; they should only be used to impress the client and then quietly disabled before production mastering.

Limiting

Limiting is often used to tame transients that have successfully passed through the compressor. It is also used to wring the last few dBs out of the song in pure volume terms, because limiting dampens the transients (typically the instrument attacks) and thus adds 3–6 dB extra headroom before audible distortion sets in. In dedicated mastering devices, this is often done by the soft limiter, which is also found in some plug-ins. As with compressing, be aware that the limiting might overly affect or even destroy transients of (particularly) acoustic instruments.

When used discreetly, soft limiting is described as having an analog character because, like analog tape, it attenuates transients.

Limiting is also used independently of the compressor in mastering, often as digital brickwall limiting, and, used in moderation, this preserves more natural dynamics than compression.

Box 30.3 The Loudness War

The Loudness War started in the 1990s and was an undeclared competition to make releases sound louder in radio broadcast and on CD. Ever since, in the pop and rock genres, many masters have been made as powerful as technically possible, the idea being that "higher than anything else" attracts attention and that louder always seems better sounding. The same mechanism has driven commercials and promos in radio and television, with ads becoming more powerful than the program content itself.

The subjective side effect is that heavily compressed music becomes tiring to listen to for long periods due to the monotonous dynamics and a constant high sound pressure level. The objective side effect is distortion, which might not be noticed because the DAW meters are not fast enough to read any signal exceeding 0 dBFS—called the intersample peaks. The harder the compression, the more intersample peaks are generated, which, when converted from digital to analog, cause D/A converters to distort (digital clipping).

The Loudness War escalated during the latter half of the 1990s and seems to have reached a peak around 2009–2011 when brickwall limiting could no longer squeeze any more dBs into the digital medium. In 2013, at the AES convention, mastering engineer Bob Katz declared the Loudness War over, basing his claim on the fact that Apple's iTunes Radio by default is regulated by the Soundcheck algorithm for a fixed maximum level of −16 LUFS (which is equivalent to an average loudness of −16 dB below 0 dBFS full scale; see p. 300). Defined in 2010 by the internationally accepted ITU-R BS.1770 standard and gradually adopted by a large part of the broadcast TV and radio media in order to normalize levels, this algorithm provides Apple consumers and others with a consistent average level without the need to turn levels up and down.

However, fixed maximum levels mean that music being mastered louder is automatically turned down 6 dB or more in iTunes and Spotify, for example, resulting in a flat and dull sound compared to tracks that utilize the dynamic range available.

Therefore, true peak meters (produced, for example, by Nugen Audio or TC Electronic) are an important tool for manufacturers in the field of broadcast media. Among other uses, the true peak meter measures the average loudness of a track.

In the CD market, the Loudness War has not yet ended, though more audio professionals are becoming aware of the drawbacks of very loud mastering. This is underscored by the fact that consumer surveys indicate that listeners do not like heavily compressed music.

However, brickwall limiting can also be used to make the music very loud, which, of course, will reduce the dynamics severely. At the same time, brickwall limiters tend to increase distortion (in drastically clipping the amplitude, square-wave distortion can be introduced), which is why many mastering engineers prefer analog-style processors.

TIPS

✓ Limiting works musically when the volume is boosted with minimal impact on the dynamics of the music. With fast attack (1–2 ms) and a fast release (depending on the musical pulse and tempo), 6 dBs of limiting can be achieved without an overly audible effect on the dynamics.

✓ With a mix that lacks impact, compression works best. First, set the threshold quite high—a ratio at 3–3.5:1—with a fast release of 250 ms. Then, when compression sets in, fine-tune the ratio and threshold (these are interdependent) and then the attack and release until the desired effect is achieved.

✓ Attack and release should match the rhythm and pulse of the music. If attack is set too short, it will cause transients to be strongly attenuated, and this sounds particularly unnatural on acoustic instruments (snare, cymbals, acoustic guitar, trumpet, piano, etc.). If the release is set too long, the compressor will not reset fast enough to let the next transient slip through uncompressed. Visually, the gain reduction meter should move rhythmically with the pulse of the music and approach 0 dB (i.e., no compression) several times per measure—otherwise the compression will sound like a special effect, resulting in evened-out dynamics and pumping effects that work against the musical pulse.

✓ Multiple compressors can be used in the mastering chain:
  • One providing width by means of MS stereo.
  • One adding top and mid.
  • One adding low end and density.
  • Finally, a limiter at the end of the chain.
These compressors can be set up either for series or parallel processing. Only the limiter should always be placed by itself and last.

✓ A high-pass side chain filter can be set to prevent the compressor responding to frequencies lower than 100–150 Hz; this lets you compress overhead cymbals and the like while preserving a powerful, punchy low end.

Mid-Side Processing

MS stereo—or mid-side stereo—as a microphone technique consists of a cardioid mic (mid) and a figure-of-eight mic (side) in conjunction with an MS decoder or three channels on the mixer. MS stereo can be decoded to L and R stereo with variable stereo width (see p. 146). The more the mid signal in the mix, the more central the content, while more side highlights the width of the mix. The mid signal alone is used to decode for mono.

In mastering, MS processors are used to control the stereo width. This is achieved by either boosting the side (or attenuating the mid) to enlarge the stereo width or by reducing the side signal to narrow the width. MS stereo should be used with great care, because it can change the mix balance between instruments and vocals that are panned.

Bit Resolution

In editing (using compression, EQ, etc.), the word length (the number of bytes [1 byte = 8 bits] used per sample) of digital is increased, and therefore the mastering should be done with the greatest possible resolution. In practice, 24-bit audio files are sufficient, since that is well over the 16–18 bits that the best speakers and headphones are able to reproduce in terms of dynamic range.

A consensus has yet to be achieved as to whether recordings at higher sampling frequencies (e.g., 88.2 kHz or 176.4 kHz—rates that certainly improve the resolution while editing) sound better, since frequencies above the audible range create intermodulation distortion (see p. 220) within that audible range and in any analog audio devices used in the studio. Currently, it is mostly 44.1 kHz that is used for audio while, 48 kHz is used for video and movies.

Box 30.4 Vinyl Mastering

Though the mastering processing is for the most part the same regardless of the end product (vinyl, digital distribution, or CD replication), there are some crucial differences between them.

The Technical Stuff

- The word length for CD has to be 16 bit, while for vinyl the optimum is 24 bit.
- Higher-resolution file formats (i.e., usually 24-bit, but also 48, 96, or even 192 kHz sampling rates) can be used. However, if hi-res files are not available, a great CD master at 16-bit 44.1 kHz will easily meet the physical limitations of the vinyl medium.
- For digital distribution and CD replication, the delivery to the mastering facility is either an individual file (WAV or AIFF) or a single DDPi file, whereas for vinyl two files (one for each side of the record) are delivered.

  Other issues are mostly due to the mechanical and physical limitations of vinyl.

The Dynamic Range

A master for CD and digital distribution can be compressed or limited to 0 dBFS (on the peak meter scale; see p. 300), while the physical constraints of vinyl make it appropriate to use the average level, the RMS level (see p. 300), measured on the VU scale. The RMS measures the average level of the total waveform (both the amplitude and the duration of peaks in the signal), thus setting a lower limit to how hot the vinyl record can be cut when being transferred to vinyl by the cutting engineer. Heavily clipped masters can only be accommodated on vinyl if they are

---

drastically reduced in level. However, the RMS level leaves plenty of headroom above the average signal for peaks and transients, which is why it is better to make a more dynamic master for the vinyl release—and the good news is that a less compressed and more dynamic master will also sound louder.

A powerful and dynamic bass and low end can cause the needle to jump, and the cutting engineer will apply compression and/or EQ to deal with this. This is an old and well-known issue that made for a lot of restrictions on the use of close-miking of the bass drum and the bass back in the early days of rock 'n' roll.

It would be fair to say that George Martin and the Beatles took part in the Loudness War way back in 1965 by experimenting with heavy compression of the bass on "Paperback Writer" to get around the restrictions of vinyl and to match the louder bottom end of contemporary American releases.

Additionally, the inner grooves of vinyl have more distortion from the tracking (becoming progressively worse as the record wears). The longer each side of the LP is, the closer together the grooves have to be, often requiring the cutting engineer to reduce the peak levels. This is why 12″ singles, with a wide groove spacing, are cut at much higher volumes than LPs.

Frequency Response

A bass-cut filter is used around 35 Hz and is often combined with a roll-off below 60–80 Hz. This is regularly compensated for by adding a bass peak around 200 Hz.

Vinyl also has problems accommodating excessive high-frequency content, such as vocal sibilance and loud hi-hats. Such content will cause distortion and necessitate limiting the overall high-frequency content of the track.

In addition, the frequency response of the disc is much better in the outer grooves, since the stylus is moving relatively much faster and so provides greater space for data per revolution; the result is a better low- and high-end response.

Stereo Separation

In the cutting process, stereo signals are separated into L−R and L+R (MS stereo; see p. 146); the L−R signal has less dynamic range than the L+R signal.

As this sets limits to the cutting levels, it is recommended that L and R channels be as identical as possible. Try to avoid pronounced stereo effects (use the phase meter in the DAW) and check the mono compatibility while mixing. Also, pan instruments with a heavy bass content to the center to make louder cutting possible.

In minimalist recordings (mostly classical and acoustic music), the phase differences between channels should be minimized if cutting to vinyl. Therefore, near-coincident techniques (see p. 144) are recommended, because spaced omnis can often create phase issues.

If the master is to be transferred to CD or converted to a MP3 file, it should be converted to 16-bit, as this is the resolution of the CD format. If 24-bit audio files are transferred to CD, the last 8 bits are simply thrown away with a noticeable depreciation heard as quantization noise in the weak passages, distortion, and a collapse of the stereo image.

Dithering is a technique used to ensure that as much as possible of the sound quality of the 24-bit resolution is preserved. An appropriate dithering algorithm produces 16-bit audio with a performance of 18 bits or better. Moreover, those dithering algorithms utilizing noise shaping also mask the quantization noise and distortion that occurs during the bit reduction. Bit reduction alone will not mask any quantization noise.

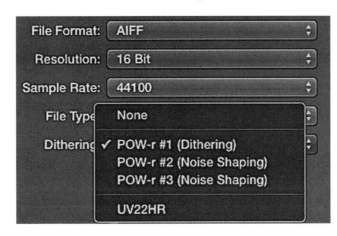

Figure 30.7

In Logic, the dithering algorithms are selected via the Bounce button (on stereo master), found in the same place as the file formats, bit resolution, and so on.

Pro Tools, Cubase, Logic, Digital Performer, and so on license various dithering algorithms, of which POW-R (Psychoacoustically Optimized Wordlength Reduction) is the most widely used and respected in the audio industry.

- POW-R Type 1 only provides dithering and can be used for most purposes and genres.
- POW-R Type 2 also adds noise shaping. Since this extends the dynamic range of the music, this algorithm is better for music that includes soft passages.
- POW-R Type 3 likewise adds noise shaping and is the one recommended by mastering engineer Bob Katz.

Apogee UV22 is also available in some DAWs and is comparable to POW-R Type 1. The UV22HR algorithm, found in Cubase, Logic, and Nuendo, also adjusts the algorithm to the selected bit resolution and optimizes dithering for data-reduced formats such as AAC and MPEG.

Stem Mastering

Traditionally, mastering engineers are only given the stereo mix, meaning that they have to work within certain constraints. Since instruments are competing for space with each other in the frequency layers of the mix (such as the kick and the toms competing with the bass, the piano with the guitar, and many midrange instruments grabbing space from the vocal), EQing will affect all instruments in the selected frequency band. EQing can also critically shift a carefully set up mix balance between instruments.

Additionally, when applying heavy compression and limiting to reach today's loudness goals, the mastering engineer might require some options to maintain clarity and transparency while at the same time maintaining the aim of the mix. By using extreme limiting on a stereo mix, the trade-offs are loss of transient detail, loss of transparency and mix detail, shifting of instrument levels, and midrange frequency buildup.

This is why stem mastering has become increasingly widespread, since it provides the opportunity to use EQ, limiting, and compression without these trade-offs. Stem mastering processes a mix by breaking it down into several manageable pieces—that is, stereo stems. The stem approach allows the mastering engineer the opportunity to make larger or smaller changes to separate mix elements before the final compression and limiting are applied to the complete mix.

Stem mastering as a technique is derived from stem mixing. Just as in stem mixing, audio tracks that have features in common or that should be processed in the same way are grouped in stereo stems or tracks to allow for individual signal processing of each stem. The kick drum, toms, and bass can be grouped and EQed and compressed differently from the stem containing the snare, the cymbals, and the acoustic guitar in order to maintain transients and clarity. Likewise, the vocals, the guitars and keyboards, and the horn section can each have their own stereo stem and processing during mastering. Thus, stem mastering makes it possible to produce a finished master with enhanced clarity, depth, and transparency while also having the sought-after perceived loudness.

As should be clear from all of the this, you cannot expect a result back from the mastering house that sounds identical to the original mix (this has long been the case—with vinyl cutting, for example, the engineer had to make changes to the mix that were largely dictated by technical limitations in the vinyl medium). Certainly, though, you should make use of the opportunity to send instructions to the mastering engineer along with your mix (and it might also be beneficial for the producer or band members to attend the final part of the mastering process).

PART V

Acoustics

31

Phase and Comb Filtering

Physically, sound spreads as a moving front of pressure through the air, a sound wave. Graphically, this can be displayed as an oscillation. Thus, a sound wave with no overtones (i.e., an oscillation having only the fundamental frequency) can be depicted as a simple sinusoidal oscillation (a sine wave or a pure tone), while a composite (or complex) tone with overtones above the fundamental frequency has a more complex waveform that looks more like the typical waveforms in the editing window of the DAW.

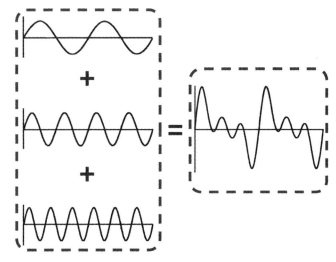

Figure 31.1
Three simple oscillations form a composite oscillation when added together (interference). The vertical axis represents the volume level and the longitudinal axis the frequency.

When shown graphically, an oscillation is regarded as having completed 360°, or a full cycle, if it passes through the 0 dB line twice when moving (graphically) in the same direction (this is easier to see when the waveform is that of a pure tone). This is called the wave cycle (or period) if plotted over time or the wavelength if plotted over distance traveled. The volume level of the oscillation is called the amplitude and is measured in dBs.

Two identical signals having their peaks and dips at the same time are said to be in phase, and so the amplitude of the two signals will be doubled when combined (for example, when they are reflected by a wall or picked up by a microphone). If a copy of a

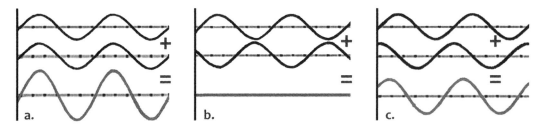

Figure 31.2

To the left, the amplitude of two sound waves in phase are added when they are combined.
In the middle, two identical sound waves, 180° out of phase, cancel out when combined (this is the fundamental principle of active noise-canceling headphones). To the right, if two sound waves that are partially out of phase are combined, the amplitude is increased in some places and reduced in others.

signal is shifted to start half a cycle later, it is said to be 180° out of phase with respect to the original signal; the one signal peaks while the other dips. This results in phase cancelation as the composite signal is canceled out completely.

Both sound and electricity are oscillations, and they both share these properties.

The Comb Filter Effect

Figure 31.3

The comb filter effect is so called because the resulting curve of the phase-canceled frequencies looks like a comb.

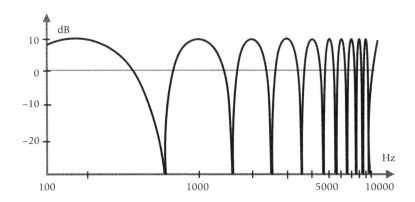

When two identical composite tones that are out of phase (other than 180°) are mixed, the result is a comb filter effect. In an acoustic space, comb filter effects are generated when the direct sound is mixed with the initial reflections from a surface. The reflected sound wave will arrive later at the ear or mic compared to the direct signal, thereby phasing out some frequencies completely while attenuating or boosting others. Comb filter effects are also generated by a monitor placed close to reflecting boundaries (walls, a mixer, etc.; see pp. 281–282). The first-order reflections are the reflections that have only been reflected by one surface; thus they still contain enough energy to have a noticeable phase effect with some frequencies from the direct signal. The resulting signal is therefore colored and does not constitute a true representation of the original signal.

The comb filter effect is easy to simulate. Combine a sound file (such as any finished mix of music) with a delayed copy of itself in the DAW. Depending on the size of the delay and the frequency content, the result can be everything from a chorus-like effect

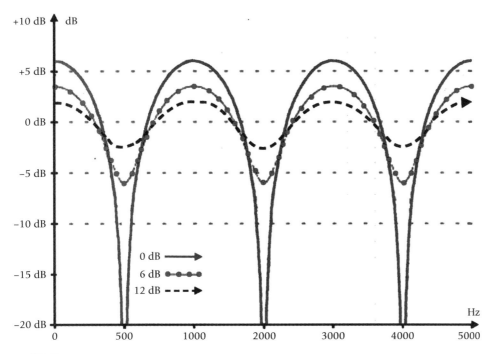

Figure 31.4

An example of the comb filter effect caused by the direct signal mixed with reflections delayed by 1 ms. In practice, this happens when a mic (or speaker) is placed 34.4 cm (the wavelength of 1 kHz) from a reflecting wall. The interference pattern resulting from the two waveforms is shown here for reflections that are attenuated by 3, 6, and 12 dB relative to the direct signal (depending on the absorption characteristics of the wall surface). 0 dB (the solid line) is strongly comb filtered, since the reflection is as strong as the direct signal. The phase-canceled frequencies are harmonically related, having dips at 500 Hz, 1.5 kHz, 2.5 kHz, and so on while being boosted at 0 Hz, 1 kHz, 2 kHz, etc.

to a thin or hollow sound. Start with a 3 ms delay and increase in 3 ms intervals. Short delays result in clear phasing in the treble range, gradually affecting the mid frequencies. At 30–40 ms, the delay assumes the character of a repeat—only creating comb filter effects in the lows and the low-mids.

Multi-Mic Recording and Phase

When we are recording music using a single mic in the ideal acoustics, we normally need not worry about phase shifts. Here, the reflections create a pleasant reverberation. However, in less than ideal acoustics, the phase of sound waves becomes critical, because the early reflections from side walls and ceilings interfere with the original signal, boosting some frequencies and attenuating others.

A mic placed close to a reflecting surface (a wall, a glass pane, or a table) picks up the direct signal and, a little later, the reflected signal with almost the same level. This results in the potential for comb filtering at some frequencies.

The same problem—the signal being picked up twice or more but time-shifted—always appears in multi-mic recordings due to spill between mics and instruments. Often, this can be solved by isolating or screening off the mics and instruments (see p. 289) or, when this is not possible, by observing some basic rules for multi-mic recording (see below—the 3:1 rule).

Box 31.1 Notes, Frequency, and Wavelengths

The wavelength of a sound is found by dividing 344 m/s (the speed of sound in air) by its frequency. Thus, the wavelength of a 1 kHz signal is 344 / 1,000 = 0.344 m or 34.4 cm. An upright or electric bass ranges across three octaves. The wavelengths of its open strings are shown below along with other relevant figures:

Note	Frequency	Wavelength
E1 (the E string)	41.2 Hz	8.35 m
A1 (the A string)	55 Hz	6.25 m
D2 (the D string)	73.42 Hz	4.69 m
G2 (the G string)	98 Hz	3.51 m
	344 Hz	1 m
	1 kHz (= 1000 Hz)	34.4 cm
	16 kHz	21.5 cm

The corresponding information for the guitar can be found by multiplying the frequency by 2 and dividing the wavelength by 2, since the guitar is tuned an octave above the bass.

The speed of sound in air varies according to a number of factors, including temperature and humidity, but 344 m/s is a good figure to use for the typical recording studio.

Critical Distances and Frequencies

A reflected frequency delayed by a whole number of cycles (1, 2, 3, 4, etc.) will have a boosted amplitude, while a delay of 1/2, 1 1/2, and so on will more or less cancel out the frequency (see figure 31.2).

In air at 20° C, the speed of sound is 344 meters per second. A composite tone with a fundamental of 1 kHz (1000 cycles per second) will therefore have a wavelength of 34.4 cm and a wave cycle of 1 ms.

Thus, this sound, if reflected and arriving at the microphone with a delay of 1 ms compared to the direct sound, oscillates in phase with the direct sound where there are overtones at 1 kHz, 2 kHz, 3 kHz, and 4 kHz, and so forth, and these will be amplified. Where there are overtones at 1.5, 2.5 kHz, and 3.5 kHz, and so on, they will be subject to phase cancelation and so will be attenuated.

In this way, reflected sound waves create comb filter effects in mic recordings (or in the control room when reflected monitor signals arrive at the listening position with a delay).

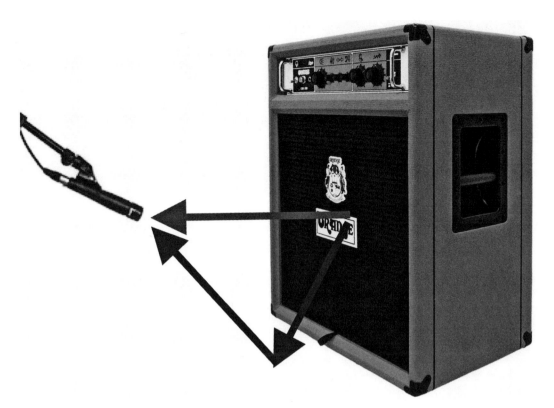

Figure 31.5
A mic placed 15 cm from the speaker and 40 cm above the floor will capture reflected sound that has traveled an extra 69 cm. This equates to a 2 ms delay, resulting in phase boosts at 500 Hz, 1 kHz, 1.5 kHz, and so on, and phase cancelations at 750 Hz, 1.25 kHz, 2 kHz, and so on in the combined signal captured by the mic. The comb filtering resulting from these reflections is clearly heard on the recorded signal.

How to Avoid Phase Cancelation

In recordings using two or more mics, phase issues are reduced first of all by pointing the mics directly at the primary source and by placing the other sources further away and, if possible, in the nulls of these mics. Phase cancelations are most evident between signals having (nearly) the same volume level, so always keep a distance away from reflecting surfaces and between instruments. For this reason professional studios have large recording spaces, giving the possibility to separate instruments and to ignore early reflections. Screens and absorbing panels greatly enhance isolation (see p. 291) and also reduce reflections.

In the following, the most commonly used precautions for multi-mic recording are described.

The 3:1 Rule

When using two or more mics to simultaneously record separate sound sources, the best results are achieved by using the 3:1 rule. If mic 1 is 1 m away from its sound source, place the second mic 3 m away from mic 1. More mics can be added following the same rule, and the signals captured by

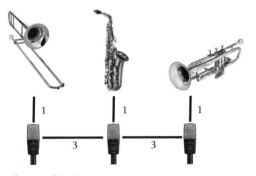

Figure 31.6
Three mics capturing three separate sound sources should be located (at least) three times the distance from each other as the distance between mic and source. This rule also applies to more than three mics.

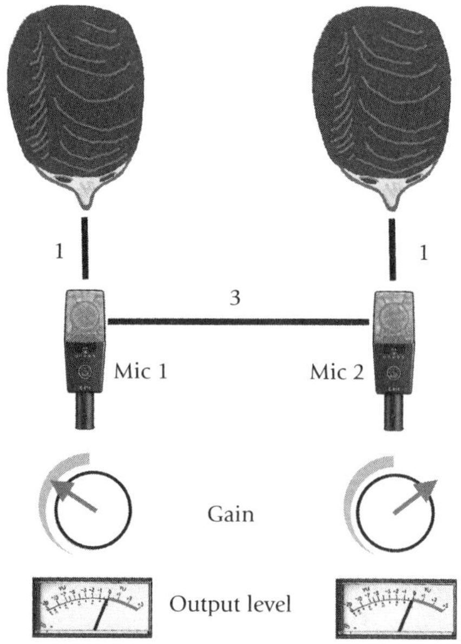

Figure 31.7
The 3:1 rule is not effective if there is a great difference in gain between the two mic preamps. If a powerful singer (mic 1) and a weak one (mic 2) are recorded simultaneously in the same room, mic 1 is reduced in gain in order not to overdrive the input stage, and mic 2 is boosted so that they both have the same signal level in the output. Thus, mic 2 will capture an increased spill from the powerful singer, resulting in phase shifts on the mic 1 signal when the two signals are mixed.

mic 2, mic 3, and so on will interfere as little as possible with the signals picked up by mic 1 when all are mixed together.

The 3:1 rule works because the distance between the mics reduces the volume level of the spill between mics. As the volume level of the delayed signal captured by mic 2 is substantially lower than that captured by mic 1, the comb filter effect is reduced accordingly. However, a slight coloring of certain frequencies remains unless screens are also used. Complete phase cancelations can only occur where the signals have equal strength.

Phase shifts are particularly audible on the transients of acoustic and percussive instruments like the snare. When recording the drum kit using two OH mics, always keep the same distance from each overhead mic to the center of the snare drum, thereby ensuring that the snare sound reaches the two OH mics at the same time. This reduces phase shifts significantly in the OH mics.

Using Track Delay to Combat the Comb Filter Effect

The time delay of a reflected signal can be calculated by measuring the distance (in meters) and dividing this by the speed of sound (assume 344 m/s).

A 34.4 cm increase in the sound wave path (e.g., traveling an extra 17.2 cm to a reflective wall and back) produces a delay compared to the direct signal path that is calculated as follows:

$$0.344 \text{ m} / 344 \text{ m/sec} = 0.001 \text{ sec} = 1 \text{ msec delay.}$$

An increase of 1 m results, therefore, in a 2.91 ms delay.

Similarly, the delay of a sound arriving at differently placed mics can be calculated. This is quite useful when recording the drum kit using OH mics, since phase shifts, if present, are clearly heard on the snare attacks as flanging when the OH and the snare tracks are mixed. By measuring the distance from the snare head to the OH mics, the delay can be calculated; if 1 m, the delay will be 2.91 ms, and if the OH mics are 70 cm above the snare drum, it takes 2.03 ms for the signal to reach the OH mics.

Usually, phase issues in the OH mics can be solved in the DAW by manually moving the OH tracks into sync so that the snare attacks on the OH tracks fit those on the snare track. If you know the exact time delay, the OH track can quite simply be moved into sync. Some DAWs require the time to be converted into tempo and time signature. In Logic, a sixteenth note corresponds to 240 ticks, one four-beat measure or bar thus being 3,840 ticks. At a tempo of 120 bpm (i.e., two beats per second), one measure lasts two seconds, and so the delay at 120 bpm is 3,840 ticks/2,000 ms = 1.92 ticks per ms—that is, approximately four ticks in 2 ms.

When using OH mics at a distance of 70 cm from the snare drum, therefore, moving the OH tracks 4 ticks to the left improves the phase between the OH tracks and the snare track. Keep in mind that anything else picked up by the OH mics will be delayed as well. Usually, a delay of 2 ms means little for cymbals and toms, but watch out for any timing issues.

However, an instrument picked up by the OH mics at 3 m distance cannot be manually moved into sync without it causing problems for the internal timing of the drums. Phase correction plug-ins are available, such as Little Labs by Universal Audio, with which the time correction can be entered in milliseconds.

A Visual Phase Check

An alternative to calculating the time delay is to move the tracks into place visually.

In the above example, the time delay of the snare in the OH tracks can clearly be seen in the waveforms when enlarged to the sample level. By comparing the two waveforms and using the attacks of the snare as reference points, the snare is easily moved into sync.

In general, the phase can be checked visually in multi-mic recordings by enlarging the waveforms of tracks on which an instrument has been picked up at different distances. However, there are plenty of circumstances in which a track cannot just be moved into place, because this would create timing issues for the instrument that is closest to mic—it is always best to guard against phase cancelation in the first instance when recording.

32

The Control Room and the Monitors

While the hardware gap between the professional and the home/project studio has been shrinking with the development of digital technology, this is not the case with the physical space and the acoustics of the sound studio. While the price of first-rate equipment has been in freefall, prices of property and space have continued to rise, exposing the differences between the great professional studios of the past and their modern replacements: the bedrooms, chicken shacks, and garages used for the home/project studio.

However, a growing understanding of the importance of the acoustics can be seen in the fact that many project studios are beginning to improve their acoustics. An increasing number and variety of acoustic panels, diffusers, vocal boxes, and so forth are available to treat often less than ideal recording spaces and control rooms in order to improve results and to avoid unpleasant surprises when the final mix is shipped out to the real world.

The acoustics of a room are determined primarily by its size, then by its shape and the materials covering its boundary surfaces. Most home/project studios are rectangular, since this is the cheapest way to build a room. Fundamentally, though, the acoustics of small, rectangular rooms are far from suitable for recording or for monitoring a

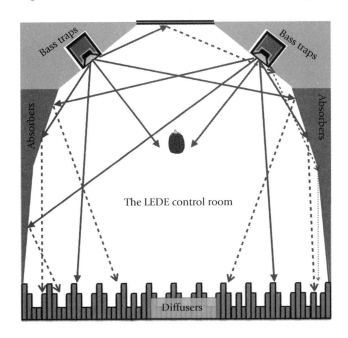

The LEDE control room

Diffusers

Figure 32.1
A control room constructed with irregular dimensions is optimal. The above measures about 8 × 9 m and is constructed following the live end / dead end principle (LEDE). Since the control room has no parallel surfaces, no early reflections are directed to the listening position, as they are directed instead toward the rear wall or are either absorbed or distributed evenly by the diffusers. The cavities next to and behind the monitors are the bass traps.

recording, and unless the acoustics are treated, even the best recording equipment will not be able to overcome the shortfalls of such spaces.

A small control room with several reflective surfaces will sound bright in itself, since it is mostly the mid and high frequencies that are reflected. The engineer might well compensate for this by attenuating those frequencies in the recorded instruments, resulting in a confined and dull-sounding mix when played back outside the control room.

If, conversely, the space is strongly dampened with absorbent materials, the room will sound dark and confined, because the absorbers mostly attenuate the midrange and highs. Compensating for this, the engineer might craft a light-weight mix that sounds thin outside the control room.

To address these common issues associated with home/project studio acoustics, an understanding of basic acoustic principles is required. These are discussed below, along with suggestions for controlling reflections and reverberation and taming standing waves.

The Control Room and the Monitors

The control room is all about acoustic balance. A mix created in the control room should transfer the same tonal balance to any other playback system in any other room—that's why it is called a control room.

The control room of the home/project studio is normally a small space, rarely measuring more than 4 × 4 × 2.5 m (length, width, and height). When the monitor sound is reflected off the walls, ceiling, and floor, a complex pattern of reflections is created that interferes with and distorts the direct sound. A space of this size and shape in an untreated state will typically have most of the following acoustic issues:

- Comb filter effects from the interference between the direct sound and the reflections from those areas of the side walls and ceiling close to the monitors.
- Standing waves in the low frequency range from the box-shaped acoustics, so that in some places low frequencies may be strongly boosted and in others attenuated or completely canceled out.
- Early reflections from the mixer, racks, tables, and other surfaces that color the sound from the monitors.
- Flutter echoes from untreated parallel surfaces and perpendicular corners.
- A nonlinear reverberation; that is, various frequency ranges behaving differently over time, some being boosted, others being attenuated by the acoustics.

Principles for Monitor Placement

The following basic rules for the placement of monitors in the control room are based on the rules of sound wave propagation in a confined space. In addition, acoustic phenomena, such as early reflections, standing waves (room modes), and the frequency response of the room, are also explained.

1. Always place the stereo monitors at a 30° angle relative to the central axis. Because of the physics of sound, this is necessary in order to create the phantom image between stereo speakers. If, for example, the vocal track is set to C (center), the vocal should be heard from the middle between the speakers. The same applies to any other panning

between the L (left) and R (right): the track is heard as if coming from somewhere between the speakers.

2. Place the monitors so that the tip of the equilateral triangle (formed by the monitors and the listener) is 20 cm behind the head of the engineer. As a result, the L monitor axis crosses the left ear and the R monitor axis crosses the right, ear thus providing the widest sweet spot (the area where the stereo image can be trusted to be true).

A 170 cm distance (C) between the L and R monitor tweeters is optimal for near field monitors. To some extent, the distance is flexible but should not be less than one meter and must not exceed two meters.

It is always the listening position that determines the placement of the speakers. The ideal position should be at 38% of the distance from the front wall to the rear wall. In theory, it is here that the least problems with standing waves are found. In a room 5 m long, the listening position is thus 1.9 m from the front wall.

3. The boundaries (the front and the side walls) must be symmetrical in relation to the monitors. Any reflective surface will create early reflections, so maintain a distance to windows, computer monitors, mixers, bald people, and so on, all of which reflect mostly the mid and high frequencies.

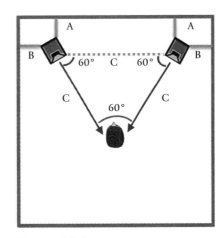

Figure 32.2

The monitors form an equilateral triangle with the listener. The distances of A, B, and C must not be the same. Neither should B and C be the same as the distance from the monitor to the floor. Equal pairs of distances will result in some frequencies being boosted or attenuated.

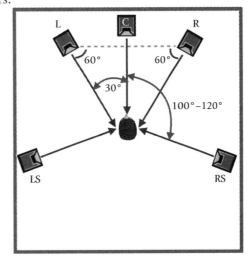

Figure 32.3

Surround speaker location. The central axis is angled 30° to the axes of the front left and right monitors. The angle to the left and right surround monitors is 100–120°.

4. Never place a monitor (or subwoofer) against walls, because any such boundary reinforces the low frequencies by up to 6 dB. The surface rule works as follows:

- A 6 dB boost from the wall (one surface).
- A 12 dB boost in a corner (two surfaces).
- An 18 dB boost on a table placed in a corner (three surfaces).

These boosts are found at frequencies below 200 Hz, since a speaker is omnidirectional in the bass frequencies. If it is placed on a table, strong early reflections are also created.

Note—each increase of 6 dB is equal to a doubling of the sound pressure!

The distances from the monitor to the floor, ceiling, and side walls should not be the same (see figure 32.2). Therefore, the best placement for nearfield monitors is freestanding on a solid stand. A distance of between 0.5 and 1 m from the walls is acceptable (the shorter distance creates phase cancelations higher in

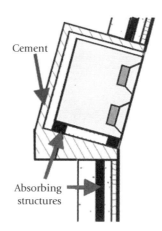

Cement

Absorbing
structures

Figure 32.4

The ideal installation of the main monitor is soffit or flush-mounting; that is, it is built into a heavy construction of cement. This tightens up the low end (with the bass range only being projected forward), while at the same time the risk of standing waves and resonances is reduced.

the frequency range), though more than 2.2 m is better. Avoid distances between 1.0 and 2.2 m.

5. Always use solid speaker stands; that is, stands with a substantial mass, such as those filled with sand. Even better is the principle behind IsoAcoustic monitor stands, which are constructed of rubber-insulated material; this almost causes them to float (acoustically speaking), so that no vibrations are transferred to the support base, and this improves the reproduction of the low-mids and the bass range.

   Never use light stands, shelves, or the mixer meter bridge, because sound transducers coupled to boundaries create resonances—just as the soundboard of an acoustic guitar amplifies the vibrations from the strings. Moreover, the stands should not add solid boundaries themselves that cause early reflections cluttering the stereo image. If the meter bridge or the table top is the only possible location, then place the monitors on dense foam (produced by Auralex, Primacoustics, etc.). If they are tilted slightly upward, this reduces both the early reflections and resonances.

6. Adjust the height of the monitors so that their acoustic center (between treble and bass unit in two-way speakers) is at ear level. They can also be placed slightly above ear level and slightly tilted down toward the listening position.

7. Experiment with moving the monitor and the listening position back and forth relative to the front wall to reduce any standing waves created between the front and the back wall. Locate these by playing back 50, 100, and 150 Hz tones, and choose the place having the least boosts and dips at the listening position. If necessary, similarly fine-tune any other position in the control room's work areas.

8. With a subwoofer connected, there is greater freedom in the placement of the L and R monitor, which are now free of bass content below the typical crossover frequency of 80 Hz. With a subwoofer, the optimal distance of 2.2 m can be reduced to between 1.1 and 2 m from the wall.

   The subwoofer should always be placed at the same distance from the listening position as the L and R monitors. If it is not at the same distance, the low frequencies will arrive offset in time relative to the L and R signal (producing phase distortion). This is less important for surround sound systems used for the movies, since Hollywood has always given priority to escapism rather than realism.

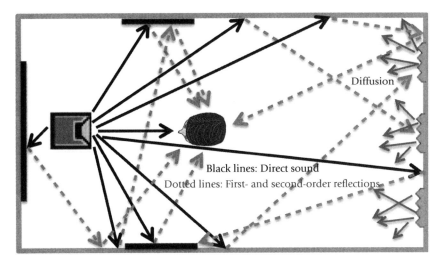

Diffusion

Black lines: Direct sound
Dotted lines: First- and second-order reflections

Figure 32.5

The reflections from a monitor in a rectangular room. Only the direct sound provides a true representation of the recording. First-order reflections are the initial reflections from the nearest walls and ceilings; they are therefore powerful and capable of distorting the sound coming directly from the monitor. The surfaces generating reflections should be treated with absorbents (the black panels), while the rear wall is treated with diffusion panels (the grey panels).

However, the subwoofer can also be placed slightly to one side of the central axis.

A subwoofer, besides improving the reproduction of frequencies below 60–80 Hz, also relieves some of the power load from the bass units of the small monitors, and this often results in a truer reproduction of the signal. It is important that the subwoofer is aligned to the levels of the L and R monitors according to the instructions in the monitor manual.

The Space and the Monitors

The room and the monitors should be perceived as one entity, both coloring what you hear. However, the interaction between the two is as important as the sound of each separately.

Comb Filter Effects

The early reflections from the side walls and the ceiling create comb filter effects in the midrange and high frequencies (see p. 272). At these frequencies, the monitors perform directionally, making it easy to calculate which surfaces should be treated with absorbers. As shown in figure 32.5, the surfaces generating first-order reflections should be treated with absorbing materials, while surfaces that are further away should be treated with a combination of absorbers and diffusers.

Room Modes

In the low frequency range, the monitor distributes sound energy in all directions (i.e., omnidirectionally). When the reflected sound waves interfere with the direct sound from the monitors, some low frequencies are reinforced while others are attenuated. Reflected low frequencies, with a particular wavelength in relation to the dimensions of the room, become standing waves.

Both ideal and more destructive ratios between the dimensions of a room (length, width, and height) exist, since these ratios determine how the waveforms interfere when reflected. Cube-shaped rooms in which height = length = width are the worst, while rooms with two equal dimensions or with a dimension that is 2, 3, or 4 times another, are nearly as bad.

On the other hand, a small space where the height is 3 m, length 4.15 m, and width 3.45 m (the proportions being 1, 1.14, and 1.39 compared to height) will counteract standing waves.

Larger spaces produce even fewer standing waves (the low-range frequency balance is of less concern in general). A large room of 3 × 6.90 × 4.80 m (the proportions being 1, 1.6, 2.33 compared to height) has dimensions that will largely eliminating standing waves.

Resonances

All mechanical constructions resonate at certain frequencies dictated by their size, shape, and material. They can be made to vibrate when struck by sound waves that have high energy levels (most often these are at low frequencies) in the same way that striking the drumhead of a snare, tom, and kick drum will trigger different resonances. Consequently, any resonant object and construction should be dampened or removed from the control room and the recording area. This does not matter for heavy or massive objects, as a large sound pressure level is required to make these vibrate (which is why flush-mounting speakers does not color large monitor sound audibly).

Fine-Tuning the Acoustics

When the control room is arranged with curtains, furniture, and a strategically placed rug, some of the room reflections are tamed. A soft couch on the back wall of the control room is an excellent absorber, and if it has legs at a certain height, the space beneath and behind it will act as a bass trap.

In addition, there are some relatively simple acoustic rules and modifications of the space that effectively reduce the audible acoustic distortion of the direct sound from the monitor and so make the monitors and the room more linear in their reproduction and reflection of sound, respectively. These are discussed below.

The Mirror Image Source Method

It is the reflections from the boundaries closest to the monitors that cause comb filter effects in the control room, with the result that you do not hear a true picture of the recorded music. The mirror image source method is used to locate first-order reflections (sound waves that have only been reflected once when they are heard) from the side walls and ceiling near the monitors and the listening position; these reflections should be attenuated.

Place yourself in the listening position and ask an assistant to go along the right wall with a mirror until you see the left monitor reflected in the mirror. Absorbers should be placed here.

Repeat this procedure for the left wall and the ceiling between the listening position and the monitors (this requires both imagination and acrobatics).

Place absorbent acoustic panels (rockwool, acoustic foam, polyester fiber, and the like) on the identified areas. Foam and polyester fiber at best dampens frequencies above 700–800

Figure 32.6

In principle, diffusers are better than absorbers, since they distribute reflections evenly around the room and maintain a degree of reverberation; in this way, the engineer is able to work for hours without listening fatigue. Diffusers can be decorative in their varying forms and dimensions—a bookcase filled with books is an efficient broadband diffuser, while uneven stone walls absorb and distribute the sound well in space, thus minimizing comb filter effects while maintaining reverberation.

Hz (acoustic panels with a proven dampening from 400 to 500 Hz do exist), but these materials become more efficient when mounted with space behind the panels. Using the better absorbers with a gap of 25–30 cm between the panel and problem surface can attenuate frequencies as low as 200 Hz. It is always more expensive to attenuate the low frequencies than the high frequencies due to both the cost of the absorbers and the space required.

A heavy treatment with absorbers might even result in the need to add in some mid and high frequency reflections using diffusers on the rear and side walls. Diffusers shift the reflections in time and distribute reflections in all directions, thereby avoiding destructive and constructive phase interference at specific points and instead providing a light and pleasing reverberation.

In addition to a more linear frequency response, diffusers dramatically improve the imaging, that is, the exact location of instruments, voices, and spatial information in the stereo image between L and R monitors.

LEDE: Live End / Dead End

In the control room, some reverberation is always needed; however, this may require a complex treatment (and an expensive one at that) to obtain a controlled and smooth reverberation across the entire frequency range.

In both a small and large room it is best to control reflections from the rear wall through a combination of diffusion and absorption. The absorbers should never absorb the entire reverberation, because working in an over-attenuated room will lead to listening fatigue. For a control room, 0.2–0.3 s of reverberation across the entire frequency range (referred to as RT-2 and representing the time it takes for the sound to decrease by 60 dB) is optimal.

A rear wall that is too dampened will be dark and lifeless sounding, and the mixes made in the space will be lightweight and thin in another space. Conversely, without dampening, the room will sound bright and the mix made in it will sound dark and stuffy outside the room.

The answer to this is the concept of LEDE—live end / Dead end. In the LEDE control room, the rear wall is alive with reflective surfaces, whereas the front wall is treated with absorbent materials. Diffusers project the sound in many directions across the entire frequency range from the rear wall (perhaps also from the ceiling and side walls), thereby eliminating problem resonances and phase issues while creating an ambient and slightly live sound.

In a rectangular room, in which the rear wall is within 2–3 m of the listening position, the diffuser panels should ideally cover about 60% of the rear wall, with the center of the panels placed at ear level.

Bass Traps

Corners generate flutter echoes that are easy to locate through hand clapping. Flutter echoes can be eliminated by using absorber panels on each of the surfaces of the corner. If the panel has a cavity, this can be filled with rockwool, thus also making it an effective bass trap. They can be made from large, half-cylindrical pipes lined with rockwool. If they have different diameters (20–50 cm), the cavity behind the panels attenuates a variety of low frequencies when they are placed in and around the corners.

A number of low-frequency absorbers might also be required around the room. Play 50 and 150 Hz tones and walk around the control room to identify the locations where there is boosting or attenuation of the low end. Experiment with placing the low-frequency absorbers in different places until this reduces the issues.

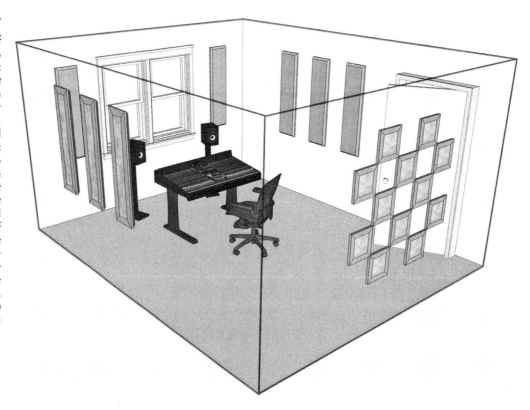

Figure 32.7
A number of manufacturers produce acoustic panels that target specific tasks such as control over early reflections, flutter echo, and bass. Primacoustic offers an all-in-one solution called the London Room Kit (shown here) that can be configured with a variety of different panels that provide diffusion or attenuate not only low frequencies but also early reflections and flutter echoes. © Primacoustic

Walls and Surfaces

If the space can accommodate it, construct non-parallel surfaces in the control room. Slightly angled, sawtooth-shaped walls (plaster board with the cavities filled with rockwool) on the side and end walls are enough to provide an improved distribution of the reflections. Generally speaking, double walls with multilayered plaster board and rockwool—preferably separated by a gap—provide the best shape for the control room. These different types of layers remove some of the impact of even the high-energy low frequencies, preventing them from being reflected back to the listening position.

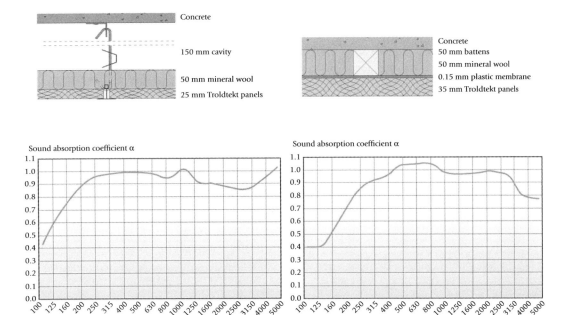

Figure 32.8
Two approaches to dampening. The right chart shows the effect of a 25 mm Troldtekt plate, 50 mm rockwool, and a 150 mm cavity in front of a concrete wall, resulting in an absorption that goes right down to 250–300 Hz. The left chart displays the result of a 35 mm Troldtekt plate with 50 mm rockwool but no cavity; the absorption only goes down to 400–500 Hz, because a cavity is essential to reducing low frequency content. Troldtekt has an uneven surface, making it effective as both a diffuser and absorber. © Troldtekt

Racks and Reflections

Never place processor racks and the like so close to the monitors that they create reflections. Any object or surface that reflects one (or both) of the monitors when a mirror is placed on it (seen from the listening position) will result in reflections of sound. The object should be moved elsewhere or acoustically treated.

Digital Correction Filters

Some loudspeaker manufacturers provide correction software that measures the interaction of the monitors with the room and so aligns the two. This is almost equivalent to an acoustician measuring the control room acoustics with respect to the location of the monitors and then treating the room acoustically to achieve a (more) linear response. There is also EQ software that uses test tones and mics to customize the monitors and control room. Using EQ to compensate for acoustic issues might be the best option in small rooms that do not have the space and resources for the required acoustic treatment. However, this approach does not remove comb filter effects and standing waves, nor does it ensure that the reverberation is linear across all frequency ranges.

EQ is thus only a treatment of the symptoms of underlying problems in the room. However, there can be good reasons for using EQ to correct acoustics below 300 Hz, given that often either it is impossible to move the listening or monitor positions sufficiently in a small control room or there is not enough space for the required bass traps and double walls that would balance the acoustics.

Often, monitors have built-in EQ to compensate for the imbalances of the room. By playing good recordings, listening, and gaining experience with how one's mixes sound outside the room, you can fine-tune the built-in EQ to compensate for some of the deficiencies of the control room acoustics.

33

The Recording Room

The acoustics of a recording room should be neither too dead nor too reverberant; the dry/wet balance depends on which instrument should be recorded and on the genre. Additionally, the frequency response (i.e., the reflected sound) should be linear across the frequency range.

Acoustics are irrelevant when a synth or an electric bass is recorded using DI. Neither is it that important when an electric guitar is recorded using close-miking with a mic right in front of the speaker. With vocals, problems begin to show if there are early reflections in the recording room (they produce comb filter effects) or reverberation (impossible to get rid of in the mix).

When it comes to the acoustic instruments—drum kit, percussion, acoustic guitar, saxophone, violin, and so forth—it all goes wrong if the acoustics are not suitable, because most acoustic instruments create their sound in interaction with the room.

This issue can be approached in two ways. The best is to use a recording space that already has the optimal acoustics for the instruments being recorded. The next best thing is to get rid of the reverberation and the reflections so that the recording captures as little as possible of the acoustics; that is, treat the recording space with absorbers and use close-miking techniques in combination with screens, isolation (iso) booths, and the like. It is this second approach that is dealt with here.

Tuning the Acoustics

Below are instructions for improving and adapting the acoustics to reduce spill when using multiple mics. The objective is to isolate each instrument on a separate track; only to the extent that the acoustics improve the sound of the instrument should they be captured by a mic.

The use of screens is the simplest technique to eliminate (poor) acoustics. A good screen effectively removes reverberation and reflections and also reduces spill from other instruments across the mid and high frequency ranges.

Iso Booths

These are the small enclosures that major studios have for loud guitar amplifiers, vocals, or weak acoustic instruments. Iso booths allow the simultaneous recording of multiple

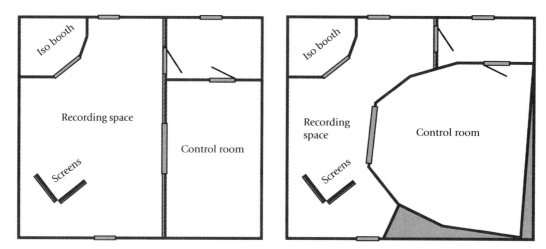

Figure 33.1

These two studio layouts share the same area and have similar features, but their approach to the acoustics is different. The recording room to the left has too many parallel surfaces. This is partially solved in the control room; however, the distance to the rear wall is too small. The one to the right has the perfect control room but suffers from short distances to the walls in the recording room.

instruments or instruments with very different sound pressures levels, for example, when the band wants to record an acoustic guitar or a grand piano together with the drum kit for the initial tracks.

Since a guitar amp sounds great when captured by a Shure SM57 placed right up to the speaker, the acoustics become irrelevant (close-miking). For this reason, the guitar amp is fine when isolated from other instruments by placing it in the iso booth (which can also be a temporary enclosure built with carpets, screens, etc.).

However, because of the booth's small size, acoustic instruments that interact with the acoustics do not sound so good when recorded in an iso booth. As reflections in the mid and high ranges are eliminated by absorbers, the iso booth produces a sound that is as if a blanket has been put over the instruments; drums and percussion become lifeless, and horns die.

The basic rule when simultaneously recording multiple instruments is to place either the noisiest instrument (or the vocal) in the iso booth or the weakest.

Box 33.1

Toto's "Hold the Line" was recorded live in the studio because the band wanted to interact like a live band rather than making overdubs. The grand piano was also in the same room as the drum kit, guitar, and bass. The problem with spill from drums and guitar was solved by wrapping the grand piano in blankets and placing the mics close to the strings inside the piano body. The shielding was so effective that it was possible to compress the grand piano very hard in the mix without enhancing the spill from the other instruments.

Screens

Screens are the alternative to iso booths. Proper studio screens (not office baffles) effectively reduce spill between instruments, though they mostly reduce the mid and high ranges (above 600–800 Hz, depending on the size of the room), while the low frequencies slip through above and beyond the screens. Placed close to a mic, the screen will always reduce spill from other instruments in the same room. This also eliminates comb filter effects from early reflections and reduces reverberation from the room.

Screens positioned in a V shape in front of the mic can be fairly effective in isolating the weaker instruments from the more powerful ones. Using the V setup and a (hyper) cardioid mic makes it possible to record the acoustic guitar in the same room as the drum kit, though it does not eliminate all of the spill. Also, take advantage of the polar pattern of the mic; place other instruments in the blind spot—that is, the rear of the cardioid—of the mic capturing the acoustic guitar.

The better you know the reflection pattern of the recording room, the more effectively the screens can be placed. It is essential that the instruments are placed with care, for example, avoiding powerful instruments facing reflective surfaces, as this will result in strong, first-order reflections distributed back into the recording space.

The Reflexion Filter and similar products provide a practical application of the rules for the distribution of sound. In a recording room with poor acoustics, screens will always improve the recording of vocals and most acoustic instruments. The Reflexion Filter eliminates room reflections above 500–600 Hz quite effectively (only reducing slightly below). However, a screen that close to the mic has its own slightly enclosed and dull sound, because the foam attenuates the high frequency range inside the enclosure as well. However, compared to the destructive consequences of early reflections and (poor) reverberation, this is a minor problem and a clear improvement of inappropriate acoustics.

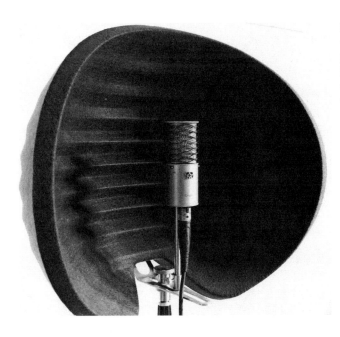

Figure 33.2
The Aston Halo Reflection Filter, in the company of an Aston Origin cardioid condenser.

The Dimensions of the Recording Space

The amount of reflections (and thus a large proportion of spill) is inversely proportional to the size of the room. Small spaces fail to distribute the energy of the sound waves evenly across a wide area, and so the early reflections slip back into the mics.

Larger spaces generate fewer early reflections and a more pleasant reverberation, since the reflections are evenly distributed in the room.

For this reason, the distance to the closest reflecting surfaces (and the types of surface) becomes important. In medium-sized spaces, a mixture of reflective and absorbing materials should be used, while in the small room (20 m² and below) it is the reflections that should be strongly minimized (using rockwool, foam, acoustic curtains, etc.). However, this will remove the ambience, and consequently the vital drive of the drums (for a pop or rock song), and reduce the sound of many acoustic instruments, and ambience can only be partially recreated using reverb and spatial effects. Also, a drum kit recorded in a small space requires a larger number of mics placed close to each drum to avoid capturing the acoustics (which would result in phase problems). To make matters even worse, small rooms typically result in standing waves, often creating powerful resonances from the individual drums (which makes the engineer reach for gaffer tape, gel pads, etc., which will affect the timbre, often resulting in a dead-sounding kit).

Concrete walls are strongly reflective and, in large rooms, enhance the low frequency range.

Raw or plastered bricks distribute the sound energy more evenly because they diffuse the sound waves (see p. 293).

Untreated wood also provides a good distribution of sound across the low to the high-mid frequencies and is therefore highly suitable for acoustic instruments.

Box 33.2

Each instrument has its optimal acoustics described in the first section of this book (pp. 5–116).

A drum kit generates powerful sound pressure levels that are distributed back into the recording space as reflections. Since a bare floor is a highly reflective surface, in particular in the midrange and the highs, a carpet beneath the drum kit reduces the sound pressure level. Furthermore, a combination of absorbent panels and bass traps on adjacent walls and the ceiling helps to even the distribution of sound in the room.

If clear resonant frequencies (or standing waves) are heard from the drum kit or any other low-end instrument, they can often be reduced by placing the instrument in a different position in relation to the surfaces of the room (in particular the corners).

Separation

In multi-mic recordings, spill is often noticeable due to delay or ambience on the spill caused by distance.

Even at quite low levels, the snare and hi-hat spill into mics more than 3–4 m away and can have a destructive impact on the drum sound. Even a small reduction of the spill by using screens might be vital in the mix. Distance reduces spill (see the 3:1 rule, p. 275). However, a weak spill in more distant mics often results in a washed-out sound compared to the direct signal, and this may sound worse than a powerful spill from a close position.

When using the close-miking technique on multiple instruments, it is worth experimenting with the mic and instrument placement to find the spot that results in the least coloration, both in terms of phase and reverberation. A test can be made by panning the tracks containing spill to the center so that when the volume levels are set in the initial mix, it becomes clear whether the spill will produce phase issues or a washed-out sound in the final mix.

Spill should not always be regarded as a problem. Spill can also provide depth to a recording, as is often the case between the mics of the drum kit. This requires, however, that the spill does not result in destructive comb filter effects. Therefore, it might be worthwhile experimenting with the placement of the mics that have obvious phase issues—often they need only be moved a couple of centimeters.

Diffusion

A bookshelf (filled with books such as this) provides an excellent solution to a reflective wall, in both the control room and the recording room, and different-sized books produce an amazing broadband diffusion. Just as with an uneven stone wall, they reflect the sound in all directions—though the bookshelf is softer sounding, since the books absorb frequencies between 2 and 6 kHz. Both bookshelves and uneven stone walls reduce comb filter effects and standing waves.

Figure 33.3
Troldtekt is made of wood wool (wood shavings, also known as excelsior) mixed with cement. The uneven surface causes the structure to act as both a diffuser and an absorber, distributing and attenuating the sound effectively if used on the ceiling or the side walls of the recording space.

Furniture with soft surfaces and of different sizes also provides absorption and a little diffusion, while heavy curtains and blankets do likewise but only absorb the mid and high frequencies. See also chapter 32, "The Control Room and the Monitors."

Box 33.3

Read more on acoustics in chapter 32, "The Control Room and the Monitors."
See also chapter 31, "Phase and Comb Filtering."

TIPS

✓ Always place the vocal mic on a rug that dampens mechanical sounds. The same applies when recording sax, trumpet, and so forth, because the musicians will move around.

✓ Always treat surfaces (those that create early reflections) that lie within 2.5 m of the mic.

PART VI

Audio Standards, Plugs, and Connectors

34

Levels and Meters

A common cause of distortion and signal degradation is audio devices that have incompatible signal voltages or impedances when connected. This chapter deals with the commonly used standards for voltage and impedance—referred to here as levels—in audio equipment, and it also presents various types of metering found in the recording studio.

Levels

Line Level

Line signals are the signals delivered by the output of a mic preamp, audio interface, effects processor, CD player, or mixer. Since line level has a higher voltage than mic level, line level signals can be sent over longer distances without noise interference.

Two standards denoting input and output levels have been defined:

- **−10 dBV** is the standard for consumer audio and home studio equipment. This also applies to most synthesizers. Often, the signal is unbalanced, using mini jacks, jacks, or RCA jacks (see chapter 35, "Plugs and Connectors"), but it can also be balanced, requiring connectors with a tip and two rings.
- **+4 dBu** is the standard used by professional audio equipment that uses XLR plugs or balanced jack plugs (1/4″ TRS with a tip and two rings). The +4 dBu signal voltage is nearly four times as high as −10 dBV and so gathers less noise from any surrounding voltage fields. A line output at −10 dBv sent to a + 4 dBu line in should normally be amplified.

Manufacturers comply with these standards, as it is a prerequisite for the equipment to work without signal degradation, and for compatibility with other equipment, many audio devices have a switch selecting between −10 dBV and +4 dBu.

Mic Level

Microphones produce a low voltage when the diaphragm is set in motion by a sound. A dynamic mic typically produces 1.5 millivolts, while a high-sensitivity condenser mic

Figure 34.1

Mic levels using XLRs and line using jack is the standard.
© Mackie

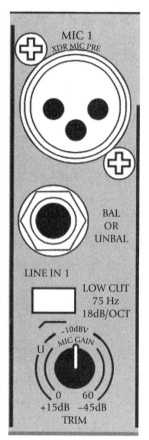

produces 50–100 millivolts. Therefore, mics are amplified with a preamp by up to several hundred times in order to reach line level voltage. However, nearby voltage fields interfering with the signal will also be amplified, which is why mics should always use balanced connectors (XLR) that cancel out such noise.

Mics have low output impedances (most between 30 and 300 ohm). A good rule of thumb is that the mic preamp input impedance should be 5–10 times higher than the mic output impedance. For this reason, some preamps have variable input impedance, so experiment with the settings.

A preamp has either clip, LED, or VU meters indicating when its input starts clipping (that is, when the signal becomes distorted). The VU meter provides the best reading of levels. Those meters that are additionally capable of displaying the output level are the best to use, as you never want to overload a signal at the line output following the preamp stage. By contrast, the gain at the input stage of some preamps can be used to shape the signal, normally by setting a "hot" signal that adds harmonic distortion (see p. 217).

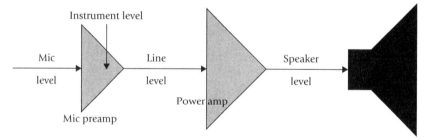

Figure 34.2

Mic level is boosted to line level in the preamp. Mixers, audio interfaces, and analog effects units also output at line level. Line level becomes speaker level in the power amp.

Instrument Level

Instrument level signals produce a voltage level that is between mic and line level. For this reason, the hi-Z input and the DI box are used to boost the electric guitar or the bass to line level when recording direct into the DAW (see p. 39).

Speaker Level

Speaker level is the level transmitted from the power amplifier to the speakers and is based on a voltage of 10 volts or more.

Audio Levels in the Signal Chain and How They Are Measured

Audio devices operate between two limits: the clipping point, at which the device starts distorting the signal, and the noise floor, at which the residual noise (hiss) becomes audible. To optimize the signal quality, the signal should be well above the noise floor and comfortably below the clipping point.

In analog audio, the nominal level and scaling of the metering was agreed upon by the audio industry to make this optimization of the signal practical.

Clipping

Clipping occurs when the signal level consumes the full power supply voltage in analog systems and, in digital systems, when the coding format runs out of numbers. This is the reason why power supplies and coding formats have a crucial impact on audio quality. An audio interface operating from its own power supply provides a higher voltage power (resulting in 6 dB more headroom when recording and mixing) than is possible with an audio interface powered by USB.

Nominal Level

This is the signal level at which line devices, effects units, and so forth are designed to work optimally (in accordance with their power supply). Nominal level is an average sound level measurement below any peaks.

If nominal level is observed, the best sound quality and the best signal to noise ratio are maintained throughout the signal chain, and it also provides the greatest dynamic range and cleanest signal. Nominal level is shown in figure 34.3 as 0 on the VU scale.

The dynamic range is reduced if the signal falls below the nominal level and, likewise, when it is transmitted from −10

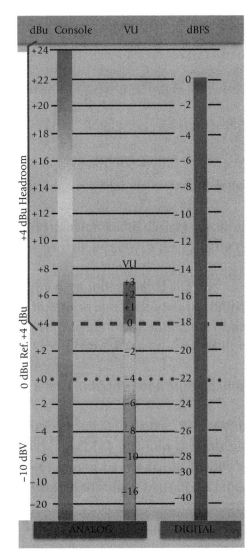

Figure 34.3

The VU scale in the middle and the dBFS scale to the right. The dBu scale to the left reflects the analog dynamic range, with analog consoles clipping at +24 to +26 dBu.

dBV to +4 dBu devices. Conversely, if sent from +4 dBu to −10 dBV devices, the signal may distort.

Headroom

Headroom represents the space available between the nominal level and the maximum level that the device can handle without clipping. Thus, the headroom is a buffer zone indicating how by many dBs the signal may exceed the nominal level without clipping. Analog metering never displays the full headroom (usually only +6 dB). On some analog devices, in particular tube preamps or compressors, overdriving the gain stage is used to color the signal.

Meters

Figure 34.4

Vintage and modern
VU meters.

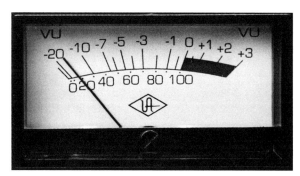

VU meter

A VU meter is used for analog audio devices and is calibrated so that 0 VU corresponds to +4 dBu, the level of the professional line signal. Thus, 0 VU is the optimal gain level for professional line devices. As can be seen from figure 34.4, the VU meter has a headroom of up to 20 dBu before clipping.

The VU meter reflects both the amplitude and duration of the signal, resulting in an accurate reading of the RMS (root mean square)—that is, the average signal voltage. This is the main reason why the readings from RMS meters are close to how our brains perceive levels.

Peak Meter

The dBFS scale used by digital devices displays the entire headroom (figure 34.3) and is therefore called a peak meter, always showing the peaks of the signal. 0 dBFS is the clipping point in digital systems, and signals exceeding 0 dBFS produce an immediate and audible distortion.

Since the dBFS scale includes the entire headroom (which is invisible in analog VU meters), many inexperienced engineers tend to record too "hot" when using digital devices, and this results in a clipping of the transients. When recording in the DAW, the dynamic range is best when levels are held between −3 dBFS and −12 dBFS (−3 dBFS being the peaks where most transients are to be found). Stay safely below 0 dBFS, as most DAW meters register peaks at the sample points. However, the actual peaks in a signal occur between the samples, and these may be 2–3 dBs higher. The new true peak meter, based on oversampling, shows the intersample peaks.

It is very important that the master bus on the mixer remains at 3–6 dB below 0 dBFS in order to avoid deterioration of the sound. Generally, a headroom of 6 dB results in a more open and natural sound and also leaves room for the mastering processing.

Also note that the signal on each track is boosted by adding EQ, compression, and so on; since each volume level fader is located after the plug-ins, this can be corrected by reducing the level fader on the channel.

The peak meter is unsuitable for assessing the perceived loudness of a signal; for this purpose, the VU meter, displaying the average sound levels over a period of 300 ms, is better.

The Loudness Meter

The newly introduced loudness meters have become important tools for audio engineers who deliver to streaming services and broadcast media after the International Telecommunication Union specified loudness recommendations in 2015 on the basis of LUFS metering (in the ITU-R document BS.1770-4, "Algorithms to Measure Audio Programme Loudness and True-Peak Audio Level").

LUFS are equal to dBs, so the loudness meter will read −14 LUFS when fed with a −14 dBFS sine tone.

However, dBFS and LUFS are calculated differently, since LUFS more accurately calculate the perceived loudness based on some extra readings:

- **Integrated loudness** measures the average loudness of the entire track.
- **Momentary loudness** (similar to the RMS/VU meter) measures the loudness of the past 400 ms.
- **Short-term loudness** measures the loudness of the past 3 s.
- **True Peak** measures peaks (intersample peaks included).

The dB(A) Scale

Level is measured in dBs. Unless otherwise stated, the linear dB scale is used. However, there is another scale, the dB(A) scale, which weights the sound pressure level relative to the sensitivity of human hearing and is nonlinear. We perceive the frequencies in the speech range (2–5 kHz) very well, while sounds below 100 Hz and above 10 kHz must be 2–3 times as strong in order to be perceived as equally loud.

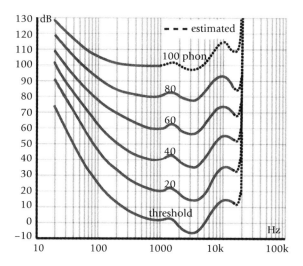

Figure 34.5

The equal loudness curve is deepest on the graph where our hearing is most sensitive and higher at the frequencies that we are less sensitive to.

The bottom solid curve (red on the companion website) is the hearing threshold for 18–25-year-olds—that is, the limit for how soft a tone at a particular frequency can be and still be heard. This is somewhat theoretical, since most young adults these days have passed through their teenage years with little regard for protecting their ears.

The equal loudness curve—also called the Fletcher-Munson curve—indicates that in the frequency range of 1–5 kHz (i.e., more than covering the range of human speech), we hear even weak sounds very well. By contrast, frequencies below 100 Hz and high frequencies above 12 kHz need to be 20–90 dB more powerful to be perceived as equally loud as frequencies lying within the 1–5 kHz range.

35

Plugs and Connectors

All audio cables have a screen that protects against noise (also called interference) from electronic equipment and voltage fields in the immediate surroundings. The screen protects against hum, crackles, and hiss, but unbalanced connections still collect some noise, particularly from computer monitors, mobile phones, and other electronic devices.

Plugs

XLR Plugs

XLR plugs are used for balanced audio signals and require a cable with a screen (1), conductor (2), and a reverse phase (3)—see figure 35.1. XLR connectors are used in professional audio because:

- They snap to the device (a jack or phono might fall out).
- The reverse phase protects against noise and signal degradation.

The additional conductor (3) carries the reverse phase to the signal (2). Since the noise collected along the cable run is added both in phase and in reverse phase, it is eliminated automatically when the balanced device correlates the difference between the transmitted and received signal.

Figure 35.1
XLR plugs are used for balanced connections.

Jack Plugs

Jack plugs can be mono or stereo. The outermost tip is the conductor while the inner is the screen.

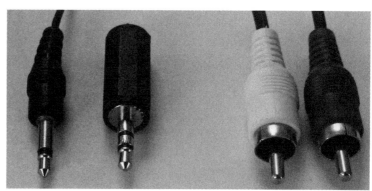

Figure 35.2

Both mini-jack and jack plugs can be mono or stereo. Mini-jacks are never balanced, but jacks can be unbalanced or balanced. RCA plugs (phono) are always mono and unbalanced.

On a stereo jack, the tip should be the L (left) channel with the intermediate ring as the R (right) channel. A stereo jack can also be used for a balanced mono signal if the jack output and input of the connected devices are balanced, the intermediary ring becoming the reverse phase. Balanced jacks are found in both outs and ins on a (high-quality) audio interface, but rarely on electronic music instruments.

Similarly, mini-jacks can be mono or stereo but they are never used in balanced equipment. RCA jacks (phono) are always mono and unbalanced. They are used in consumer equipment where they often fall out or are inserted incorrectly.

Balanced Connectors

Balanced is the professional standard for microphone cables and connections between audio equipment. If balanced connectors are to work, both the sending and receiving device must be balanced in output and input.

Balanced connectors can have long cable runs without adding signal degradation and without collecting RF (radio frequencies) and noise from the AC voltage fields they

Figure 35.3

Balanced XLR female to XLR male connector. 1 is the screen, 2 the conductor, and 3 the reverse phase.

Figure 35.4
Balanced XLR plug to stereo jack. 1 goes to the inner ring, 2 to the tip, and 3 to the middle ring.

pass through. Balanced cables, therefore, are particularly important to mics, as the mic signal is amplified by up to 700–800 times in the mic preamp.

The cabling between the different types of balanced connectors can be seen in figures 35.3 and 35.4.

Unbalanced Audio

Figure 35.5 shows how phono and jack connect to XLR. This is used when connecting consumer to professional audio equipment. The result is an unbalanced connector that must be kept as short as possible, a maximum of 3–4 meters. Remember, to switch from −10 dBV to +4dBu (p. 297) if selectable on the pro device.

Figure 35.5
Unbalanced jack or RCA to XLR. If a two-wire and screened cable is used, connect both screen (1) and reverse phase (3) to the same pin in the jack or RCA plug. When using a cable with only one conductor and screen, pin 1 is short-circuited to pin 3 at the XLR connector.

Cables vary in quality—and hence their price differential. Prices are determined by the quality and thickness of the copper conductors and the quality of the shielding that rejects magnetic and voltage fields. High-quality cables reduce the amount of noise and interference picked up from the surroundings through which the cable passes. Also, they are reliable (here, particularly the quality of connectors is crucial) and they last (almost) forever.

TIPS
✓ Never use cables longer than necessary.
✓ Use labeled or different colored cables. This helps to stay organized in a crowded session.
✓ Acquire a stock of connectors that converts between the different plug types.

Inserts

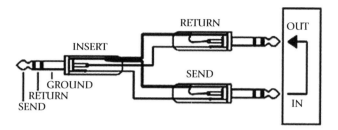

Figure 35.6

The soldering of the insert using three stereo jacks. At the send/return jacks (the effects processor), the middle and the inner rings are short-circuited using a small wire.

For outboard equipment, specific types of connectors are used. In the case where an external processor (like an analog compressor or a vintage echo unit) is inserted on a mixer channel, the insert both sends and receives the processed signal. A stereo jack is always used for the insert, which means that the signal will be unbalanced. Thus, the tip carries the send signal to the input of the external processor, the middle ring carries the return, and the lower ring provides the screening.

On the analog mixer, the insert point is always before EQ (pre-EQ) and after the high-pass filter (post-HPF). Only a few audio interfaces have inserts for external processors and instead the outputs and inputs of the audio interface are used to connect to external processors.

Digital Audio Formats

FireWire, USB, and Thunderbolt are common formats for the transfer of digital audio between a computer and an external peripheral such as an audio interface. In addition, there are also other formats that transfer two or more channels of digital audio:

- **AES/EBU** (Audio Engineering Society / European Broadcast Union). The professional format for the transfer of two channels of digital audio between digital devices through a balanced cable using XLRs (pin 1 screen, with 2 being the signal and 3 the reverse phase). Since AES/EBU is intended for stereo signals, the two channels are interleaved. AES/EBU is low-impedance, typically 110 ohms, and 10 volts, which allows for cable runs of up to 100 m with no signal degradation or interference pickup.

- **S/PDIF** (Sony/Philips Digital Interface Format). Consumer standard for transmitting two channels of interleaved (stereo) digital audio between devices. S/PDIF uses RCA/phono jacks and a two-wire cable. The signal is low impedance, typically 75 ohms, and 0.5 volts, which allows up to only 10 m of cable run without signal degradation. The format is also called coaxial, and on some devices it can be made to transfer the optical format.

- **ADAT** (also called ADAT Lightpipe). A format transmitting up to eight channels at 48 kHz sampling rate and 24–bit audio between digital devices (or four channels of 96

kHz, 24 bits). Using an optical fiber cable with TOSLink connectors, it has become the standard in audio interfaces for adding preamps and other external devices digitally.

Though S/PDIF and the ADAT have different protocols—two and eight channels, respectively—on some devices ADAT can be switched between the two formats. ADAT also interfaces with FireWire.

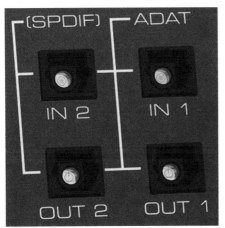

Figure 35.8
ADAT was developed by Alesis with the modular, digital eight-track multitrack recorder in 1992, which recorded and played back eight separate audio tracks on Super VHS video tapes. ADAT Optical carries eight channels on a single light pipe, four channels at 88.2/96 kHz, or two channels at 176.4/192 kHz. ADAT is compatible with S/PDIF. © rme

- **Ethernet-networked audio.** A format designed to distribute multiple audio channels in live sound, multiroom recording studios and post production. It can also be used to expand I/O channel count and to interface digital peripherals. Ethernet is scalable and boasts near zero latency.

Synchronizing Digital

Digital sync is required if multiple digital devices are to be interconnected. Word clock locks the transmitter to the receiver in order to synchronize the digital signal (i.e., to keep the samples timed and constant).

In simple setups, sync is assured by making one device the master with the others as slaves. The internal clock of the master (often the audio interface) thus controls the slave

Figure 35.9
The RME ADI-4 DD interfaces the digital formats of ADAT, AES/EBU (found both as XLR or as D-Sub multipin connector), and S/PDIF. Word clock will enable the ADI-4 DD to sync with any other digital device. © rme

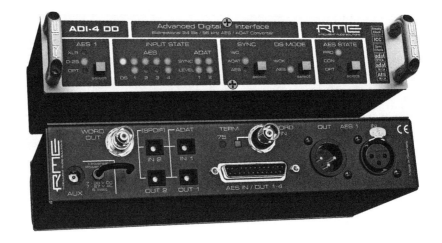

digital devices through a clock pulse embedded in the audio signal sent via the AES/EBU, S/PDIF, or ADAT outputs to the digital input of each slave.

The computer automatically syncs USB, Thunderbolt, and FireWire audio interfaces if it is set to master and the connected digital devices are each set to slave. Lack of synchronization is heard as high frequency jitter or crackles.

Word Clock

For more complex setups, a central sync device is required that distributes the clock via the word clock connectors to each unit (labeled Word Out and Word In). This is also called house sync.

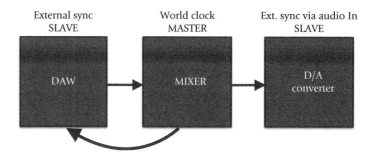

Figure 35.10
In this setup, the digital mixer is the word clock master, and the DAW is the slave. The D/A converter is synchronized via the digital output to the digital input (AES/EBU or S/PDIF) of the converter.

GLOSSARY

0 dBFS: 0 dBFS, or "zero decibels relative to full scale," refers to the maximum possible volume level that can be represented by a digital signal. Values that are beyond the maximum value cause clipping.

additive EQ: Boosting a selected frequency band.

ADSR: Attack-decay-sustain-release, describing the typical four phases of an amplitude envelope that plots the amplitude of a sound wave against time.

air: The frequency content of the upper harmonics of (certain) instruments. A high-shelf filter can be used to add air in the 12–16 kHz frequency range, that is, to boost the upper harmonics.

ambience: The reflections in an acoustic space. Ambience usually represents the shorter reverb times.

aux: Auxiliary channel. An extra line in/out bus on the mixer that can be assigned different functions such as a sub-group or send/return from an effects processor.

bass: The 60–250 Hz frequency range. Most instruments' deepest notes are found in this area. The male voice goes down to about 80 Hz and the female voice to approximately 160 Hz. The lowest note on the guitar is the E string at 82.41 Hz. The basic "bottom" of the rhythm section is located here, as is fullness and that "warm analog sound." If all instruments are allocated fullness in the bass, the mix becomes boomy and muddy.

bounce: A stereo mixdown of a multitrack session. The term is also used for the final mix.

brickwall limiter: A limiter abruptly cutting a signal that exceeds the threshold.

bus: A signal path feeding, for example, an audio signal to a sub-mix, sub-group, or an aux channel.

clipping: Overload due to the signal exceeding the maximum level that an audio device can handle. Digital clipping occurs over 0 dB and exhibits obvious distortion, while in analog equipment the overload occurs gradually, which is why it is often used to deliberately color a signal.

compressor: A device that automatically controls amplitude levels of an audio signal over time. A compressor decreases dynamic range by attenuating segments of the signal that are loud. The compressor can also be set to increase parts of the signal that are weak.

cue: A cue vocal is a preliminary and temporary vocal providing cues for the musicians during recording.

DAW: Digital audio workstation. Sequencer software used to record and edit audio and MIDI. Plug-ins provide further processing abilities to the DAW.

dB(A): Sound pressure level in decibels. "A" in the brackets, means that the measurement is weighted according to human perception—that is, using a filter that matches the frequency response of the human auditory system.

DDPi: A Disc Description Protocol image is a pre-master containing four files. Commonly used as a format for specifying the content of optical discs, including CDs and DVDs. Used by the mastering houses for the delivery of pre-masters for duplication to the CD plant (on a data CD-R or DVD or uploaded directly to a CD plant's server).

decibel (dB): A unit used to indicate the levels of sound waves and audio signals. Increasing the level 6 dB is a doubling in sound pressure, because the decibel scale is logarithmic, similar to the way we perceive sound waves.

ducking: When a compressor is set to attenuate a particular part of a track, the track at that point is said to be ducked. The triggering of ducking is often frequency-dependent and therefore controlled by a side chain signal. (See also side chain.)

dynamic range: Describes the difference between the weakest and strongest audio signals that an audio device is capable of handling, Generally, describes the distance between the self-noise and the maximum SPL that the device can reproduce without distortion. Sixteen-bit digital audio systems have an objective dynamic range of 96 dB, but the perception of the dynamic range can be extended using techniques such as noise-shaped dithering.

filter: A circuit that boosts or cuts certain frequency ranges to specified levels.

formants: The formants are fundamental to giving each voice its unique character (also helping to identify the gender and age of a singer) and are determined by the resonances added in the vocal tract, the strength of the vocal cords, the breathing and singing technique, and so forth. The more advanced pitch processors display the formants, making them editable.

frequency response: The ability of a device to reproduce the input frequency range.

fullness: The low-end frequency content of instruments below 300–400 Hz.

gain: This controls the amount of amplification of a signal.

harmonics: Partials of a complex, harmonic tone. The fundamental is considered the first harmonic, while overtones count from above the fundamental; that is, the second harmonic is the first overtone.

high: The 6–20 kHz frequency range. Except for the largest church organs, no instruments have their fundamentals here, but quite a few have harmonics in this area. The high range controls definition and clarity on most instruments. If it is exaggerated, though, the instrument's sound might become thin and piercing. Air is in the 12–20 kHz range, but above 16 kHz it is only felt rather than heard due to the limitations of the human auditory system.

high-mid: The 4–6 kHz frequency range. Most instruments (except some bass instruments) have frequency content here because of their harmonics. The high-mids give definition, presence, and clarity to the mix. Vocal sibilance is also found here.

Hz: Hertz. The number of cycles per second in sound waves and electric signals. One kilohertz (1 kHz) is 1000 Hz.

interference: When two or more electrical signals or sound waves are combined, a new waveform is produced. This process is called interference, resulting in new amplitudes and/or frequencies in the signal.

insert: A signal path that makes it possible to connect external processors in series with a mixer channel or a device.

jitter: Time-based errors in transferring data between digital audio devices, resulting in a metallic and distorted sound, which is particularly evident in the collapse of the stereo perspective.

latency: The delay that occurs from the input to the output in a digital circuit.

limiter: A compressor set to a high ratio (from 10:1 to ∞:1). Often used to control peak levels of a signal that might otherwise result in clipping. Limiting the peaks of a mix allows the overall volume level to be raised (gain makeup). The result is an increased loudness and a reduced dynamic range.

LFO: Low frequency oscillator. Used in synths and effects units to produce modulation effects.

low-mid: The frequency range between 250 Hz and 2 kHz. Quite a few instruments have their highest fundamentals in the low-mid range. The low-mid controls the impact of an instrument in the mix. Attenuation might be needed in the lower parts of the range in order to reduce boominess and in the upper parts of the range in order to suppress a tinny sound.

matched (stereo) pair: Two mics used to record in stereo that are matched in terms of frequency range, sensitivity, polar response, and so on.

midrange: The 2–4 kHz frequency range. Any instrument will have frequency content here because of the harmonics, but only the whistle, the church organ, and the piano have fundamentals reaching that high. Therefore, EQing above 2 kHz only affects the harmonics on most instruments. The midrange area highlights the attacks of the instruments in the mix, and too much attenuation here produces a sharp and metallic sound.

muddiness: This is created in the mix when the frequency range of 200–500 Hz is overrepresented, normally from many instruments having (too much) content in this range.

multiband compressor: A device that splits the signal across multiple compressors into frequency bands that can be compressed independently. Thus, multiband compression can be used to compress the frequency layers differently, thus serving as a form of broadband EQ by using gain makeup.

nominal level: Designates the level at which an audio-processing device is designed to operate for optimal sound reproduction.

null: The figure-of-eight polar pattern on a microphone captures virtually nothing from the sides; these positions are called "nulls." This is useful when it is necessary to eliminate sound from the sides during recording.

octave: The octave doubles the frequency of a tone. Also used to describe the steepness of EQ filters (as in a 12 dB/octave roll-off or attenuation).

overdubbing: The process of adding new tracks to a session or replacing (parts of) existing recordings.

pan: The functionality on the stereo mixer that places an individual track somewhere between L (left) and R (right).

peak: The highest volume levels of the audio signal. (See also transient.)

PFL: Pre-fade listen. A monitor function that lets you hear a single instrument or group of instruments before the channel fader without affecting the headphone mix or the stereo mix.

phantom image: A phantom image is created when monitoring sound in stereo if the system is well designed and set up. The phantom image creates the illusion of hearing a sound as if it were coming from a place between the speakers, even though the speakers are placed out to the sides. When panning somewhere between L (left) and R (right), any position should create a phantom image.

phantom power: Supply voltage through a balanced mic cable (XLRs required) to feed the condenser mics that contain active electronic circuitry. Usually 48 DC.

polar pattern: The microphone's directional characteristics for capturing sound.

post-fade: A signal sent post-fade will reflect changes in level, EQ, and so on that are set on the channel fader. Post-fade is normally used with aux sends, sending to effects units.

preamp: Used to boost (gain) a mic or instrument signal to line level.

presence: Resides in the 4–6 kHz range, which, when boosted, brings clarity to an instrument.

proximity effect: A directional mic (cardioid and figure-of-eight) exhibits a bass boost in the 100–250 Hz range; at 10 cm and under, this can be as much as 10–15 dB. The proximity effect decreases with distance, and at 30 cm the cardioid is almost linear.

punching in/out: Shifting into and out of record on a track of a multitrack recorder while the track itself is playing previously recording material. A technique that in the days of reel-to-reel tape required lighting reflexes and a good ear if desired parts of the previous recording were not to be irrevocably lost but that today, with digital devices, can be easily programmed and, if mistakes are made, undone.

resonance: An acoustic amplification of particular frequencies. It is caused by the physical dimensions of an enclosed space corresponding integrally to the wavelengths of the sound's harmonics. An acoustically resonant space usually has many resonant frequencies, and this what colors a sound and provides the particular, often recognizable characteristic of the space. Such spaces can be rooms, formed by the inner surfaces of musical instruments, or the cavities of the human body. (See also formants.)

reflection: All surfaces absorb and reflect sound according to the frequency content of the sound and the qualities of the surface material. Any sound that is reflected contributes to the reverberation of that sound.

reverb time: The reverb time is the time it takes for a signal to attenuate by 60 dB (via the effects of absorption) from the initial level of the direct signal through its reverberant tail. Cladding, carpets, curtains, and so forth determine how different frequencies are absorbed.

roll-off (filter): A filter that gradually attenuates frequencies below or above a selected frequency.

room modes: The resonant frequencies of a resonant room (also known as standing waves). Usually just referring to the lower, more dominant frequencies.

side chain: A side chain allows a process to be controlled by another signal other than the one being processed. As an example, a side chain on a compressor only controls the compressor action, having no effect on the input signal itself.

signal-to-noise ratio (S/N ratio): The S/N ratio describe the ratio between the self-noise of an audio device and the strongest signal that the device can handle. (See also dynamic range.)

SMPTE: A signal code that contains an absolute time reference visualized in terms of hours: minutes: seconds: frames. SMPTE is used to synchronize audio and video equipment.

sub-bass: The 20–60 Hz frequency range. The sub-bass is more physically felt than heard (although any harmonics will be heard). Most instruments have no frequency content in this area, and therefore it is better to attenuate it (low-cut or low-shelf filter) to avoid rumbling in the mix. Reaching down to 27.5 Hz at A0, the concert piano (together with the organ) possesses the lowest pitch. The low E1 on the electric and double bass is 41.2 Hz.

subtractive EQ: Attenuating a selected frequency band.

transient: Short-term peak from the attack of an instrument or any other sound. Transients often have more high frequency content relative to the rest of the ADSR envelope that follows. (See also peak.)

unity gain: 0 dB at the fader of a mixer channel is often marked U, meaning that the output level is the same as the input level. When recording and mixing, unity gain should be established between the connected devices, such as mixers, outboard effects, dynamics processors, and so on, and this results in a cleaner signal, preventing signal degradation.

waveform: A graphic representation of sound as shown in the recording window of the DAW.

INDEX